T0302025

The Covid-19 pandemic has fundamentally shaped strategic HRM priorities and operational HR practices. It has proven to be a catalyst for many organisations by showcasing how flexible working practices can be better incorporated and utilised, and how people can be led and managed remotely, in many cases while working from home. However, with this comes HRM challenges too, for example, concerning employees' sense of identity, teamwork, psychological contract, and health and wellbeing, to name but a few. Hence, the timing of this book is excellent in providing practical guidance for HRM as we navigate through what is rapidly becoming the 'new normal'.

– Dr Kirsteen Grant, Associate Professor in HRM, Edinburgh Napier University, UK.

The move to hybrid working will arguably define the future of work. Practical examples of implementation from organisational contexts, and discussion of key concepts and the issues surrounding them, will both provide solutions and inform the debate. This book will be welcomed by present and future people management practitioners and by academics seeking texts that tackle this most topical issue.

– Christine Daley, Course Director – Postgraduate Courses in Human Resource Management, and Learning & People Development

This book provides rich resource on HR in the current changing context for both academics and practitioners. It fills in the gap between theory and application.

– Dr Lujia Feng, Programme Director MSc Human Resource Management and Development (Distance Learning), Lecturer in Human Resource Management, Global Development Institute, School of Environment, Education and Development, University of Manchester

Offering a nuanced depth of insight into the changing nature of strategic people management practices in contemporary hybrid organisational contexts, the text chapters provide well-rounded insights for both students and practitioners alike to critically think through. Newer fields of contemporary debates in the people profession including people analytics, employee well-being practices, employee experience, risk-based people management approach, sustainability in people management practice and aspects of managing EDI in a hybrid workspace are also concisely introduced.

– Dr Adetola Adekunle (Senior Lecturer in Human Resource Management), Course Leader MSc Strategic People Management & Course Leader MSc Strategic People Management with Extended Practice

Dr Maddox-Daines provides considered and thoughtful insight into contemporary issues arising around the management of people within a hybrid working environment. A key text for anyone studying Human Resource Management and one I would recommend to my students.

– Michelle Maunder (MD Temesis Limited)

This text effectively encapsulates the strategic purpose, benefits and complexities of agile and hybrid working for organisations across a range of sectors and industries. As well as providing an excellent guide, with informative practical examples, to people and business practitioners wishing to develop agile and hybrid working to benefit their organisations, it also provides invaluable in-depth discussion to aid those studying at undergraduate and postgraduate level.

– Tristan Callaghan, HR Tutor & Business and People Consultant

Managing People in the Hybrid Workplace

Managing People Effectively in the Hybrid Workplace is designed to ensure that both aspiring and experienced people professionals are equipped with in-depth knowledge of how workplace structures are being disrupted by new technology and working models. It explores analytics and capability to provide evidence-based insights that can shape employee experiences, support adaptation to changing business conditions, navigate risk, drive workplace performance, harness collaboration and open up new possibilities for HR and the organisation.

The book has been designed both as a text to support students studying HRM on university programmes and as a handbook for professionals wishing to update their knowledge in contemporary HRM. The book also supports the core and specialist knowledge and core behaviours in the CIPD Profession Map.

Kay Maddox-Daines has worked in higher education and professional development for over 20 years. Something of a 'pracademic', Kay balances her research and teaching with consultancy in order to keep abreast of rapid changes in the people profession. Kay is Visiting Fellow at the University of Suffolk, Fellow of the Chartered Institute of Personnel and Development (FCIPD), Fellow of the Higher Education Academy (FHEA), Fellow of the Staff and Education Association (FSEDA) and Registered Career Development Professional (RCDP) with the UK Career Development Institute.

Managing People in the Hybrid Workplace

Kay Maddox-Daines

Routledge
Taylor & Francis Group

LONDON AND NEW YORK

Designed cover image: metamorworks

First published 2023
by Routledge
4 Park Square, Milton Park, Abingdon, Oxon OX14 4RN

and by Routledge
605 Third Avenue, New York, NY 10158

Routledge is an imprint of the Taylor & Francis Group, an informa business

© 2023 Kay Maddox-Daines

British Library Cataloguing-in-Publication Data
A catalogue record for this book is available from the British Library

ISBN: 9781032380001 (hbk)
ISBN: 9781032379999 (pbk)
ISBN: 9781003342984 (ebk)

DOI: 10.4324/9781003342984

Typeset in Bembo
by Deanta Global Publishing Services, Chennai, India

Dedication

To Alastair, you are my rock.

Contents

Illustrations

FIGURES

TABLES

INTRODUCTION

The coronavirus pandemic led to a rapid shift in working from home for many people.

As the restrictions were lifted, some workers were reluctant to return to the office after becoming accustomed to the flexible benefits offered by home working. However, despite savings on commuting costs and improved work and life balance, some staff were feeling isolated and disconnected from the workplace as a result of the virtual environment. Limited opportunities for collaboration can have an impact on well-being resulting in lower levels of productivity, higher absenteeism and even higher employee turnover.

Organisations too have recognised the benefits of remote working including the potential for cost savings arising from a reduced requirement for large commercial space. However, they have also noted the costs associated with low engagement, and there are concerns relating to staff retention. Since the pandemic there has been a shift in the way workers evaluate work in relation to the rest of their life with a greater focus on personal well-being and life outside of work. The challenge for organisations, therefore, has been to retain the benefits of remote working on the one hand, whilst finding ways in which to promote connections to enable engagement on the other.

Hybrid working presents a solution to this dilemma of balance. Hybrid refers to a type of flexible working whereby the employee splits their time between their workplace and usually (but not necessarily) their home. Hybrid working is likely to take many forms, depending on the nature of the organisation, the needs of the role and the preferences of the individual. The hybrid working model provides both organisations and employees a number of benefits. For organisations, it helps to maintain company culture and identity. For example, as a remote worker changing roles, it may be difficult to get a grasp of the company culture in the new organisation if culture clues are missing between logging off on the Friday at the old

DOI: 10.4324/9781003342984-1

organisation and logging on to the new role on the following Monday. For employees, the hybrid model provides flexibility.

Maintaining an office space to support meaningful collaboration provides the opportunity for staff to develop closer connections and a sense of organisational identity along with some variation to the work environment. Offering a hybrid work environment helps to open up a much larger candidate pool. Hybrid working is also critical to diversity. It enables organisations to work across languages, time zones and countries, encouraging a wide range of experiences and skills. The hybrid working environment has the potential to remove obstacles for workplace participation for those with caring responsibilities, the disabled, the neurodiverse and those who cannot afford to commute at the start of their contract.

However, hybrid working also presents challenges for inclusion. For the model to work effectively, it is important that no matter when and where someone is working they still feel a sense of belonging through robust communication channels and regular meetings so that they are supported to be a productive and valued member of the team. If some sections of the workforce are invisible there is the worry that they might be forgotten, impacting progression opportunities. Managing staff effectively in a hybrid work environment is necessarily different from managing in an office. Forward-looking organisations are focusing less on where people work and more on how they work with a focus on outcomes and impact rather than activity. Managing in a hybrid work model demands different skills with leaders having to adjust their style so that they provide the right balance of autonomy and support to both teams and individuals. The new hybrid working environment is built on trust, fairness and inclusion.

With no template to follow, people professionals have tweaked policies and implemented initiatives in reaction to events. Every single aspect of the employee lifecycle is being challenged by the hybrid working model, from resourcing to induction, learning and development, reward and recognition, performance management, well-being, the employee experience and communication at every level. Hybrid working requires new ways of working, policies and procedures, many of which challenge traditional beliefs about work and high performance. The biggest challenge for HR professionals is how to create an equitable work environment for everyone.

Introduction

This is a journey and regular staff feedback will be invaluable in navigating the new normal.

The idea for this book was conceived during the revalidation of the MSc Strategic People Management that I wrote in 2022. I was looking for a text that would provide not just a contemporary look at the profession but one which would prepare learners for the next stage of people management. There are some excellent theoretical HR textbooks available but I was seeking something that was more practice based and that would provide a a holistic approach to the fast-changing nature of the profession. I couldn't find a suitable text so this book, therefore, fills that gap. I have aimed to use a number of case examples in each chapter to contextualise the discussion so that key points can be easily applied. At the end of each chapter is a summary of key points for ease of reference. There are also some self-test and reflection questions. The book can be read as a stand-alone text or used as a basis for structuring teaching and learning sessions. I plan to use the text as a basis for discussion with students so that we are able to gain both breadth and depth of insight into next practice.

You will note throughout the book that I have used the terms 'HR' and 'people professional' interchangeably. This has been for ease of writing and for the purposes of this text does not imply any difference in meaning.

One of the challenges of writing a book based on next practice is finding sources that are both robust and contemporary. Geopolitical and social changes are moving so quickly that it is taking time for books and journal articles to catch up. As a result, it has been necessary to draw on some of the grey literature, which includes reports, conference presentations and articles that may have been produced outside of traditional publishing and distribution channels. The advantage of this is that it has been possible to capture emerging themes from a global and diverse perspective. The disadvantage is that not all grey literature is subject to the scrutiny of peer review, and I have had to make a judgement on the value of the source used to provide context.

This book explores how the profession is changing, now requiring expertise in digitalisation, analytics and value-based decision-making. It covers all aspects of the employee journey from candidate attraction to employee exit and beyond. The book consists of 16 chapters and each is described briefly below.

Chapter 1 introduces the key stages of the employee lifecycle and discusses the framework that will be used throughout the book. Each stage of the lifecycle is explored, providing the reader with an introduction to the areas that will be developed in later chapters. A candidate case study is provided to support insights into the employee experience from the candidate's perspective.

Chapter 2 explores how strategic planning and sustainability and ethics can be reconciled. Ethical decision-making is introduced and the component parts of strategic planning explored. Strategic management tools are introduced together with case study examples to contextualise discussion. The importance and challenges of aligning HR strategy to organisation strategic goals are discussed with opportunities for reflection included.

Chapter 3 discusses the increasingly dynamic and highly unpredictable environment that we must now navigate. It explores the intricacies of organisation life with a focus on culture, change and organisation development and design. The chapter introduces a range of theories, models, frameworks and interventions to support the build of effective structures that drive performance. Detailed case examples are used throughout the chapter to explain how theory is applied.

Chapter 4 focuses on resourcing talent and the challenge and opportunity of planning and resourcing in a dynamic labour market. Key labour trends are explored with an examination of their significance for strategic planning. Each stage of the recruitment process is discussed in relation to contextual examples including candidate attraction and employer branding. Technological developments are explored together with metrics for evaluating success.

Chapter 5 highlights the importance of the onboarding stage of recruitment. It explores the similarities and differences between onboarding and induction and considers the challenges of both through the lens of a hybrid working model. The implications of poor practice in onboarding are discussed and how this can be avoided. Measurement is key, and the chapter discusses ways in which feedback can be collected and when.

Chapter 6 explores people development from the perspective of the individual, team and organisation within the context of a learning culture. The chapter highlights the importance of aligning learning and development activity with organisation strategic goals and what to include in a learning and development policy. The rationale for people development is explored along with the variety of activities that support learning. Digital learning is introduced and the possibilities examined. The importance of social collaboration learning activities in a hybrid world is discussed with examples.

Chapter 7 introduces reward and its constituent parts. The notion of total reward is discussed and the complexity of designing a reward strategy for a hybrid workforce explored. Reward at individual, team and organisation levels is considered through a variety of contextual examples. Fair, equitable and reasonable reward is considered in relation to the legal framework and pay gap reports. The future challenges and direction of reward are examined.

Chapter 8 introduces the employment relationship within a global economy facing considerable challenges. It assesses external market conditions and how they impact employment relations. The psychological contract is examined with the elements required for a positive contract considered. Trust is an overarching theme throughout this book as it is integral to effective hybrid working models. The psychological contract is a key element of this. Employment relations frames of references are explored through the framework of employee involvement, collectivism and employee voice.

Chapter 9 examines the benefits and challenges of emerging technologies and how to embrace these within the people profession. The chapter introduces AI and machine learning, automation and virtual reality and how each can be used in the employee journey. The concept of technology as an enabler is introduced, freeing the HR team to focus on more strategic and project-based work. The risks and challenges of AI are explored through case examples, and the role of regulation in protecting users is considered.

Chapter 10 introduces people analytics and descriptive, predictive and prescriptive analysis. It provides an insight into the opportunities analytics provides and the challenges for the people team. Terminology is explained and an examination of how to use people analytics through the employee lifecycle provided. Data analysis tools are introduced, and consideration of how to present data to different stakeholders is undertaken through dashboards and storytelling. Data privacy, transparency, security and ethics are discussed within the context of a case study.

Chapter 11 proposes that well-being works most effectively when it is built as an integral part of organisation culture. It considers the role of leaders and managers in promoting well-being and the role of the people professional in formulating and implementing well-being strategies. The chapter is built on the premise that if people are well, they are likely to perform effectively. With this in mind, the notion of performance is explored at both job and organisation level. Case study examples are included to highlight how organisations can create a culture of well-being that promotes high-performance working.

Chapter 12 explores how design thinking can be used to reconceptualise the employee experience in a hybrid working model. In order to implement an effective hybrid working strategy, it is necessary to revisit every policy and practice within the employee journey and to understand what changes are required to ensure an inclusive culture where everyone feels they belong. Evaluation of the employee experience is critical for progression, and a number of measures and feedback tools are examined.

Chapter 13 introduces contingency planning and crisis models as a way to identify the strategic vulnerabilities of an organisation. The rationale for business continuity is explained along with the types of risk to plan for. Business continuity is a strategic tool to support the management of resources in times of disruption. Consideration of the role of the people professional in planning, communicating and managing through the employee lifecycle framework is undertaken addressing key areas of risk.

Chapter 14 explores how to build an organisation that is inclusive and where everyone feels that they belong. This is a challenge for the hybrid workforce. The chapter explains the differences in terminology, introduces the Equality Act and suggests how to manage natural bias. Building a diversity and inclusion strategy, culture and values is explored through case examples, and the challenges of managing diversity and inclusion in a hybrid workforce are examined.

Chapter 15 explores climate change and the business case for sustainability. It explains the difference between corporate social responsibility (CSR) and environment, social and governance (ESG) and introduces the United Nations 17 Sustainable Development Goals (SDG). It discusses the role of people professionals and how taking a lead can support good work. There are a number of measures for monitoring and evaluating progress, and these will be considered in relation to the strategic context of the organisation and the role of HR.

Chapter 16 completes this book with a focus on international HRM strategy and the convergence and divergence approach to employment relations. Hybrid working models have enabled organisations to extend their recruitment activity, potentially on a global scale. This presents both opportunities and challenges and will certainly impact the decisions made in relation to international staffing in the future. Cultural diversity brings both innovation and flexibility, and training and awareness can promote harmony and understanding.

Introduction to the employee lifecycle

Chapter 1

INTRODUCTION

This chapter introduces the reader to the key stages in the employee lifecycle, including brand attraction, recruitment, onboarding, development, retention, offboarding and alumni. It links each of the stages to people processes and how they are used to support good practice in agile and hybrid workplaces. A candidate journey case study is included following the experience of an individual through each of the lifecycle stages in order to capture the employee perspective. The people practitioner role is introduced to highlight how effective people processes support each stage of the lifecycle together with examples. Situating the employee lifecycle within the hybrid working model is explored, emphasising the strategic positioning of work and noting that there is no single way to manage hybrid working in an organisation context.

THE EMPLOYEE LIFECYCLE FRAMEWORK

The employee lifecycle refers to the journey that every employee takes, from prior to joining an organisation until the day they leave and beyond. The employee lifecycle model was conceived from the customer journey mapping which explores the overall journey that customers experience in relation to company brands. Lemon and Verhoef (2016) conceive that the customer journey is a multidimensional construct which focuses on a

DOI: 10.4324/9781003342984-2

customer's cognitive, emotional, behavioural, sensorial and social responses to a firm's offerings during the customer's entire journey. Taking an employee view of the journey allows organisations to measure and assess the experience of staff during the stages of their employment. Journey mapping allows organisations to gather information that will help them better understand 'the frustrations and experiences of their customers' (Boag, 2015). It provides the HR team with the opportunity to determine the challenges employees are facing and eliminate, fix or help solve those challenges, with the goal of improving performance and engagement of employees (McKelvey and Frank, 2018).

There is no one model or employee life cycle theory as such. Indeed, as Kwon and Park (2019) found, although the current proliferation of employee engagement research has advanced theoretical understanding, there is still a scarcity of practical knowledge of how to assess, boost and sustain employee engagement in the workplace with employee engagement still in its initial stages of becoming a formal theory. Newell (2019) purports that the employee lifecycle might include the stages of attract, recruit, onboard, develop, retain and offboard. Qualtrics (2022) identifies seven stages in the employee lifecycle, including brand attraction, recruitment, onboarding, development, retention, exit and advocacy. Some organisations use a comprehensive cycle with smaller steps, while others combine steps and so create a framework with fewer steps.

In this chapter, we define employee lifecycle as the journey that every member of staff will undertake in their engagement with the organisation. This starts before they formally join the company, through employer and/ or customer branding and can be ongoing after the employee leaves the organisation. The stages that we will use include attraction, recruitment, onboarding, development, retention, offboarding and alumni.

ATTRACTION

The employee lifecycle is likely to commence as soon as a potential candidate hears about the organisation. This might be through a product or service they purchase from the organisation or through a job posting that they read. Arguably, industry leading organisations may find it easier than smaller local businesses to attract candidates. Candidate attraction refers to the approach that an employer uses to attract potential applicants to fill a vacancy. It is important to have a long-term strategy that makes the organisation attractive to the people that you are looking to recruit. The strategy will include a range of activities that align candidate attraction with workforce plans. Consideration needs to be given to the channels that the organisation will use to target potential candidates. It is important to remember that candidate attraction is a two-way process, and sufficient information should be made available about the organisation and the role to enable a candidate to self-select. Armstrong and Taylor (2020) report that the process of attracting candidates requires the organisation to develop an employer brand and employee value proposition. Employer branding is an important part of candidate attraction, enabling employers to market their value proposition to potential candidates. The employer brand is the image presented by an organisation as a good employer and 'a great place to work' (ibid.). The 'employee value proposition' describes what an organisation stands for, requires and offers as an employer (CIPD, 2021). For example, Recurly is a subscription and billing platform aimed at businesses that offer subscription-based products (Recurly, 2022). Their employee value proposition looks like this:

GROW YOUR CAREER

At Recurly, you are empowered to iterate and solve elegantly, helping our company thrive and our customers succeed. Equipping you with professional development and tuition reimbursement, we celebrate your accomplishments.

NURTURE YOUR INTERESTS

As your career grows, so does the circle of people you care about. Recurly offers office-location freedom, unlimited time off, generous parental leave and opportunities to make a difference through our community-building efforts.

DEEPEN YOUR RELATIONSHIPS

Intangible Recurly culture benefits – like the balance between delivering meaningful work and driving kids to school, Google Meet and track meets – are important. We're here for it.

Organisations regularly review their candidate attraction campaigns to target specific candidates. The case study below provides an example of how Goldman Sachs has updated its attraction strategy to emphasise ecology, technology and purpose.

CASE EXAMPLE: GOLDMAN SACHS

Goldman Sachs is a global investment banking, securities and investment management company with just over 40,000 staff. The company spent time researching potential candidates before launching its recruitment campaign aimed at attracting the next generation of bankers. It found that young professionals didn't want to work somewhere like Wall Street. The organisation was keen to showcase the firm as an employer of choice, and it was keen to attract talent by showing the culture of the company. Goldman Sachs launched a campaign in 2022 aimed at recruiting younger applicants. The aim was to promote the organisation's ecological and technological strengths in response to younger workers' desire to be working for a cause. Its career website promotes 'make things possible at Goldman Sachs'. The company promotes the potential of its people and teams and states that 'we're dedicated to providing programs and resources that support growth goals. In order to be the best place for talent to work, grow and thrive, we support our people and their families with world-class offerings'. The company highlights its commitment to diversity and inclusion, health, well-being and development in its statement:

> We believe who you are makes you better at what you do. We're committed to fostering and advancing diversity and inclusion in our own workplace and beyond by ensuring every individual within our firm has a number of opportunities to grow professionally and personally, from our training and development opportunities and firmwide networks to benefits, wellness and personal finance offerings and mindfulness programs.
>
> *(Goldman Sachs, 2022)*

RECRUITMENT

The recruiting stage is often the first direct contact that a prospective candidate will have with the organisation. This is the first time the candidate will learn about the organisation, its culture and the advertised role. The focus in this stage of the lifecycle is on designing the advert and deciding which channels to use to attract candidates. Compiling the advertisement is a key element of the process. It should not only detail the core attributes and skills set for the ideal candidate but also entice people to apply through a well-articulated employer brand. Advertising internally is an important element of the recruitment campaign in order to offer progression opportunities or horizontal moves for current staff seeking to extend their experience. This stage of the lifecycle involves the selection of candidates, which means choosing people who have the right qualifications to fill a current or future job opening. The selection process will likely feature the interview and perhaps tests might also be incorporated ranging from aptitude and personality tests to assessment centres. The organisation will be assessing whether the candidate is a good fit and the alignment of experience to the vacancy, whilst the candidate will be evaluating whether the company aligns to their needs and values.

ONBOARDING

Onboarding starts as soon as a candidate accepts a job offer and only ends when the new employee is fully integrated and performing in the organisation. Onboarding is focused on welcoming the new recruit to the organisation and this is an important element of the lifecycle process, impacting employee engagement, performance and retention. The process is likely to involve collaboration with the HR team, the line manager, the IT team and other departmental managers as relevant to the position. A key part of this process is promoting company culture, helping new staff to understand the organisation vision, mission and values. The aim is to help new staff to become part of the team as quickly as possible, getting to know colleagues, creating confidence and trust. The onboarding process should set expectations, introduce performance management measures, set goals and explain rewards. Many organisations have an onboarding process that is limited to a number of weeks or perhaps a month but to be effective and to ensure that new staff have sufficient time to get to know the organisation and to complete any required training the process is likely to take at least 90 days and sometimes up to a year. A buddy system provides new employees with a trusted advisor who can support them, share information and be a reference point for any questions.

The following case example provides a step-by-step approach to the candidate journey from the application to the onboarding stage of the employee lifecycle.

CASE EXAMPLE: RECKITT

Candidate journey mapping

Reckitt is a global organisation, founded in 1819, employing 40,000 people specialising in hygiene, health and nutrition brands, and its purpose is a cleaner, healthier world (Reckitt, 2022). The organisation is transparent in its candidate journey, and it outlines the process clearly on its website. This includes:

1. The process: the organisation is committed to keeping things transparent so it will keep you informed at every stage of the process. With your permission, it will even suggest other roles that you may be interested in as well as the one you have applied for.

2. Application: using your social profile (and any device that you choose) you will create an account. They outline that they are bias free and will only ask you for information that they can use.
3. Initial screening: this is where the organisation will look at your application, and if there is a good match between your application and what the organisation is seeking, a member of the team will call you on the phone. After that, the hiring manager will review your application and this might lead to an interview over Skype.
4. Face–to-face interviews: if everything has gone well, you will be invited to meet the hiring manager and a member of the HR team at one of the company offices. Depending on the role, there might be a second interview and some sort of presentation. You may also be asked to undertake some online testing.
5. The offer: if you are successful, you will receive a verbal offer soon after the interview. This will be accompanied by a written, online offer with e-signature capabilities.
6. Onboarding: you'll be sent all the information required to get you set up and ready for your first day including arranging access to systems. You'll feel part of the team before you have joined.

DEVELOPMENT

Opportunities for ongoing professional development should be offered for staff at every level of the organisation. This might involve internal or external learning, conferences, seminars, 'lunch and learn', webinars, mentoring, coaching, for example. Developmental opportunities occur at individual, team and organisation level. At an individual level, development needs analysis might be identified through a performance review process. For example, the employee and the manager might identify a need for a financial skills-based management training to support budget management responsibilities. At a team level, the head of department might consider that the team would benefit from training on a new HR system that is about to be implemented. At an organisation level, mandatory training might be required for all staff in areas of health and safety, compliance, equality and diversity in order to meet legal requirements and strategic priorities.

RETENTION

It is much less expensive to retain your current people than to recruit new staff. The most important stage of the retention process is ensuring that the right people are recruited at the beginning. The focus in this stage of the lifecycle is on engaging staff to optimise productivity and developing employees so that they are effectively equipped to contribute to business success. It is important to foster good relationships with the team and gain feedback from employees about their experience in the organisation through engagement surveys, focus groups and personal conversations. If they feel valued, accepted and included in the organisation, they will want to stay. Retention strategies should align to organisational values and be effectively communicated. Employees stay with organisations for many reasons which may include challenging work, rewards and recognition, work-life balance, career growth and development, career path progression routes and more.

OFFBOARDING

This stage occurs when an employee leaves the organisation. The main goal is to achieve a smooth transition and to ensure that the remaining time with the organisation is positive with a planned exit that might involve finishing projects, training others, providing information about the end of their contract and benefits. Wilton (2022, p.438) describes the exit interview where 'interviews are conducted with departing employees to discuss the reason for their departure and to better understand drivers of employee turnover and potential organisational problems'. People leave organisations for many reasons, for career progression, to retire, for self-employment or they might even be headhunted by a competitor. It is important to find out the reasons why an employee is leaving the organisation and ask them for honest feedback about their time with the company. The offboarding process provides an opportunity for the organisation to improve the overall employee experience. When a colleague leaves the company, team morale can be negatively impacted so it is important to communicate the action that will be taken to replace the team member and to confirm the value of the team to the organisation.

ALUMNI

Maintaining good relations with ex-employees is effective for the employer brand and can be an integral element of an organisation's attraction strategy. This does require a positive exit experience, however. The departing employee may promote or denounce the company depending on the leaving experience. Happy ex-employees can become brand advocates whilst unhappy ones may damage the employer brand, impacting the organisation's ability to recruit, disrupting team morale and may even leave reputational damage. Recognising and thanking staff who are leaving for their contributions and hard work is key. The organisation may wish to keep in touch through email and social media, potentially inviting ex-staff to corporate functions. This can be beneficial for candidate attraction where the departing employee may be able to recommend new hires via their network presenting a cost-effective and efficient way to secure new staff.

THE EMPLOYEE LIFECYCLE FROM THE CANDIDATE PERSPECTIVE

Working through the employee lifecycle from the perspective of the candidate can provide deeper insights into what is working and what potentially needs updating. The following perspective explores the experience of Jacob, a graduate in economics.

Jacob graduated with a degree in economics three years ago and found his first position as a junior financial analyst in Makeit Bank. Jacob has a strong interest in the digital economy and last year opened a bank account with Quontic Adaptive Digital Bank (Qunontic, 2022). One of the features that Jacob was really interested in was the fact that Quontic is now in the Metaverse's new digital location in Decentraland. Jacob has just seen an advert for a senior-level analyst at Quontic. He is looking for progression but is not keen on the traditional banking culture that he has experienced so far. Quontic looks different, it's a digital bank with a commitment to growth and empowerment. With 65 per cent women and 60 per cent from diverse backgrounds, the company culture is very different to that found in traditional banking. In addition to being able to fulfil his career aspirations, Jacob has also found that the company offers health, dental, vision and life insurance, financial wellness planning and coaching, counselling support services and resources and pet insurance in addition to a competitive salary. Jacob is eager to apply.

As an organisation that is keen to provide an excellent customer experience, Quontic applies the same to its prospective employees through the recruitment process. Jacob first had a call with a recruitment advisor within the organisation so that he could explain more about his work experience. He was then invited to attend an interview online with the hiring manager and the team leader. After this, Jacob was asked to attend a second interview with the vice president of the business division. The process in all took three weeks. The salary range was provided in the first call with the recruiter; however, Jacob was offered only the very lowest point in the range. Jacob's experience is in line with the reviews on Glassdoor which reveal that 90 per cent of candidates enjoy a positive interview experience with the bank.

Jacob has been impressed with the employee onboarding programme which started on day one of his new role. The fully remote workforce enjoy an immersive onboarding experience where they are able to learn about the company values and how these are adapted for work in the community. Jacob has been offered a mentor and has learned about opportunities in leadership development for aspiring and existing leaders. There are company events happening every week including water cooler informal chats, virtual meditation and yoga and opportunities to meet others through participative events and projects. Quontic is keen to receive feedback about Jacob's experience and he has been asked to review his first 7, 30 and 90 days within the organisation. Going forward, he will be asked twice a year for feedback about his experience in the company. As an organisation committed to hybrid working, staff are able to work in regional offices whenever they choose. All staff are encouraged to initiate, participate and cultivate change.

Jacob is happy at Quontic at the moment although he is aware that the salary scale is lower than what he would like to earn. He is planning to stay for about three years and then he will seek a leadership role in a bank which has cultivated a culture similar to Quontic. He will be able to stay in touch with colleagues as he feels appreciated, respected and valued. As such, he will recommend the bank to his network if the opportunity arises.

THE EMPLOYEE LIFECYCLE AND HYBRID WORKING

The focus of this book is how to manage effectively in a hybrid world. The employee lifecycle provides a framework for visualising the stages that the company and employees progress through during their relationship. There is no single way to manage hybrid working as this will be dependent upon the organisation context and may include several types of hybrid working even in one organisation (CIPD, 2022). Hybrid working impacts every aspect of the employee lifecycle, from recruitment activities to talent acquisition, to onboarding, learning and development, performance management, reward and recognition, inclusion and diversity. In order to be effective, organisations must first agree on their strategic position in relation to hybrid working. The strategic plan will set the context and action against each of the stages of the employee lifecycle. It will also need to explore how the risks of hybrid working can be managed. For example, although in many cases hybrid working supports inclusion and diversity through better work and life balance and a more tailored employee experience, there is also evidence that more people from underrepresented groups, including workers from the LGBTQ+ community and people with disabilities who choose to work from elsewhere may suffer from psychosocial risks such as exclusion, increased work demands and social isolation (Parker, 2022). Hybrid work creates the potential for inequality and may strengthen already established groups for those that are 'in' and 'out' in organisations. These out groups may miss out on promotions and pay awards (Hamouche, 2021).

The employee lifecycle will be used throughout this book as a framework for assessing systems, practices and processes throughout the employee journey.

SUMMARY POINTS

- The employee lifecycle is a model that organisations use to explain the stages that each employee will journey through during their time with the company and beyond.
- There is no one model as organisations will adapt the framework to suit their specific needs. Some models will be detailed with a large number of stages whilst others will summarise activities into fewer headings.
- In this book, the employee lifecycle is defined as the journey that every member of staff will undertake in their engagement with the organisation. The stages include Attraction, Recruitment, Onboarding, Development, Retention, Offboarding and Alumni.
- When designing their employee lifecycle, organisations should consider the journey from both the employee and employer perspective.
- Hybrid working impacts each stage of the employee lifecycle which will necessitate changes to organisational policies, systems and practices. Organisations will need to equip managers to lead effectively in a hybrid world.

SELF-TEST QUESTIONS/REVIEW QUESTIONS

- You have been asked by your senior team to explain what is meant by the employee lifecycle. What key points would you make?
- Assess how taking an employee perspective to the lifecycle journey can support the overall experience for staff.

A CASE EXAMPLE: GOLDMAN SACHS

Review the Goldman Sachs case example discussed in this chapter. Assess the focus of the employee attraction campaign. Explore the benefits and potential drawbacks of the campaign in relation to the target group of candidates.

REFLECTION

Consider a role that you have applied for and assess your experience as a candidate through the attraction and recruitment stages. What was positive? What might have been better?

References

Armstrong, M. and Taylor, S. (2020). *Armstrong's Handbook of Human Resource Management Practice*. 15th ed. London: Kogan Page.

Boag, P. (2015). All you need to know about customer journey mapping. Available at: https://www.smashingmagazine.com/2015/01/all-about-customer-journey-mapping/ (accessed 1 September 2022).

CIPD (2021). Employer brand. CIPD. Available at: https://www.cipd.co.uk/knowledge/fundamentals/people/recruitment/brand-factsheet#gref (accessed 1 October 2022).

CIPD (2022). Planning for hybrid working. CIPD. Available at https://www.cipd.co.uk/knowledge/fundamentals/relations/flexible-working/planning-hybrid-working#gref (accessed 22 September, 2022).

Goldmansachs (2022). Available at: https://www.goldmansachs.com/careers/ (accessed 20 October, 2022).

Hamouche, S. (2021). Human resource management and the COVID-19 crisis: Implications, challenges, opportunities, and future organizational directions. *Journal of Management & Organization*, pp.1–16.

Kwon, K. and Park, J. (2019). The life cycle of employee engagement theory in HRD research. *Advances in Developing Human Resources*, 21(3), pp.352–370.

Lemon, K. N. and Verhoef, P. C. (2016). Understanding customer experience throughout the customer journey. *Journal of Marketing*, 80(6), pp.69–96.

McKelvey, H. and Frank, J. L. (2018). Improving onboarding with employee experience journey mapping: A fresh take on a traditional UX technique, 1(9). Available at: https://quod.lib.umich.edu/w/weave/12535642.0001.903?view=text;rgn=main. (accessed 22 October 2022).

Newell, C. (2019). The employee lifecycle is about an experience. *Forbes*, 21 Oct. Available at: https://www.forbes.com/sites/forbeshumanresourcescouncil/2019/10/21/the-employee-life-cycle-is-about-an-experience/?sh=f24f181248c7 (accessed 13 October 2022).

Parker, S.K. (2022). The future of work: Emerging risks and opportunities for health and well-being. *Safety and Health at Work*, *13*, pp.S10–S10.

Qualtrics (2022). Available at: https://www.qualtrics.com/uk/experience-management/employee/employee-lifecycle-model/ (accessed 1 October 2022).

Quontic (2022). Available at: https://www.quontic.com/ (accessed 30/10/2022).

Reckitt (2022). Available at: https://www.reckitt.com/ (accessed 22/10/2022).

Recurly (2022). Available at: https://recurly.com/ (accessed 24/10/022).

Wilton, N. (2022). *An Introduction to Human Resource Management*. 4th ed. London: Sage.

Strategic planning and ethical decision-making

Chapter 2

INTRODUCTION

This chapter provides an in-depth exploration of the factors and complexities involved in strategic management and how the continuously evolving environment impacts the strategic formulation and implementation process, particularly in relation to ethical decision-making. A predominant theme throughout is the reconciliation of an organisation's overarching 'commercial' aims whilst embedding ethics and sustainability, employee well-being, equality, diversity and inclusion.

The chapter aims to promote strategic thinking so that readers are able to provide a critical review of strategic models, tools, theories and frameworks and determine how these can help provide informed evidence-based decision-making. The practical application of strategy will be explored in a range of organisational contexts. Readers will evaluate environmental trends and developments in public policy and their impact on organisational and people management strategies.

ETHICAL DECISION-MAKING

Decision-making is the action or process of thinking through possible options and selecting one. Elbanna et al. (2020) define decision-making as a dynamic and interactive process. Ethical decision-making is defined by Jones (1991, p. 367) as 'a decision that is both legal and morally acceptable to the larger community'. The law is rarely enough sufficient to regulate ethical decision-making as it is concerned only with the bare minimum in terms of human rights and safety. For example, the

DOI: 10.4324/9781003342984-3

minimum wage indicates the bare minimum your workers need to be compensated, however, this does not always equate to a living wage. There are a number of ethical frameworks that support decision-making. Lloyd and Aho (2020) note that moral relativism offers a local solution to making ethical decisions. Utilitarianism focuses on maximising the greatest good for the most number of people. The justice view emphasises the relationship between members of the organisation. Corporate social responsibility encourages consideration for all stakeholders affected by the decision-making of an organisation (see Chapter 15). In this chapter, we will focus on the CSR model and examples of how this is used in strategic planning.

CSR as an ethical framework takes into consideration all of the stakeholders that are impacted by a business decision including the shareholders, the employees, communities, creditors, suppliers, environment and government. Klein (2012) argues that every corporation has an overarching social purpose that goes beyond the operations of corporate social responsibility and when effectively integrated this can have a positive impact on the business and beyond. The underlying premise with CSR is that businesses need to do more than simply make money. They need to advance the agenda of the social good as well.

Developing a people management strategy provides a focus on longer-term issues so that internal resources can be matched to the future needs of the business. It provides a planned approach to organisation structure, culture and values across each element of the employee lifecycle. Strategy will be tailored to the specific needs of each business recognising that people are integral to sustainable value creation meaning that organisations should invest in and use employee knowledge, skills and abilities to create sustainable value for the organisation and its stakeholders (CIPD, 2021). One example of this is Danone, a world leader in four businesses: essential dairy and plant-based products, early life nutrition, medical nutrition and waters. The vision of the company states that the economic goals and social goals are interdependent. With 100,000 employees in 57 countries, the human resource management strategy is built around four key pillars: health and safety, inclusive diversity, employee training and development and social dialogue. The company is committed to strengthening its business model through its dual economic and social projects. They seek to balance their business and financial agenda, as well as create and share sustainable value for all (Danone, 2022).

Strategic planning is a critical aspect of organisational survival and growth. Armstrong and Taylor (2020) define strategy as the approach *selected* to achieve specified aims in the future. Note the word 'selected'. There may be many ways of achieving the aim and the approach taken will depend on organisational goals. Corporate strategy is about putting a plan in place for the longer term, perhaps three, five or even ten years or more. Taking a longer-term approach provides the organisation with the direction to move forward and drive growth in relation to organisational goals. Strategic people management planning provides the framework for developing and implementing HR strategies in relation to organisational plans, goals and priorities within the changing context in which the company operates. Essentially, strategic people management is about having a plan. Without a destination in mind, it is not possible to plan a route to get there. Strategies are useful for individuals as well as organisations of all sizes as they provide the basis for action planning.

Strategic management is best described as 'a process of strategy making, of forming, and if the firm survives, reforming its strategy over time' (Boxall and Purcell 2008:44). Truss et al. (2013:49) define strategic management as 'the process that enables organisations to turn strategic intent into action'. Managers who think strategically will be better placed to focus on longer-term planning and resource allocation. This will support alignment of activities to the organisation's strategic priorities.

A strategy usually consists of the organisation's vision and mission, an introduction to its values and its strategic objectives that will guide the company to meeting its strategy.

WHAT DOES A STRATEGY INCLUDE?

Strategic plan introduction

The introduction describes priority themes and commitments and how they will be delivered. It might also say how the plan has been developed, including a mention of the various parties that have contributed to the strategy.

The Chicago State University strategic plan (2020) begins with the following introduction:

> As the University works to reach higher levels in all aspects of teaching and learning, we recognise that our human capital are the key to propelling this exceptional academic institution and its constituents to levels of success.

THE VISION STATEMENT

A vision statement focuses on tomorrow and how an organisation wants to develop.

For example, Chicago State University (ibid.) will be recognised for innovations in teaching and research, community development and civic engagement. We will promote excellence, ethical leadership, entrepreneurship, and social and environmental justice. We will embrace, engage, educate, propel and elevate our students and community to transform lives locally and globally.

THE MISSION STATEMENT

A mission describes the purpose of the organisation – why it exists. The focus is on the here and now of what the organisation is doing.

For example, Chicago State University (ibid.) transforms students' lives through innovative teaching, research and community partnerships through excellence in ethical leadership, cultural enhancement, economic development and justice.

COMPANY VALUES

Company values provide a guide as to how the company should be run. They can set a company apart from its competitors. Essentially, an organisation's values define its brand and its reputation. Clear values not only form part of the unique identity of the organisation but they also influence decisions about what and how you do business.

For example, Chicago State University (ibid.) values include:

Personal and academic excellence
Personal, professional and academic integrity
Diversity, Equity, and inclusion
Leadership, service, philanthropy, social justice, and entrepreneurship
Creative and innovative thinking and learning
Pride in self, community, and the university
Lifelong learning.

STRATEGIC OBJECTIVES

Objectives provide the big picture. They are statements that indicate what is crucial for your organisational strategy. Objectives are the goals that the company is trying to achieve in a given period, most likely three to five years.

Let us compare the vision, mission and values of Chicago State University with Twitter.

Twitter presents 'our company' as the vision of the organisation (Twitter, 2022). Twitter is an open service that's home to a world of diverse people, perspectives, ideas and information.

Twitter explains its purpose (mission) as: 'we serve the public conversation'. It matters to us that people have a free and safe space to talk. That's why we're constantly improving our rules and processes, technology and tools. We're not perfect, that's why we listen to you, the people on Twitter. It's also why we work to be as transparent as possible.

Twitter is committed to the following principles (values):

Promoting health: freedom of speech is a fundamental human right – but freedom to have that speech amplified by Twitter is not. Our rules exist to promote healthy conversations.

Earning people's trust: Twitter is what's happening. To stay reliable and credible, we must always be earning your trust.

Making it straightforward: simple is good, but straightforward is better. Our product, our behaviour and our work habits should all be transparent and to the point.

Uniting profit and purpose: Twitter is a purpose-driven company that does good. Twitter ties philanthropy to its business objectives.

Being fast, free and fun: we should move fast, feel free to be ourselves, and have fun. That's Twitter.

Although the two examples included above are very different, they essentially include the same structure. The compilation of the strategic planning process is relatively straight forward but without effective management, the strategic objectives are unlikely to be delivered. That is why strategic management is so important. Strategic management is about the management of an organisation's resources to meet its goals and objectives. It involves the setting of objectives, analysing the competitive environment, analysing the internal environment, evaluating strategies and making sure that the management team delivers the strategies across the organisation. Farnham (2015) identified two key elements in strategic management: strategy formulation and strategy implementation. Firstly, strategy formulation is about developing a strategic plan based on organisational goals and market conditions. Secondly, strategy implementation involves planning and control systems which provide the means by which strategic objectives and policies are translated into specific, measurable, attainable goals and plans.

RESPONSIBLE STRATEGIC PLANNING

Responsible leadership is based on ethical, inclusive principles that can build trust with stakeholders. This requires a long-term commitment to company interest and success. Strategic planning through a sustainability lens requires organisations to embed commitment to environmental, social and governance (ESG) through their corporate purpose and communicate this in relation to the company's vision, mission and values. In strategic planning discussions a key question for organisations is what success looks like in terms of ESG. For example, exploring performance and productivity in relation to reducing environmental and resource footprints and aligning purpose, goals, objectives and activities to the UN Sustainable Development Goals (SDGs) will provide direction.

CASE STUDY: DANONE (DANONE, 2022)

We discussed the company's human resource management strategy above. Now let us explore in more detail its approach to responsible business through strategic planning.

Danone is a world–leading food and drink company built on three businesses: essential dairy and plant-based products, specialised nutrition and waters. It is committed to sustainable shared value creation. A new CEO was appointed in 2021 after a slowing growth, a flat market share, falling profitability resulting in 2,000 job cuts. *The Financial Times* commented that the former CEO was ousted because of his inability to interweave sustainability and profitability (FT, 2021). They argued that shareholders are supportive of the purpose-driven company but not at the cost of profits (ibid.), particularly when its competitors, Nestle and Unilever, were managing to produce higher returns whilst also pursuing progressive, purpose–led business. A revised strategy was devised with the following vision:

One Planet. One Health. These words reflect our vision that the health of people and the health of the planet are interconnected. It is a call to action for all consumers and everyone who has a stake in food to join the food revolution: a movement aimed at nurturing the adoption of healthier, more sustainable eating and drinking habits.

This vision is built on four strategic pillars: to restore Danone's competitiveness in core categories and geographies; expand in terms of segments, channels and geographies; seed future growth avenues; and manage portfolio. These pillars are supported by four key enablers: culture, capabilities, sustainability and cost competitiveness.

The people management strategic headlines highlight the organisation's commitment to 'entrust Danone's people to create new futures'. The company allows each of its employees to co-own the agenda and goals both at a global and local level. Since 2018 each of Danone's 100,000 employees is invited to actively engage and shape the future towards the 2030 goals. This is achieved through a digital platform with sharing and learning resources related to the company's vision and goals.

The company is committed to realising its goals through an innovative governance framework, which seeks to foster engagement and action inside and outside the company. The framework provides the 100,000 employees with the power to co-own the company agenda. It includes collaboration with partners such as the United Nations Institute for Training and Research (UNITAR). All Danone employees are provided with the opportunity to learn and build on the issues, challenges and opportunities that come with the goals. Employees are also provided with the opportunity to voice their point of view on both company agenda and the definition of the 2030 goals roadmaps, at local and global levels. Through its 'one person, one share', each employee receives one Danone share to deepen the ownership mindset in combination with an annual dividend-based incentive scheme. In addition, staff are provided with the opportunity to invest in the company at a discounted price and to increase a sense of ownership.

A key dilemma for strategic management is the extent to which managers should concentrate their attention on the external market position and the extent to which they should focus on their internal capabilities. Indeed, for Danone, it was necessary to refocus its priorities in relation to its financial objectives. Balancing environmental, social and governance issues is a challenge. Kim and Mauborgne (2009) argue that environmental factors are what matters most in driving strategy and therefore strategy development should be about exploring attractive opportunities in the marketplace. Martin (2010) contends that it is the internal approach that matters most and strategic development should be driven by an organisation's internal strategic capabilities.

Effective strategic planning involves taking both an external and internal approach, and there are various models of strategic planning that can be used, for example, the PESTLE analysis, SWOT analysis and Porter's Five Forces. Strategic management consists of finding answers to the following questions:

- Where are we?
- Where do we want to get to?
- How can we get there?
- What do we have to do to get there?

Before organisations are able to develop their strategy, they need to assess both the external and internal marketplace. Using models such as PESTLE, SWOT and Porter's Five Forces can support organisations in their decision-making.

PESTLE

PESTLE stands for Political, Economic, Social, Technological, Legal and Environmental. It provides the basis from which organisations are able to analyse their position at a macro level and can be helpful for developing strategy in relation to products and services and different geographies. A PESTLE analysis informs decision-making and can help organisations to assess opportunities as well as minimise threats (CIPD, 2021). The most important aspect of the PESTLE analysis is analysing the information that is collected. As a manual process this can be time consuming and to be undertaken effectively requires sufficiently skilled staff to undertake the review (Peterdy, 2022). To be valuable the process needs to be repeated on a regular basis and should be based on sufficient data to provide evidenced–based decisions. Indeed, one of the key disadvantages of this model is that although substantial research might have been collected to inform the analysis, the data might quickly become outdated due to the fast rate of change (Johnson et al., 2014).

QUESTIONS TO SUPPORT THE PESTLE ANALYSIS

Political: what is happening at national and international levels that may impact the business? How will a change in government policy affect the organisation? For example, changes in tax?

Economic: how is the economic environment impacting the business? Consider high inflation, interest rates and the impact on consumer disposable income.

Social: how are social and demographic changes likely to impact the business? Consider work-life balance, consumer buying habits, career attitudes and lifestyle.

Technological: how will artificial intelligence, robotics and disruptive technologies such as the Metaverse impact the business? Consider cybercrime, data storage and confidentiality, employee expertise and further investment requirements.

Legal: consider employment law and health and safety regulations in the countries where the organisation operates.

Environmental: explore ethical sourcing, corporate social responsibility, supply change management and environmental restrictions.

An example of a PESTLE analysis for Nike, an American multinational corporation that designs, develops and manufactures footwear, apparel and accessories is included below. The company was founded by Bill Bowerman and Philip H. Knight in the 1960s originally under the name of Blue Ribbon Sports with the Nike shoe brand launched in 1978. It is an American sportswear company headquartered in Oregon. By the early 21st century, Nike had retail outlets and distributors in more than 170 countries (Nazario and Roach, 2015).

A SWOT analysis is a planning tool to understand key factors, strengths, weaknesses, opportunities and threats to support the strategic planning process. The model might be written as a TOWS to emphasise the opportunities and threats as a starting point for analysis or a WOTS up analysis (CIPD, 2021). The technique is credited to Albert Humphrey, who led a research project at Stanford University in the 1960s and 1970s that explored long-range planning processes in a range of leading organisations. A SWOT analysis can support strategic planning, prompt group discussion about strategic issues and help management uncover opportunities. The framework is simple and is useful for anticipating business threats and for matching the organisation's goals to the environment in which it operates. As with the PESTLE analysis, undertaking a SWOT analysis is time consuming and requires access to quality data. There is a tendency to oversimplify the situation, to focus too much on the current environment and historic customers and competitors and is prone to bias (Gurel, 2017). SWOT is a static instrument to use, a one moment in time review of the organisation's position in a world of change and there is no guarantee that an organisation's strengths and capabilities will lead to competitive advantage.

Strategic planning & ethical decision-making

Table 2.1 PESTLE Analysis for Nike

Political	Geopolitical volatility, particularly in US and China relations, and the potential impact on supply chains impact the exports of finished goods and the import of raw materials. The Russia–Ukraine war has meant that Nike cannot currently guarantee delivery of goods to customers in Russia. As a result, merchandise purchases on nike.com and the Nike app are temporarily unavailable in this region. Nike's move is the latest in the series of sanctions imposed by US companies condemning Russian President Vladimir Putin's invasion of Ukraine (Nike, 2022). Other political factors might include trade barriers.
Economic	The US sporting goods industry has witnessed a growth of 5.9 per cent (IBISWorld – Industry Market Research, Reports, and Statistics, 2022). Inflation is higher than predicted worldwide especially in the United States and major European economies at 6.6 per cent in advanced economies and 9.5 per cent in emerging economies. This will impact household purchasing power (IMF, 2022).
Social	There is an increasing preference for e-commerce channels as online shoppers are anticipated to increase to 300 million by the end of 2023. Customers are expecting footwear and apparel to focus on sustainability and the planet using recycled materials. Millennials and Generation Z place great value on popular global brands, and there is a positive trend towards sports and apparel.
Technological	Technologies in the sporting goods industry include wearable technology, influencer marketing, digital marketing including SEO strategies, artificial intelligence, augmented reality and so on. In the apparel and footwear industry, the latest technologies include traceability in the supply chain, buy now pay later mechanisms, augmented reality in e-commerce, novel fabrics, data analytics, lean manufacturing, clean and alternative sources of energy and so on. Technologies will drive key players to invest in order to retain and attract new customers.
Legal	The organisation must comply with anti-competitive activities, employment and labour laws, workplace safety regulations, minimum wage regulations, various consumer protection laws and product safety norms. In addition, Nike must carefully focus on its supply chains in emerging countries to avoid child labour, slavery and labour exploitation in countries like India, China, Vietnam and so on which are becoming manufacturing hubs for the industry.

(Continued)

Table 2.1 Continued

Environment	Greenhouse gas emissions, wastage of water, water pollution and packaging issues are widespread in the industry. The world is now moving towards sustainability with the view of creating carbon-neutral industries, cleaner alternatives of energy, sustainable apparel, accessories and sporting goods. Furthermore, the United Nations has laid down a framework of 17 Sustainable Development Goals that the global community needs to meet by 2030. Among these 17 goals, the goals pertaining to climate action, responsible production, clean energy and protection of ecosystems directly concern most industries.
	Most governments are now bringing stricter environmental laws for the industry which are also aligned with the commitments under the Paris Agreement and COP26. In 2021, the United States rejoined the Paris Agreement after withdrawing from it under the Trump Administration. In the United States, the Environmental Protection Agency lays down various environmental regulations that the industry needs to follow. The Clean Air Act, Clean Water Act, Toxic Substances Control Act are some of the major environmental laws in the United States under EPA that the industry needs to follow (EPA, 2022). Furthermore, even the leading companies in the industry are proactively developing sustainable products and packaging alternatives to acquire new customers who are ready to pay premium prices for sustainable products.

Taking Nike again as a case example, let us examine the company in relation to the SWOT model.

PORTER'S FIVE FORCES FRAMEWORK

Michael Porter identified five key factors that significantly impact the profitability of an organisation. These are competitive rivalry, bargaining power of suppliers, bargaining power of buyers, threat of new entrants and the threat of substitutes. Organisations can create, modify and update their strategy based on these five competitive forces. The framework provides a simple but powerful model which is easy to use (Johnson et al, 2014).

The framework provides a structure for analysing the external marketplace with competitive rivalry as the central focus and it aligns helpfully to PESTLE. It has been criticised for being too simplistic (Grundy 2006) and its static approach, providing a snapshot of the wider

Table 2.2 NIKE SWOT Analysis

Strengths	Weaknesses
Nike is globally recognised for being the number one sportswear brand in the world. It is a global brand. Nike has a strong brand reputation and is known for its high-quality products. Revenue grew 19 per cent in 2021. The company was ranked 83rd in the Forbes list of 500 companies in 2022. Nike factories are outsourced resulting in a lean organisation.	Nike has a limited network of company-owned retail outlets meaning that it relies on other retailers to sell its goods. The company has limited diversification of production locations and facilities that are mainly located in Asia meaning that the business is subject to the economic and socio-political trends in the region. Nike was reported to have used child labour in Pakistan and Cambodia to produce soccer balls and this impacted brand image, consumer perception and investor confidence.

Opportunities	Threats
The strength of the Nike brand provides the opportunity to move into fashion apparel. The company might consider establishing additional company-owned retail outlets to increase more customers. The company might focus on improving customer perception and stakeholder relations through a focus on labour policy and employment practices. This includes negotiating further control in the manufacturing process.	Market competition is very strong and there is a growing threat of imitation products. Rapid technological investment and development from competitors may impact the effectiveness of the current technological assets. The textile industry in general impacts the environment and the organisation must address sustainability issues or suffer from adverse public feedback.

environment at one point in the past (Beattie, 2019) and prone to blind spots. It has also been accused of being too abstract and analytical to be used by practising managers (Grundy 2006). Nonetheless, let us explore an analysis of Porter's Five Forces in relation to Nike.

PORTER'S FIVE FORCES MODEL

Porter's Five Forces analysis of Nike

Competitive rivalry: the company has multiple international rivals including Adidas, Reebok, Puma. Nike holds 18.3 per cent of the market share for apparel in the United States and 21.1 per cent for sports footwear (Tighe, 2022). Intense rivalry will impact the long-term profitability of the organisation.

Bargaining power of suppliers: due to its size and the strength of its international brand, suppliers are keen to work with Nike. Suppliers hold low bargaining powers as Nike as the client holds the dominant position. Innovating new products will likely induce customer appetite for the latest product. By building efficient supply chains with multiple suppliers, Nike will continue to hold control of the bargaining power with suppliers.

Bargaining power of buyers: Nike has a strong brand name and loyal customers with a limited choice of companies offering high-end sportswear in the sector which provides only moderate bargaining power for buyers.

Threat of new entrants: it is relatively easy to enter the industry on a smaller local level but difficult to compete with Nike due to its size. New entrants are likely to have a different target market in mind. Over time any new entrant may pose a threat to Nike.

Threat of substitutes: the threat of a substitute product is only high if it offers something different from what is on offer in the sector. Brands that offer new innovation or lower pricing strategy and that can offer a new value proposition to customers will present the biggest threat to Nike.

STRATEGIC PEOPLE MANAGEMENT

Before people professionals can develop an appropriate people management strategy for the business they necessarily need to understand the business strategy and then how the HR function can support the organisation in achieving its objectives. This will require consideration of how the people management team can contribute to the development of a high-performance culture and ensure that the organisation has the talented, skilled and engaged people it needs.

The development of an HR strategy for Nike will depend on the decisions made in relation to the challenges and opportunities identified in the marketplace. If the company decides to expand through its own retail outlets the HR team will need to consider how this will be resourced. HR need to create a positive employment relationship between management and employees and a climate of mutual trust and encourage the application of an ethical approach to people management. Ethical practice is a core behaviour in the CIPD HR Profession Map (CIPD, 2021). It requires HR professionals to consider different ethical perspectives in decision-making, challenge others on their decision-making, be transparent and role model professional values (ibid.). As is evident in the strategic models discussed above, environmental sustainability concerns and climate change need to feature strongly in strategic planning to effect change and mitigate risk. People professionals are uniquely placed to support the organisation to deliver on these aims.

HR strategy is an integral part of business strategy and HR policies are designed to support the achievement of wider organisational objectives (Kew and Stredwick, 2016). Morris and Snell (2009) identify that the focus of HR strategy today is based on value creation where learning and innovation are key to business survival and human capital and social capital relationships are prioritised. Previously, HR strategy tended to focus on efficient behaviours, emphasising routine and output-based incentives.

THE CHALLENGE OF ALIGNING HR STRATEGY TO ORGANISATIONAL STRATEGY

Developing an HR strategy is not easy due to the often evolutionary and incremental way in which strategies develop in many organisations. It is difficult to ensure that business and HR strategies are aligned when the organisational strategy is changing rapidly in response to the internal and external context (for example in response to the Coronavirus pandemic). Another challenge is how to measure the impact of HR policy on organisation performance. Increasingly, HR teams are recognising the value of data, and metrics typically define the measures for quantifying areas such as resourcing and skills acquisition, engagement and retention.

There is no absolute agreement on what constitutes an 'ideal' HR strategy or what works in every circumstance. Leatherbarrow and Fletcher (2016) identify three key perspectives to strategy formulation.

THE BEST PRACTICE MODEL

This model argues that some HR practices are just much better than others and all organisations should adopt these best practices to ensure that they maximise their overall performance and gain competitive advantage. This perspective is sometimes discussed in terms of 'high-performance work systems', high-commitment HR or high-involvement HR and depicted through 'bundles' of HR practices that are considered to help achieve competitive advantage. HR policies incorporated within this model include selection processes that emphasise attitudes and skills, open and participative appraisals, learning and development for core employees and reward systems aligned to both individual and group performance-related pay. Key HR policies in the effective management of people might include hiring selectively, self-managed teams/teamworking, high compensation linked to organisational performance and extensive training.

THE BEST-FIT MODEL

In this perspective, HR practice must align with other aspects of the organisation, most importantly the organisation's strategy. This suggests that how HR practices impact organisational performance depends on their 'fit' or alignment with the firm's internal and external environment, its product markets, size and structure. Organisations should focus on designing HR systems that develop employee skills, knowledge and motivation so that employees' behaviour is aligned to the needs of the business. HR strategy choice will vary according to whether the organisation is operating in a start-up, growth, maturity or decline stage. For example, when considering the recruitment and selection of staff, the focus will be to attract the best talent at the start-up stage. In the growth stage, the focus will be to recruit adequate numbers and manage the recruitment pipeline so that the right person is in the right place at the right time. At the maturity stage, the focus will be encouraging turnover to minimise layouts and to encourage mobility. At the decline stage it will be necessary to plan and implement workforce reduction.

THE RESOURCED-BASED VIEW OF THE FIRM

This inside-out approach starts by considering the organisation's internal resources to more fully understand how organisational performance can be maximised. In this model, the workforce may have skills that are rare and not easily imitated or duplicated. The corporate strategy might be designed around its workforce, for example in research and development where scientific and technological development shape the future of the industry rather than responding to developments. From an HR perspective, the focus in this approach will be on developing employee behaviours, skills, knowledge, attitudes and competencies to promote sustained competitive advantage for the business.

Although helpful from an academic perspective, these models are unlikely to form the basis of HR strategic planning on a practical level. In reality, it is helpful to be aware of them, and HR will likely take a mix of all three strategies as they both plan for organisational goals and respond to environmental challenges.

Summary points

- Ethical decision-making is one that is acceptable to the wider community, going beyond minimum legal compliance.
- Strategy is the approach selected to achieve the aims of the organisation. It will include a focus on vision, mission, values and strategic objectives.
- Responsible leadership is based on ethical principles that build trust with stakeholders. This generally requires a change in mindset from short-term planning to longer-term thinking.
- Effective strategic planning involves taking both an external and internal approach and there are various models of strategic planning that can be used, for example, the PESTLE analysis, SWOT analysis and Porter's Five Forces.
- HR strategy is an integral part of business strategy and HR policies are designed to support the achievement of wider organisational objectives.

SELF-TEST QUESTIONS/REVIEW QUESTIONS

- To what extent is it ever possible to balance the needs of all stakeholders in a purpose-driven organisation that needs to make a profit for its shareholders?
- How useful are strategic planning models in supporting the formulation of an organisation's strategic plan?

STRATEGIC PLANNING IN PRACTICE

A case example: Danone

Review the Danone case study discussed in this chapter. To what extent do you consider that it is ever possible to balance the goals of sustainability and profit? How will the launch of the company's revised strategic plan support the goals of the organisation. How does the company's HR strategy support the delivery of the organisational strategy?

REFLECTION

A SWOT analysis can be very helpful as an organisational strategic tool but equally, it can be used to support our own strategic positioning.

Undertake a personal SWOT analysis to help you identify your talents as well as your developmental areas.

References

Armstrong, M. and Taylor, S. (2020). *Armstrong's Handbook of Human Resource Management Practice*. 15th ed. London: Kogan Page.

Beattie, A. (2019). The pitfalls of Porter's 5 forces. *Investopedia*. Available at: https://www.investopedia.com/articles/investing/103116/pitfalls-porters-5-forces.asp (Accessed 3 October, 2022).

Boxall, P. and Purcell, J. (2008). *Strategy and Human Resource Management*. 2nd ed. Basingstoke: Palgrave Macmillan.

Chicago State University (2020). Strategic plan 2020. [pdf] Available at: https://www.csu.edu/strategicplanningresources/documents/Strategic_Plan.pdf (accessed 22 September, 2022).

CIPD (2021a). Explore the profession map. Available at: https://peopleprofession.cipd.org/profession-map#gref (accessed 3 October, 2022).

CIPD (2021b). PESTLE analysis. Available at: https://www.cipd.co.uk/knowledge/strategy/organisational-development/pestle-analysis-factsheet#gref (accessed 2 September, 2021).

CIPD (2021c). SWOT analysis. CIPD. 7 Dec. Available at: https://www.cipd.co.uk/knowledge/strategy/organisational-development/swot-analysis-factsheet#gref (accessed 3 October, 2022).

Danone (2022). Available at: https://www.danone.co.uk/ (accessed 30 October, 2022).

Elbanna, S., Thanos. I. C. and Child, J. (2020). Strategic decision making process and outcomes. Available at: https://www.researchgate.net/project/Strategic-decision-making-process-and-outcomes (accessed 13 October, 2022).

EPA (2022). Laws and regulations. Available at: https://www.epa.gov/laws-regulations (accessed 4 October, 2022).

Farnham, D. (2015). *Human Resource Management in Context: Insights, Strategy and Solutions*. 4th ed. London: CIPD.

Financial Times (2021). Danone: A case study in the pitfalls of purpose. 18 March. Available at: https://www.ft.com/content/668d9544-28db-4ad7-9870-1f6671623ac5 (accessed 29 October 2022).

Grundy, T. (2006). Rethinking and reinventing Michael Porter's five forces model. *Strategic change*, 15(5), pp.213–229.

Gürel, Emet (2017). SWOT analysis: A theoretical review. *Journal of International Social Research*, 10, pp.994–1006. 10.17719/jisr.2017.1832.

IBIS World (2022). Available at: https://www.ibisworld.com/ (accessed 23 October 2022).

IMF (2022). Available at: https://www.imf.org (accessed 1 September 2022).

Johnson, G., Whittington, R., Scholes, K., Angwin, D. and Regner, P. (2014). *Exploring Corporate Strategy*. Harlow: Pearson.

Jones, T. M. (1991). Ethical decision making by individuals in organizations: An issue-contingent model. *Academy of Management Review*, 16(2), pp.366–395.

Kew, J. and Stredwick, J. (2016). *Human Resource Management in a Business Context*. 3rd ed. London: CIPD.

Kim, W. and Mauborgne, Renee (2009). How strategy shapes structure. *Harvard Business Review*, 87, 1–14.

Klein, P. (2012). Defining the social purpose of business. *Forbes*. Available at: https://www.forbes.com/sites/csr/2012/05/14/defining-the-social-purpose-of-business/?sh=7a4339b1cacd (accessed 30 August 2022).

Leatherbarrow, C. and Fletcher, J. (2016). *Introduction to Human Resource Management: A Guide to HR in Practice*. 3rd ed. London: CIPD.

Lloyd, Robert and Aho, Wayne (2020). The four functions of management: An essential guide to management principles. *Management Open Educational Resources*. Available at: https://scholars.fhsu.edu/management_oer/1 (accessed 3 July 2022).

Martin, R. (2010). Five questions to build a strategy. *Harvard Business Review, 88*(5). Available at: https://hbr.org/2010/05/the-five-questions-of-strategy (accessed 3 September, 2022).

Morris, S. and Snell, S. (2009). The evolution of HR strategy: Adaptations in increasing global complexity. in: A. Wilkinson, N. Bacon, T. Redman and S. Snell eds. *The Sage Handbook of Human Resource Management*. London: SAGE. Ch. 6. pp.84–99.

Nazario, M. and Roach, D (2015). Nike's incredible road to becoming the world's dominant sneaker retailer. 5th October. Available at: https://www.businessinsider.in/nikes-incredible-road-to-becoming-the-worlds-dominant-sneaker-retailer/articleshow/49220193.cms (accessed 30 October 2022).

Peterdy, K. (2022). What is a Pestel analysis? 27 October. Available at: https://corporatefinanceinstitute.com/resources/management/pestel-analysis/ (accessed 22 October, 2022).

Tighe, D. (2022). Sportwear marketshare in the United States. 27 July. Available at: https://www.statista.com/statistics/896595/sports-apparel-market-share-by-company-us/

Truss, C., Alfes, K., Delbridge, R., Shantz, A. and Soane, E. eds. (2013). *Employee Engagement in Theory and Practice*. London: Routledge.

Twitter (2022). Available at: https://about.twitter.com/en (accessed 26 September 2022).

Organisation development, culture and change

Chapter 3

INTRODUCTION

Organisation development is typically enacted in organisations through formal and planned change systems that are aligned to the strategic priorities of the institution. The coronavirus pandemic required a very different approach through a sudden and unplanned change that required adaptation at speed. This chapter introduces readers to organisation development and design, culture and change within the context of a hybrid workplace. It discusses the opportunities and challenges for organisation design and culture and discusses the role of organisation development in supporting change. A case example is used to analyse the culture and to demonstrate the application of organisation development models. The chapter explores the future of the workplace through the reimagining of workspace which is capable of connecting employees through adapting structures.

A CHANGING WORLD

Over the last two decades, advances in digital technology have led to the emergence of a new work paradigm and the fundamental transformation of many traditional job roles (Orlikowski and Scott 2016). Prior to the

DOI: 10.4324/9781003342984-4

coronavirus pandemic, most businesses favoured the office as a place where work was undertaken. The pandemic has had a huge impact on institutions across the globe and, despite in many cases governments removing all guidance to work from home where possible, there is an indication that the pandemic has prompted a lasting shift to more remote working for many. In fact, Taylor et al. (2021) research into the impact of hybrid working for different worker groups conducted by the Work Foundation and Chartered Management Institute found that 9 in 10 workers do not wish to return to pre-Covid working patterns. Indeed, Gratton (2021) found that flexible work arrangements had been on the agenda at Fujitsu for some years but managers in the Japan offices favoured the long office hours (as indeed did their staff with 74 per cent reporting that the office was the best place to work in the internal survey undertaken shortly prior to the pandemic). By the middle of March (2020), the majority (80,000) of Fujitsu's Japan-based employees were working from home. By May of the same year in a follow-up internal survey, only 15 per cent of Fujitsu employees considered the office to be the best place to work with 30 per cent stating that their homes were the best place and the remaining 55 per cent favouring a mix of home and office, a hybrid model.

Marston et al. (2021) define hybrid as a world that embraces the flexibility that remote working and virtual interaction can offer, with the recognition that people desire both public and private spaces to meet face to face, to deepen relationships and socialise with friends and relatives. Fayard et al. (2021) argue that post-pandemic the office will become a focus for productive collaboration. They contend that people still need in-person touchpoints that provide opportunities to clarify and align expectations and to build trust. Kumar and Das (2022) found in their research that in a hybrid model, individuals have more opportunities to improve their quality of life because of increased flexibility and more sustainable workloads including better meals, more time with family and the ability to take breaks, exercise more and recharge through proper rest. Managers have found that flexible working conditions are possible without necessarily affecting workers' productivity or increasing costs (Grzegorczyk, et al. 2021).

Nevertheless, hybrid working is not without its limitations and although more flexible working conditions are desired by workers it should not put remote workers at a disadvantage or negatively affect their well-being (ibid.). Ipsen et al. (2021) found that the main disadvantages of working from home included home office constraints, work uncertainties and inadequate tools. Working remotely for a sustained period can weaken social ties and lead to loneliness, isolation and disengagement. Another challenge is making time for regular feedback. Sometimes managers struggle to find the balance between caring and control, with either too many or not enough meetings scheduled. Managing a back-to-back online meeting culture and the distractions arising from working at home can also impact on well-being.

One of the main challenges for employers today is encouraging employees back to the office. One of the arguments from employees is that office environments with their open-plan and flexible offices and non-assigned work stations are often not conducive to uninterrupted work. Offices of the future need to explore a space that encourages the building of relationships and creative forms of collaboration and this may mean redesigning both physical and digital workspaces to fit the needs of employees in the hybrid working world. Strengthening opportunities for shared purpose are integral to the culture of the organisation. This necessitates some thought in relation to developing the organisation, managing culture and implementing change.

ORGANISATION DEVELOPMENT AND DESIGN

Beardwell and Thompson (2017) purport that organisation development today is typically enacted in organisations through formal, planned change efforts (which can be related to strategic planning, organisational redesign or leadership development) and this is led by both internal or external consultants with behaviour change and/or performance improvement as the primary goal. Cummings and Worley (2015) highlight the link to performance improvement and organisational effectiveness in their definition of organisation development as a system-wide application and transfer of behavioural science knowledge to the planned development, improvement and reinforcement of the strategies, structures and processes that lead to organisation effectiveness. These definitions support Burke and Bradford (2005) earlier definition where they suggest that for a process to be called organisation development firstly it must focus on or result in the change of some aspect of the organisational system, secondly there must be learning or the transfer of knowledge or skills to the organisation and thirdly there must be evidence of improvement in or an intention to improve the effectiveness of the organisation. Essentially, organisation development should be focused on value creation so that a measured improvement is evident. This is summarised effectively by the CIPD (2022) as a planned and systematic approach to enabling sustained organisational performance through the involvement of its people. As discussed in the last chapter, all activity should align to the organisation's strategy, goals and core purpose in order to maximise value for the organisation.

The relationship between organisation design and organisation development is often confused with the terms used interchangeably. For example, Armstrong and Taylor (2020) include organisation design as an activity or intervention that is included under the umbrella of organisation development. The CIPD (2020) describes organisation design as the holistic review of everything from systems, structures, people practices, rewards, performance measures, policies, processes, culture and the wider environment. It argues that people professionals are gatekeepers of the organisation's people data with a system-wide view that informs the way to organise the work and people in a company in order to best achieve its purpose (its goals, aims or strategy). Cumming and Worley (2015) identify organisation design as a strategic change intervention which addresses the architecture of the organisation including the structure, work design, human resources practices and management processes. Organisation design aligns these components with the organisational strategy. In this chapter, we identify the interrelationship between organisation design and development in that they are interweaving and complementary.

Organisation development and design is included as specialist knowledge in the CIPD HR profession map (2021). It focuses on the following characteristics:

Organisation design: developing operating models, structures, frameworks, systems and metrics.

Organisation development: using behavioural science to design and deliver change, focusing on culture, values, capability, behaviours, relationships and ways of working.

Designing organisation models and systems and developing behaviour and culture to meet organisational strategic goals and performance targets requires practices that deliver sustainable strategies and workforces that are able to respond effectively in a VUCA world. The term VUCA (which stands for volatility, uncertainty, complexity and ambiguity) is a common phrase used in the corporate world and was initially developed in the US Army).

ORGANISATIONAL DEVELOPMENT INTERVENTIONS AND ACTIVITIES

Organisation development is usually described as an 'intervention' where skilled practitioners acting as change agents apply established techniques in a process that responds to identified issues, problems and challenges (Beardwell and Thompson, 2017). There are a number of models to achieve performance improvement that are included under the organisation development heading. These can be helpfully framed according to individual, team and organisation needs. At an individual level, such activities might include coaching, mentoring, training, critical reflection, 360-degree feedback, action learning and leadership development. At a team level, interventions might include cross-team development, equality, diversity and inclusion and sustainability projects for example. At an organisation level, surveys, culture change projects, succession planning and scenario planning might be used.

Some years ago, I worked in organisational development at BAE SYSTEMS. During my time there, I led on two organisational development initiatives with the support of the senior team. The first was called 2020 with the objective of meeting 20 per cent return on capital employed and the second, Target 10 which was an organisation commitment to reduce waste by 10 per cent in every operation across the organisation. 2020 was a cross departmental initiative providing staff with the opportunity to work with new colleagues, to explore new ideas and to present back at large all staff meetings and conferences. The second was departmentally led so that teams worked together to assess where processes and systems could be revised to achieve the 10 per cent reduction in waste.

Armstrong and Taylor (2020) note that organisational development programmes were originally behavioural science based and focused on interpersonal relationships, organisational processes and culture change. Today, anything can be included under the organisation development umbrella as long as it contributes to organisational effectiveness. The following list provides an indication of the types of interventions and activities that may be included.

HIGH-PERFORMANCE WORKING

Developing work system processes and practices and policies to enable employees to perform at their full potential. This might involve a focus on quality, customer service, growth and profits.

CULTURE CHANGE

Changing the organisation culture through its values, norms and beliefs, and people policies or practices.

CHANGE MANAGEMENT

Using a range of techniques that consist of processes to manage change (see section on change below).

ACTION RESEARCH

Seeking transformative change through the simultaneous process of taking action and doing research linked together by critical reflection.

SURVEY FEEDBACK

Collecting data through attitude surveys and workshops to support action planning.

APPRECIATIVE ENQUIRY

A methodology that focuses on a positive approach of identifying what is working well and using that information to plan for change.

GROUP DYNAMICS

Exploring ways to improve the effectiveness of groups through training to improve sensitivity, diagnostic and action skills.

PERSONAL INTERVENTIONS

Using processes such as transactional analysis (an approach to understand how people behave and express themselves through transactions with others), behaviour modelling (using positive reinforcement and corrective feedback to change behaviour and neurolinguistic programming or NLP) (helping people to organise their thinking, feeling, language and behaviour to develop their interactions).

In addition, employee engagement, performance management, lean process improvement, organisational learning, total reward, team building and agile working might also be included (and covered elsewhere in this book).

Organisation development is often misunderstood as a consequence of the wide-ranging interventions and activities that might be included in this specialism. Ortenbled (2013) a contemporary philosopher, contends that organisation development is one of a group of both value and attractive management ideas which include the learning organisation, total quality management and business process reengineering that may be popular because of their vagueness. Legge (1995: 212) is critical of organisation development initiatives due to insufficient evidence of success suggesting that 'many of the initiatives were in retrospect, … inward looking involving schemes of management development, work system design, attempts at participation … without close attention to how they were to deliver against market driven organisational success'. Marsh et al. (2010:143) also note that one of the problems of organisation development is that it is 'orientated to process and tools rather than results … where techniques are considered to be ends in themselves rather than a means to deliver organisational performance'. The success of any organisation development intervention depends on the extent to which it drives performance improvement. To be effective any intervention needs to focus on enabling growth and must be relevant within a business.

ORGANISATIONAL DEVELOPMENT IN A HYBRID WORLD

To create an optimal work environment for employees it is necessary to consider both individual outcomes (such as productivity, satisfaction, well-being etc.) and the performance of the organisation as a whole (knowledge sharing, organisation culture). Organisation development specialists play an important part in creating the systems that support hybrid working, for example through the development of digital communities, cross-functional teams, well-being support, collaboration, communication and training. Essentially, the design of the hybrid working environment presents an opportunity for organisational development experts to create direction and connect people through facilitating meetings, coaching and developing and managing and communicating change.

Jacobs (2021) found that hybrid working is inducing changes to office space. Where previously people were working in large open-plan spaces and using meeting rooms to collaborate there is now a focus on designing space that allows the exact opposite. Workplaces are being redesigned to promote group work. For example, at Spotify office spaces are being reconfigured to provide not only collaboration space but also quiet rooms, where distraction free work can be undertaken as well as adding more phone booths to allow staff to jump on a call (ibid). Managers are key to supporting a change to hybrid working. They need to support, guide and role model organisational values and behaviours. Organisation development and design is key to supporting the development of new models for a hybrid future by reimaging workspace, connecting with employees and adapting structure and roles. This can be achieved through a review of organisational culture and purpose to drive performance.

ORGANISATION CULTURE

Organisation culture refers to the shared values, beliefs and standards that characterise the company. Balogun and Johnson (2004) simply refer to culture as 'how to do things round here'. Schein (2004) suggests that organisation culture should include a successful strategy, effective leadership, excellent employee performance and ethical philosophy. In an effective organisational culture, members of the organisation understand how to interact with various stakeholders and each organisation has a different organisational culture that covers a wide range of behaviours in the organisation (ibid).

Organisational culture has been defined in various ways by scholars incorporating formal and informal systems and environmental factors that impact the attitudes, beliefs, values and motivation of people who work in a particular organisation. Culture might be referred to as the personality of an organisation, the atmosphere of the work place, including the complex mixture of norms, values, expectations, policies and procedures that influence individual and group patterns of behaviour. The CIPD (2020) argues that culture matters because it offers a way for employees to understand their organisation, to voice their views and to develop connections and common purpose. It is also important to continually assess the culture, as the organisation's purpose and values will affect the standard of its customer service and influence the engagement and retention of its people.

Berger et al. (2021) argue that corporate culture and remote culture is a key challenge in hybrid working models. Johnson and Scholes (1999) formulated the concept of the culture web with core beliefs and assumptions focused at the centre of the organisational paradigm. These guide the other elements of organisational culture representing the visible, tangible aspects (structures and controls systems) and the less tangible ones such as myths and stories, symbols, routines and rituals and power structures. Deal and Kennedy offer additional elements such as ideologies, symbols, heroes, rites and rituals (Deal and Kennedy, 1982).

The shift in working culture from the workplace to hybrid and remote models has required a number of modifications to achieve and embed change. From concerns regarding onboarding to mental health awareness, effective collaboration and managing teams, organisations are facing new challenges. Organisational culture is linked with the behaviour of the people working within an organisation. Companies exist in a particular culture, which affects the way their employees perceive, feel and behave (Wziątek-Staśko et al., 2020). A survey by Deloitte that studied over 7,000 executives from 130 countries shows that over 80 per cent deem culture a top issue they face and a driver of strong financial performance, while only 12 per cent think that they foster 'the right' culture (Deloitte 2016). But to what extent should organisations be managing culture? Schein (2004) purports that organisational culture matters because cultural elements determine strategy, goals and modes of operating. Therefore, creating good, strong culture is vital for business in long-term success.

Kiziloglu (2022) identify that the two most important elements of organisational culture are adaptability and mission, which significantly affect organisational performance. Paying attention to adaptability and mission is important as organisational culture has a significant impact on the attitude and performance of its staff. For employees, organisational culture can provide either the glue that brings people together or the catalyst for driving them apart. Toxic cultures can significantly impede productivity and induce people to leave the organisation. This needs to be managed and employees need to shape the redefining of the culture through agreement of the essential pillars. Schein (2004, p. 11) highlights that

> the only thing of real importance that leaders do is to create and manage culture and that the unique talent of leaders is their ability to understand and work with culture; and that it is an ultimate act of leadership to destroy culture when it is viewed as dysfunctional.

The people team are well placed to drive culture change through values and behaviours. A set of values provides the moral compass from which organisation culture must follow and this includes an agreement of behaviours (supporting, communicating, teamworking etc.). Culture is about a set of norms and standards by which employees' behaviour is prescribed in a workplace.

A cultural web analysis (Figure 3.1) is a useful tool for exploring the current culture of an organisation and also to identify any gaps and

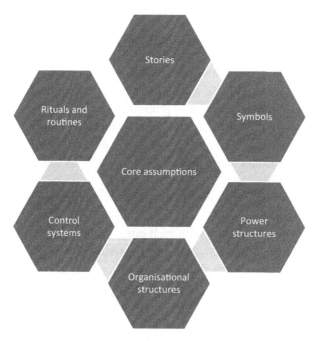

Figure 3.1 The culture web (adapted from Johnson et al., 2014).

assumptions that impact the implementation of change. The cultural
web (Johnson et al., 2014) shows the behavioural, physical and symbolic
manifestations of a culture that inform and are informed by the taken-for-
granted assumptions, or paradigm of an organisation.

Stories: Stories refer to past events and things people have talked about both
   internally and externally. What stories are commonly told, for example
   to newcomers? How do these reflect assumptions and beliefs?
Symbols: Symbols refer to visual representations of the organisation, for
   example, logos, offices, dress codes. What objectives, events or people
   do employees in the organisation particularly identify with? Which
   aspects of strategy are highlighted in publicity?
Power: Where does the power and influence in the institution reside?
   Consider status, claims on resources and symbols of power. Who makes
   things happen or stops things from happening?
Organisation: What is the structure of the organisation, formally (as defined
   on the organisation chart) and informally (recognising where highly

valued contributions are made)? How rigid are the structures? To what extent does organisation structure encourage collaboration or competition?

Controls: What systems are in place to control the institution, for example, quality, financial. What is most closely monitored or controlled? Is there an emphasis on reward or punishment?

Rituals and routines: What behaviour do routines encourage? What are the key rituals? What do training programmes emphasise? How easy are rituals and routines to change?

The cultural web assumes a strong organisational culture. In practice, an organisation is likely to have a number of sub-cultures. The cultural web relates to how people interact with each other in the organisation and the shared values. Each of the areas needs to be studied to find out what is and isn't working, what needs to change and what can stay the same.

I have used the cultural web a number of times as a structure for facilitating discussions about culture. I outline below a few highlights from an organisation I worked with several years ago. I have changed the name of the institution for reasons of confidentiality.

CASE STUDY: UNIVERSITY OF HOPE

University of Hope is a small university based in the UK. Prior to the coronavirus pandemic, all staff worked at the main campus with occasional remote working. As a relatively new university, established about 30 years ago, stories were told about its rapid growth and the numerous senior managers that have come and gone and the impact. The senior leadership team have a strong female representation and stories are told about how this influences the chances for promotion depending on your gender. Stories are told regarding extramarital affairs and inappropriate behaviour at the senior team level towards younger and junior members of staff. There is some indication that engaging in such relationships is 'good for career prospects'. The university logo is promoted all over the city and railway station. The office is open plan with an allocated closed office for the heads of department. Not all heads use their offices. Some men wear jeans with a shirt and women tend to dress smart casual. The heads of departments are in charge and there is a degree of micromanaging.

Academic departments each have a senior management team who make decisions regarding individual allocation of funds for research development and conferences. Programme leads have little power. The organisational structure is hierarchical both departmentally and organisationally and centralised decision making takes place through committee structures. A consequence of this process is the lengthy time it takes for decision-making. Strict control mechanisms are in place such as quality assurance and governance at the university level. To advance in the organisation requires approval from your line manager and their line manager and it is a difficult and lengthy process and many applications are unsuccessful. This is demotivating for staff and some decide not to pursue their aspiration for advancement within the university, deciding either to leave or to remain in their current post for the long term. University routines are designed around university semester structures. It is a long hours' culture with some degree of presenteeism. There are many meetings held every week, many of which are not productive or considered necessary by the staff. The organisation is very student focused. Colleagues are supportive to each other and regularly bring cakes and sweets when it is a birthday or if someone returns from holiday. Core assumptions of the university focus on the student experience and the fact that there is no money for anything. There is a drive towards innovation to generate more students that will bring income.

Using the cultural web can help to crystallise what works in an organisation and what needs to be improved. It can help to facilitate strategic planning.

IN A HYBRID WORLD

Referring to the same case study, how will stories be shared when connections with colleagues are reduced to transactional virtual meetings? The 'water cooler' chat had brought support and friendship and this social connection has now disappeared. How do managers feel about their loss of status in the physical office sense? Do they have the skills to manage in a hybrid world? Managers have implemented regular 'check-ins' but is this supportive or surveillance? How will the roles and responsibilities of colleagues across the organisation be understood without the physical distinctiveness of different offices and campuses? How can technology be used to collaborate and communicate and what additional investment is required? Will the long hours' culture and presenteeism continue in a hybrid world? Will these factors impact the core assumptions in the cultural web?

The university has recognised that some elements of the culture need to change in order to build trust between managers and staff, to reduce presenteeism both in the office and virtually, to hold a meeting only when necessary and to use technology more effectively to enhance collaboration and innovation. In the next section, we examine organisational change and how this might be managed.

ORGANISATION CHANGE

The world of work is experiencing considerable change and change management is an ongoing organisation wide priority. Organisations are required to keep up with the ever-changing demands of customer preferences, technological development, globalisation, institutional and political change, demographic and cultural shifts. Armstrong and Taylor (2020, p.66) discuss change management as 'the process of leading and facilitating change, initiating and achieving the smooth implementation of new developments and initiatives by planning and introducing them systematically and allowing for the possibility of their being resisted or misunderstood'.

Johnson et al. (2014) distinguish between incremental and transformational change, with a small change being incremental and a large change transformational. Change is most effective when it is planned, adaptive and transformational.

The classic model of change was identified by Lewin (1951) which set out three stages in change management. Firstly, unfreezing, creating a readiness for change by creating an anxiety of the current environment and so presenting the rationale for the change. Secondly, movement by taking action that will develop new responses or behaviours based on the new information available. Thirdly, refreezing, which seeks to embed new ways of working. Lewin (ibid.) also developed the concept of force field analysis whereby an analysis of both driving and restraining forces is used to understand proposed change and the supporting or opposing arguments.

Early change plans were designed in relatively stable environments and they have been criticised for their assumptions which are based on a static state which is less likely to be effective in dynamic and changing environments such as the VUCA environment we now work in. Most change models propose a process for implementation. For example, Judson (1991) suggests that it is necessary to follow a five-step model that includes analysing change priorities, communicating the change, gaining acceptance of new behaviour, changing from a status quo to a desired state and consolidating and institutionalising the new state. Kanter et al. (1992) propose a ten-point list for planning change including analysing the need to change, creating a shared vision, separating from the past, creating a sense of urgency, supporting a strong leadership role, lining up political sponsorship, crafting an implementation plan, developing enabling structures, communicating and involving people and reinforcing and implementing change. John Kotter's (2012) eight-step change model builds on Kanter's, it is both simplified and easier to use in practice. The steps are as follows:

1. Establishing a sense of urgency (examining the market, competitive realities, identifying and discussing crisis or major opportunities).
2. Creating the guiding coalition (putting together the group to lead the change).
3. Developing a vision or strategy (developing a vision to direct the change effort).
4. Communicating the change vision (using every channel to constantly communicate the new vision and strategy. The guiding coalition should role model the behaviour expected of employees).
5. Empowering the broad-based action (removing obstacles, changing systems or structures that undermine the vision, encouraging risk taking and non-traditional ideas, activities and actions).
6. Generating short-term wins (planning for wins and recognising and rewarding people).
7. Consolidating gains and producing more (using increasing credibility to change systems, structures and policies in alignment with the vision, recruit and promote staff to implement the change vision, focusing on new projects and utilising change agents).
8. Anchoring new approaches in the culture (achieving better performance through customer and productivity focus, communicating relationship between new behaviours and organisation success, implementing leadership development and succession planning).

Let us examine the model in practice through the Lego change transformation.

CASE STUDY: LEGO

From 1932 until 1998, Lego was a profitable organisation. By 2003, sales had dropped by 30 per cent year on year and the brand was $800 million in debt. Lego hadn't added anything of value to its portfolio for a decade. CEO, Jørgen Vig Knudstorp, admitted that the brand was running out of cash after a period of expansion. Lego decided it was time to commence a restructure. The new CEO, Vig Knudstorp, decided it was time not to put the company's sole focus on physical toy products. Lego is now increasingly concentrating on bridging the physical and virtual augmented reality (AR) experiences. It has implemented a digital transformation. By finding new sources of revenue, LEGO has managed to transform its brand and keep up with the requirements of its target audience. The company has worked in partnerships to create new entities, movies and TV shows over the last ten years. It recognises that it might not make as much money but the product is better (Davis, 2017).

ANALYSIS OF LEGO USING KOTTER'S MODEL

In order to restructure the business, it was necessary to organise the sales force to meet new targets. The restructure focused on new markets and new opportunities. Leadership was required to persuade all stakeholders of the need for action. They formed a new powerful guiding coalition in the form of a change of CEO to lead on the new vision. The change leader needed to ensure that all employees understood the end vision and goal through open discussion and communication of the improvements necessary. This ensures that people understand what the improvements are, how change is being implemented and the rationale for doing this. In some areas, Lego was able to adapt existing software and systems without additional investment. It focused on what was already in place and assessed how this could be adapted. Using key performance metrics is a robust way of measuring the progress of an initiative and to build an organisation-wide improvement attitude so that short-term wins can be recognised and celebrated. Continuous improvement requires that the organisation's set of values reflects the purpose of the organisation and these need to be understood by all stakeholders. This will support all stages of the employee lifecycle, from resourcing new staff to engaging them and working with the wider community.

In the change management literature, there is considerable disagreement regarding the most appropriate approach to changing organisations. Change is increasingly rapid and complex, and senior management do not always have the time to identify, plan and implement every action required. The responsibility for change is, therefore, more devolved and, as a result, requires great changes in the roles played by senior management, from controller to facilitator. Therefore, it is sometimes difficult to plan for change and an emergent response may be more appropriate.

Emergent change occurs 'in real time' (Burns, 2006:363) and therefore fosters ongoing re-alignment with the environment, ongoing learning and strategy making. Emergent change is more unpredictable, often unintentional, can come from anywhere and involves relatively informal self-organising (Weick and Quinn, 1999). Responding to the pandemic can be evidenced as both an emergent and planned response to the management of change. It required a response in 'real time' but management teams are now planning how to sustain the working models introduced through hybrid working models. Managers tend to react to the influences of their organisation and in respect to a specific or perceived problem, usually an external threat. Managers develop plans from their own direct experience or through external consultancy services. In the above case study, we can see that Lego has responded to changes in real time, through consultation and collaboration, through an emergent and planned response that balances bottom-up preferences with organisation strategy.

HYBRID WORKING AT LEGO

Lego has launched its 'Best of Both' to allow individual flexibility over working preferences and a strong focus on company culture through the physical workplace. Lego recognises that whilst everyone is an individual, they are also part of a group. Lego has updated its mission for the workplace experience to not only encourage employees to be the best versions of themselves but also be the best colleague. In the research undertaken by Lego throughout the pandemic, it found that the most important workplace activities according to employees were social interactions, creating thinking, collaboration, group learning and connecting to the company and its values (Lego, 2022). The Lego team mapped individual tasks to understand where and how the workplace can add value to these activities. Originally, Lego built its physical workplace on the model of 70 per cent desk and focus space, 15 per cent collaborative and meeting space and 15 per cent social space. Following the research undertaken, it now recognises that it will need to split the model evenly across all three (Lego, 2022).

LEADING ORGANISATION DEVELOPMENT AND CULTURE CHANGE

HR professionals, organisation development and design specialists are usually expected to support and lead on change projects and this has been the case during the pandemic (Maddox–Daines, 2021). Ulrich (1997) identified the role of change agent as a difficult role to play. Armstrong and Taylor (2020) identify that organisations often contract people from outside an organisation to lead change but people inside the organisation who are well respected and credible can add extra value. Leading change effectively requires professionals to be clear on what needs to change, how it can be changed and what the intended result will look like. Measuring the effectiveness of the change is critical. It is important that managers are included in the design of the change and that the project has the commitment of the senior management team.

SUMMARY POINTS

- Hybrid working offers individuals increased flexibility and an improved quality of life. It does have limitations however and these need to be carefully managed. Careful consideration of well-being, integrating appropriate opportunities for collaboration and ensuring staff have the right equipment for the job is critical.
- The terms 'organisation design' and 'development' are often used interchangeably. Organisation development uses behaviour science to focus on organisation culture, values, capability, change, development, behaviour and relationships. Organisation design relates to strategic change in relation to structure, work design, HR and management practice and metrics.
- Culture should be aligned to strategy. It consists of formal and informal aspects, attitude, beliefs, values, motivation and standards. It is the atmosphere and the personality of the organisation and it should be continually assessed.
- Change and change management is an ongoing organisation wide priority. Change can be considered in relation to a series of steps. The rationale for the change must be clear and communicated to all stakeholders effectively. It is critical that metrics are used to measure the success of the change.

SELF-TEST QUESTIONS/REVIEW QUESTIONS

- To what extent are organisational development interventions and activities helpful in implementing change?
- To what extent is it possible to change organisation culture? How can culture change be effectively embedded?

STRATEGIC PLANNING IN PRACTICE

A case example: Lego

Review the Lego case study discussed in this chapter. What are advantages and disadvantages of the Lego 'Best of Both' hybrid working model? Evaluate the design of the hybrid working model from both employee and organisation perspective.

ACTIVITY

Using the cultural web explore each of the factors to analyse the current environment of your organisation or one with which you are familiar. What improvements would you like to make to the culture? How might you address the gaps?

References

Armstrong, M. and Taylor, S. (2020). *Armstrong's Handbook of Human Resource Management Practice.* 15th edn. London: Kogan Page.

Balogun, J. and Johnson, G. (2004). Organizational restructuring and middle manager sensemaking. *Academy of Management Journal,* 47(4), pp.523–549. https://doi.org/10.2307/20159600.

Beardwell, J. and Thompson, A. (2017). *Human Resource Management: A Contemporary Approach.* 8th edn. Harlow: Pearson.

Berger, S., Weber, F. and Buser, A. (2021). *Hybrid Work Compass: Navigating the Future of How We Work.* [pdf] Available at: https://www.alexandria.unisg.ch/264298/1/2021_Hybrid%20Work%20Compass_Report.pdf. (Accessed 12 September, 2022).

Burke, W. and Bradford, D. (2005). The crisis in OD. In Bradford, D. and Burke, W., eds. *Reinventing Organisation Development.* San Francisco: John Wiley & Sons. pp.1–14.

Burns, B. (2006). Kurt Lewin and the planned change approach to change: A Reappraisal. In *Organizational Development.* San Francisco: Jossey-Bass Publishing, pp.133–157.

CIPD (2020). Organisation design. CIPD. 25 Nov. Available at: https://www.cipd.co.uk/knowledge/strategy/organisational-development/design-factsheet#gref. (Accessed 22 October, 2022).

CIPD (2022). Organisation development. CIPD. 4th April. Available at https://www.cipd.co.uk/knowledge/strategy/organisational-development/factsheet#gref. (Accessed 22 October, 2022).

Cummings, T.G. and Worley, C. G (2015) *Organisation Development and Change.* 10th edn. Andover: Cengage Learning.

Davis, J., 2017. How Lego clicked: The brand that reinvented itself. [online] *The Guardian.* Available at: https://www.theguardian.com/lifeandstyle/2017/jun/04/how-lego-clicked-the-super-brand-that-reinvented-itself. (Accessed 13 October, 2022).

Deal, T.E. and Kennedy, A.A. (1982) *Corporate Cultures: The Rites and Rituals of Corporate Life.* Reading: Addison Wesley Publishing Company.

Deloitte. (2016). Shape your culture, drive your strategy. [pdf] *Deloitte.* Available at: https://www2.deloitte.com/content/dam/Deloitte/us/Documents/strategy/us-cons-culturepath-infographic.pdf. (Accessed 1 September, 2022).

Fayard, A.L., Weeks, J. and Khan, M., 2021. Designing the hybrid office. *Harvard Business Review, 99*(2), pp.114–123.

Gratton, L., 2021. How to do hybrid right. *Harvard Business Review, 99*(3), pp.66–74.

Grzegorczyk, M., Mariniello, M., Nurski, L. and Schraepen, T. (2021). *Blending the Physical and Virtual: A Hybrid Model for the Future of Work* (14/2021). Bruegel Policy Contribution.

Ipsen, C., van Veldhoven, M., Kirchner, K. and Hansen, J.P. (2021). Six key advantages and disadvantages of working from home in Europe during COVID-19. *International Journal of Environmental Research and Public Health, 18*(4), pp.1–17. https://doi.org/10.3390/ijerph18041826.

Jacobs, E. (2021). The new frontiers of hybrid work take shape. [online] *Financial Times.* Available at: https://www.ft.com/content/f568997c-513c-48b0-8422-fabacda46418. (Accessed 13 August, 2022).

Johnson, G. and Scholes, K. (1999). *Exploring Corporate Strategy.* 5th edn. Essex: Prentice Hall.

Johnson, G., Whittington, R., Scholes, K., Angwin, D and Regner, P. (2014). *Exploring Strategy.* 10th edn. Harlow: Pearson.

Judson, A.S. (1991). *Changing Behavior in Organizations: Minimizing Resistance to Change.* Cambridge, MA: Blackwell Business.

Kanter, R.M., Stein, B., and Jick, T.D. (1992). *The Challenge of Organizational Change: How Companies Experience It and Leaders Guide It.* New York: Free Press.

Kiziloglu, M. (2022). The effect of organisational culture on organisational performance: The mediating role of intrapreneurship. *The Irish Journal of Management, 41*(1). pp.20–36. https://doi.org/10.2478/ijm-2021-0008.

Kotter, J.P. (2012). *Leading Change.* Boston, MA.: Harvard Business School Press.

Kumar, A.S. and Das, J.B. (2022). The impact of 'hybrid-work-model' on job satisfaction. *International Journal of Business Management & Research (IJBMR), 12*(1), pp. 71–82.

Legge, K. (1995). *Human Resource Management: Rhetorics and Realities.* London: Macmillan.

Lego (2022). Available at: https://www.lego.com/en-gb. (Accessed 30/10/2022).

Lewin, K. (1951). *Field Theory in Social Science.* New York: Harper.

Maddox-Daines, K.L. (2021). Delivering well-being through the coronavirus pandemic: The role of human resources (HR) in managing a healthy workforce. *Personnel Review.* https://doi.org/10.1108/PR-04-2021-0224

Marsh, C., Sparrow, P., Hird, M. (2010). Integrated organization design: The new strategic priority for HR directors. In P. Sparrow, A. Hesketh, M. Hird and C. Cooper (eds.) *Leading HR.* London: Palgrave Macmillan. Ch.8, pp.136–161.

Marston, H., Wilson, G., Morgan, D.J. and Gates, J. (2021). Beyond digital: Planning for a hybrid world. [online] Covid-19 Committee: 1st Report of Session 2019-21. Available at: https://oro.open.ac.uk/76051/.

Orlikowski, W.J. and Scott, S.V. (2016). Digital work: A research agenda. A Research Agenda for Management and Organization Studies, pp.88–95 In Czarniawska, B. ed. (2017) *A Research Agenda for Management and Organization Studies*. Cheltenham, UK: Edward Elgar.

Ortenblad, A. (2013). Vague and attractive: Five explanations of the use of ambitious management ideas. *Philosophy of Management*, 5(1), pp.45–54. https://doi.org/10.5840/pom20055130.

Schein, E.H. (2004). *Organizational Culture and Leadership*. 3rd ed. London: Wiley.

Taylor, H., Florisson, R. and Hooper, D., 2021. Making hybrid inclusive - Key priorities for policymakers. Policy Brief, Chartered Management Institute and Work Foundation. [online] Available at: https://www.managers.org.uk/wp-content/uploads/2021/10/wf-cmi-making-hybrid-inclusive-policy-brief.pdf.

Ulrich, D. (1997). *Human Resource Champions. The Next Agenda for Adding Value and Delivery Results*. Boston: Harvard Business School Press.

Weick, K.E. and Quinn, R.E. (1999). Organizational change and development. *Annual Review of Psychology*, 50(1), pp.361–386. https://doi.org/10.1146/annurev.psych.50.1.361.

Wziątek-Staśko, A., Stańczyk, I, and Stuss, M.M. (2020) Organisational culture as a stress determinant in SME sector organisations. *European Journal of International Management*, 14(6), pp.955–975.

Resourcing talent in the hybrid workplace

Chapter 4

INTRODUCTION

To be a top-performing organisation, employers need to attract and retain high-potential staff with a talent management strategy that is aligned to the business strategy. This chapter explores issues associated with talent planning and management in an increasingly dynamic and diverse labour market and hybrid working models. Methods and techniques to inform talent planning and management activities are discussed along with the tools to understand and analyse key labour market trends and their significance to inform talent planning and management. By managing talent strategically, organisations can build high-performance workplaces that are able to deliver on organisational priorities and goals. This chapter assesses job analysis techniques, job design, candidate attraction, employer branding and recruitment and selection as the essential ingredients to formulate an effective resourcing strategy.

TALENT PLANNING, MANAGEMENT AND RESOURCING

Interest in talent management in the business context came in the 1990s with the ground-breaking study entitled 'The War for Talent' by McKinsey

DOI: 10.4324/9781003342984-5

(Michaels, Handfield-Jones, & Axelrod, 2001). This study suggested that demand for talented employees exceeded the available supply, thus leading to the problem of talent shortages. Talent management is future orientated and focuses on resource planning and projecting employee needs. Put simply, organisations need to know how many people and what sort of people they need to meet present and future business requirements. It is an integral part of business planning.

The CIPD defines talent as individuals who can make a significant difference to organisational performance which may be through their immediate contribution or, in the longer term, by reaching their highest levels of potential (CIPD, 2020). It refers to talent management as the systematic attraction, identification, development, engagement, retention and deployment of those individuals who are of particular value to an organisation. This may be through their high potential or because they fulfil critical roles. Talent management is a strategic endeavour determined through a set of processes, programmes and cultural standards with the goal of attracting, developing, unfolding and keeping talent in order to meet future business challenges (Silzer and Dowell, 2010).

THE STRATEGIC LEVEL

Talent management addresses how an organisation can attract candidates who can secure organisational goals in a competitive business environment. With skills shortages and a shrinking talent pool, organisations must focus on both resourcing and retaining staff so that they are able to achieve a competitive edge. Identifying positions and attracting candidates who offer high potential and high performance can be viewed in terms of the resource-based strategic perspective (discussed in Chapter 2) where organisations compete on their internal resources and capabilities to gain a competitive advantage. High-performance working practices include rigorous recruitment and selection procedures supported with tailored training and development. Regular development prepares employees for further responsibility and can support staff retention through motivation and engagement. One of the ways in which organisations achieve this is through a talent pool whereby high-potential employees are developed for key positions.

Some organisations focus their efforts on the development of a succession plan (Leatherbarrow and Fletcher, 2016) whereby the organisation plans for the replacement of key senior management and other critical positions within the company. For example, who will replace the director of finance when she retires or moves to another organisation? The CIPD (2020) argues that fairness is integral to the success of any succession plan and all candidates must be assessed objectively. Some organisations use succession planning committees to review and challenge decisions and advise on improving the process.

In many firms, the process of talent management has broadened to focus on talent management of the workforce rather than a pool of talent, in recognition that all staff are integral to gaining competitive advantage. Chahal and Kumari (2013) suggest that a holistic approach to talent management is most effective where it focuses on all phases of the employee lifecycle supporting the high performance and potential of the workforce as a whole. This ensures that all staff benefit from the advantages of employee development and helps the organisation to reduce staff turnover and the associated costs of resourcing and onboarding.

INFORMING TALENT PLANNING

Demography looks at populations, their sizes, characteristics and the way they change. Population growth or reduction is important in determining economic, development and social change. The industrial revolution in the UK was made possible by the surplus labour from the countryside and this was the same for China in its rapid growth and industrialisation since the 1980s. There are two factors that control population change across the world: the birth rate and the death rate. The United Nations Population Fund (2022) states that the world population today stands at 7.6 billion. People between the ages of 15 and 24 make up almost 21 per cent of the world's working-age population (ILO, 2020), and only 36 per cent of people (429 million) in this age group are employed (ibid.). There will be more people over age 55 than children under 15 by 2035 and more people over 55 than people under 25 by 2080 (Harasty and Ostermeier, 2020). By 2030, only 38.8 per cent of the global population will be 24 years old or younger, down from 41 per cent in 2020 (United Nations, 2019). Migration is also an important factor in the rise and fall of population levels by country. The United Nations estimates that 191 million people live outside their country of birth or citizenship (ibid.). Political, social, economic and environmental impact have led to large-scale movements. There is divided opinion of projected scenarios for 2050 with estimates of population to 10 billion but population growth is projected to slow with an ageing population and an estimated 9.2 million over their 50s are predicted to leave the workforce in the next 20 years. This will lead to skills shortages across different sectors (Kew and Stredwick, 2016).

THE SKILLS GAP

The CIPD Resourcing and Talent Planning report (2022) suggests that competition for well-qualified talent has increased over the last year with 77 per cent of organisations experiencing difficulties attracting candidates which is an increase of 49 per cent since the 2021 survey. Recruiting for senior and skilled roles has been most challenging at 58 per cent although 26 per cent reported challenges with recruiting low-skilled candidates. Sixty per cent of organisations in the survey report that it is more difficult to retain staff now compared to 2021, and over a third have engaged in initiatives to improve employee retention in the same period (compared to 29 per cent in 2021). Around two-fifths of organisations expect to increase their recruitment and talent management budgets going forward.

The Edge Foundation (2022) found that 1.7 million people aged 15+ across the UK lack the 'essential digital skills' needed for day-to-day life online and that the top 5 skills sought by employers in the UK are auditing, nursing, accounting, business development and an understanding of key performance indicators. Severe skills shortages in 'workplace skills' are reported with at least 2.1 million workers likely to be acutely under-skilled in at least one core management area (ibid.). With the reopening of the economy, the UK has indeed seen a record number of vacancies, while the supply of candidates has been restricted for a variety of reasons, including low unemployment, early exit from the labour market by older workers and non-UK nationals returning to their home countries. Attracting and recruiting individuals into the right role at the right time and cost is both a challenge and a priority for people professionals.

CLOSING THE SKILLS GAP

The UK government offers a range of initiatives to help close the skills gap. The apprenticeship levy is one initiative established to create long-term sustainable funding for apprenticeships and to give employers more control to provide their staff with a range of opportunities (GOV.UK, 2019). Governments can also legislate to support access to migratory skills in the form of right to work legislation, working visas and through the creation of trade initiatives to encourage job creation. Employers can support skills shortages through graduate development and early careers pathways. For example, the Dyson Institute of Engineering and Technology is the first education provider in the UK to be given new degree-awarding powers founded as an alternative to a traditional degree education during which time Dyson has invested £31.5 million (Dyson, 2022). Trade unions too offer learning and development for their members.

In order to recruit the right people into the right roles at the right time, organisations require a resourcing strategy that is fit for the future. In the next section, we explore some essential components of a resourcing strategy.

THE RESOURCING STRATEGY

Candidate attraction

Candidate attraction is an important step in the resourcing of talent. Candidate attraction is about drawing potential candidates to view the job advertisement. It is about the tools and techniques an employer uses to attract potential candidates. An organisation will need to develop an employer brand and an employee value proposition.

EMPLOYER BRANDING

The employer brand is a term generally used to describe the employment offering and environment of a particular company and how it differentiates itself from its competitors. It is the process of building a unique proposition to candidates. Effective employer branding leads to competitive advantage and assists in employee retention. Edwards (2010, p.6) suggests that employer branding involves identifying the unique 'employment experience' by considering the totality of tangible and intangible reward features that a particular organisation offers to its employees. Over and above this, however, a central element to employer branding involves the identification of elements of the character of the organisation itself; features such as the organisation's key values and the guiding principles underlying how it operates as a collective entity (ibid.).

In order to develop an employer brand, it is necessary to define which organisational features are likely to be desired by potential candidates. The employer value proposition conveys what the company has to offer (see below) and social media is used to present information on what the company is like as an employer (linked to the website and career sites). It is also necessary to benchmark the approaches of other organisations such as the Sunday Times 100 Best Companies to ensure that the proposition is competitive and to check review sites such as Glassdoor for feedback from ex-employees.

The following Heineken case study provides an insight into the process of employer branding.

CASE STUDY: HEINEKEN

Heineken is a global brewer and distributor of beer and cider founded in 1864 with headquarters in Amsterdam in the Netherlands. The company has just under 85,000 employees and a revenue of 21.94 billion euro in 2021.

Heineken has rejuvenated its employer brand through its campaign 'Go Places' with a new focus on showcasing employee stories and driving awareness and engagement.

The campaign features the stories of 33 Heineken employees, from Carlos who heads up Heineken's e-commerce business, The Sub, to Marcel trying to sell cider into the competitive South African market. The 45-second films show staff from all roles, levels and departments including marketing, sales, finance, supply chain and HR and details how they turned a challenge into an opportunity. All the videos end with a question 'Ready to ...', for example 'Ready to turn a no into a yes?' or 'Ready to work some miracles?'

Heineken conducted research in 15 of its markets around the world to understand what the brand and a new campaign should focus on. From that research, it found three core pillars. The first pillar is authenticity, which Heineken felt it needed to evolve the brand with a focus on real stories. The second is transcendency, which looks to ensure the brand means something to more people. The third is longer-term management of the brand so that there is a consistent increase in the quality and quantity of job applicants, rather than just a spike when the campaign is live. HR and marketing worked closely to evolve the brand. The company has recruited a global HR social media manager to ensure that the employer brand is appropriately managed.

The company measured the employer brand through qualitative and quantitative results, for example, the impact it has on the industry and the 56 per cent increase in applications during the campaign period. The company is now working on improving the interview process and the interactive website, bringing the global and local careers websites onto the same platform. Metrics focus on both the quantity and quality of new hires.

Internally, the company is raising awareness, engagement and pride, the three pillars of its communication strategy both internally and externally.

THE EMPLOYEE VALUE PROPOSITION

Prospective employees evaluate employee value propositions (EVPs) (defined here as the brand promises of organisations) by considering aspects such as 'what's in it for me to work here?' (Erickson, 2009). Hein (2015) defines employment value propositions (EVPs) as the summation of all the characteristics and contents of a job and the employment characteristics that can attract, retain and motivate employees. According to Erickson (2009), EVPs should contain detailed information about compensation, benefits, affiliation, career pathing and work content to attract and retain talented employees.

The nature of the employer value proposition will differ across organisations. The only real way to find out what employees value is of course to ask them. Many organisations conduct annual surveys to gain insights to inform reward practice and link this to the employer brand (Leatherbarrow and Fletcher, 2016). Measuring the employee value proposition is not just about what provides staff with job satisfaction; it is rather more akin to a customer survey whereby the employee considers what they pay for in relation to what they get (in terms of work-life balance, progression opportunities, learning and development, pay and benefits, hours of work, holidays, additional benefits, organisation culture and more). However, employees tend not to think about the absolute benefits but the benefits they get relative to what they believe they could receive elsewhere.

The following case examples provide an insight into some EVPs across different organisations.

CASE STUDY: BAIN & COMPANY

In 2021, Bain & Company achieved first place in the Glassdoor Best Places to Work and in 2022 they came third. The company is a global consulting firm and was founded in 1973 with over 10,000 employees. Their EVP is:

> Bain & Company attracts and retains top talent for our clients. And we are proud to be recognised around the globe as a great place to work. We're competitive for our clients but very supportive of each other. Our people love what they do, making them great to work with. We champion the bold to achieve the extraordinary Bain & Company (2022).

CASE STUDY: NASA

The National Aeronautics and Space Administration is an independent agency of the US federal government responsible for the civil space programme, aeronautics research and space research. Their EVP is:

> Explore the Extraordinary, Every Day. NASA is more than astronauts. We are scientists, engineers, IT specialists, human resources specialists, accountants, writers, technicians and many other kinds of people working together to break barriers to achieve the seemingly impossible.
>
> *(NASA, 2022)*

CASE STUDY: UNILEVER

Unilever is a British multinational consumer goods company with headquarters in London. The company employs 148,000 people across the world and has over 400 brand names in 190 countries. Unilever products include food, condiments, ice cream, cleaning agents, beauty products and personal care. Their EVP is:

> Unilever is the place where you can bring your purpose to life through the work that you do, creating a better business and a better world. You will work with brands that are loved and improve the lives of our consumers and the communities around us. At the heart of our value proposition is that we build leaders. We develop leaders for Unilever, and Unilever leaders go on to be leaders elsewhere in the world.
>
> *(Unilever, 2022)*

Following the pandemic, two-fifths of companies are now re-evaluating their EVP according to a survey of 332 HR professionals undertaken by Aon Benefits and Trends survey (Aon, 2021). The research indicates that 28 per cent companies now have a clear EVP, up from 23 per cent in 2020 with another 43 per cent reporting that they are planning to develop one. In the new normal, employers must drive a sense of purpose so that the values of the employee and organisation align. This will drive employee engagement and loyalty. Providing flexibility and autonomy to employees and cultivating a culture of trust are non-negotiable.

TECHNOLOGICAL TRENDS

Employee recruitment and selection has been heavily affected by the emergence of technology, influencing all aspects of the recruitment and selection cycle (Woods et al., 2019). Online recruitment has been used by organisations for some time, and job sites and job boards have proved to be highly effective for both recruiters and job applicants. Indeed, the CIPD reports that nearly three-quarters of respondents to the CIPD (2021) Resourcing and Talent Planning Survey confirm that technology has enabled them to expand their pool of suitable candidates. Technology provides organisations with the capability to engage in website tracking to assess how many visits they receive to their career site. Company career sites serve to support employer branding activities where candidates can view video-testimonials of current employees describing their experience with the company. It has never been easier to network through social media and to apply for vacancies. One of the drawbacks of accessibility, however, is the high volume of respondents to some advertisements. The CIPD (2022) found that two-thirds of respondents reported that technology has increased applications from unsuitable candidates. However, the increasing sophistication of technology is helping employers to screen out candidates who do not meet the criteria.

Artificial Intelligence (AI) can be used for sifting through CVs, assessing suitability of candidates for positions, helping to reduce the time-intensive task of sifting applications. Applicant tracking systems such as Team Tailor can reduce the time it takes to screen and they can store information allowing for keyword search which is helpful for large numbers of applications. However, for all its convenience, technology can also be used inappropriately, for example by employers who extract informal and personal information about candidates or current employees through cybervetting of profiles on Facebook and Instagram (Nikolaou, 2021).

Beyond online testing, companies are also now using asynchronous video and digital interviews, particularly for initial screening. This opens up the international job market for candidates. The interviews might be viewed by several different managers who rate the candidates and then collectively reach agreement. Companies with sophisticated data analytics in place are able to measure word speed, changes in body temperature and seconds between responses through the use of sensor devices (e.g., HireVue) (Langer et al., 2017). Some participants consider digital interviews to be less personal, however, and they are concerned regarding privacy (ibid.). Negative candidate perception of the digital interview is problematic to organisations, despite the advantages offered, as it is very easy for candidates to share negative feedback of the interview through social media platforms, for example Glassdoor.

The CIPD (2022) reports that organisations' use of technology has improved candidates' experience, at least to a small extent (in 2022, 78 per cent of respondents confirmed that this was the case in comparison to 68 per cent in 2021). Additionally, technology has sped up the recruitment process (with 72 per cent of candidates responding that this was the case in 2022 compared to 64 per cent in 2021). Technology has also helped organisations to reduce unconscious bias, increase the diversity and quality of their hires, and improved their understanding of jobseeker behaviour (ibid.). These advantages are challenged by Miller (2019) as AI does not always eliminate bias as it has to be taught what to look for and candidates with non-traditional backgrounds might get overlooked due to rigid AI decision-making.

JOB ANALYSIS AND DESIGN

Job analysis is undertaken with a systematic assessment of the organisation's recruitment needs. The first question is whether or not a job exists. When someone tenders their resignation, it is a good idea to assess whether a new incumbent is required or whether the job can be undertaken differently and indeed whether the role still exists in its current form. Job analysis and design is the process of assessing and defining the components of a post with a focus on responsibilities, accountability, skills and knowledge, equipment required, working conditions, where the job sits within the organisation and outputs or performance measured. The information required may be carried out through direct observation, interviewing, critical incident techniques (which focus on key aspects of the job essential to achieve the outcomes) or sometimes work diaries undertaken by the current role holder (Wilton, 2022). Job analysis can be used to support pay differentials, training needs, performance targets, promotion, redundancy and disciplinary action for poor performance. The main problem with job analysis is that the methods used to analyse a job can be subjective (for example, a current role holder may exaggerate tasks).

Job analysis provides the basis for the design of the job description, person specification and/or competency framework. Job descriptions summarise the key responsibilities and accountabilities of the post. Person specifications are derived from job descriptions and set out the experience in relation to knowledge, skills and attitudes and the qualifications required for the role.

Competency frameworks are used by some organisations in place of or in alignment with the person specification. Competencies are not specific to the job and instead they are designed at organisational level in relation to what the organisation requires as the key skills to drive performance. Organisations that design competency frameworks use these across the employee lifecycle to support development, promotion and performance management. Post the pandemic and in a hybrid world, we are more likely to see competency frameworks requiring adaptability, creativity, critical thinking, resilience and self-management.

RECRUITMENT AND SELECTION

Recruitment is the process of finding and hiring the best candidate for a role in the most timely and cost effective manner. The aim is to attract as many applications as possible from suitably qualified candidates thus maximising the organisation's ability to employ the best person. The process of selection focuses on which of the candidates to appoint.

Jobs need to be advertised in such a way as to reach the intended target audience and to encourage them to apply. Recruitment methods vary from corporate websites, to commercial job boards and specialist trade press. A good practice approach to recruitment is a commitment to fairness which encourages applications from everyone who is qualified to do the job irrespective of their personal characteristics. The Equality Act 2010 protects people from discrimination in the workplace and in wider society (GOV.UK, 2015). The Act outlines nine protected characteristics including age, gender reassignment, being married or in a civil partnership, being pregnant or on maternity leave, disability, race including colour, nationality, ethnic or national origin, religion or belief, sex and sexual orientation.

It is the role of the people professional to ensure that all aspects of resourcing strategy comply with the Equality Act. They are also required to ensure that workers are engaged on appropriate and compliant contracts of employment, and this involves undertaking right to work checks. All data must be handled, recorded and stored in line with the GDPR regulations (CIPD, 2021).

Recruitment

Social media tends to be highly favoured by employers today with respondents to the CIPD Resourcing and Talent Planning report (CIPD, 2021) stating that LinkedIn and the company website are the most favoured methods of recruiting for a role (see Table 4.1). Whilst this is good for reaching large numbers of potential candidates quickly and cost effectively (including perhaps passive seekers who are not looking for a new role), this method of recruitment may attract too many names and the employer does have to manage their own profile carefully.

Whilst posting adverts on corporate websites is a low-cost option, it does depend on a strong employer brand in the marketplace and may not be an effective option for smaller organisations who do not have the budget for branding campaigns. Additionally, in a tight labour market (where vacant jobs are plentiful and workers scarce), employers will need to strengthen employment offers to attract and retain staff.

Recruitment consultants are also one of the preferred methods of recruiting staff. This can be an effective option to source candidates as it is possible to tap into a market of passive candidates (for example, through social media). Recruitment consultants are often expensive when compared to other options, however.

Table 4.1 Most Popular Recruitment Methods: CIPD Resourcing and Talent Planning Report (2022)

	Private sector services	Public sector	Non-profit sector
Base	565	147	66
Own corporate website	44	54	52
Professional networking sites, e.g., LinkedIn	48	34	44
Recruitment/search consultants	49	32	30
Internal advertising to existing talent pool	35	53	35
Advertising roles as open to flexible working arrangements	26	39	40
Professional/employee referral schemes (e.g., 'refer a friend')	37	12	8
Social networking sites, eg Facebook	26	26	61
Commercial/industry-specific job boards	23	18	32
Encourage speculative applications/word of mouth	26	13	19
Apprenticeships	20	25	16
Links with schools/colleges/universities	20	29	9
Specialist journals/trade press	13	28	18
Directly targeting passive jobseekers	18	6	7
Job fairs (including virtuals)	12	17	10
Secondments	8	23	8
Newspapers (online or print, local or national)	9	13	9
Collaborating with other employers/sectors	7	13	8

It is a good idea to analyse each of the recruitment methods for their advantages and disadvantages on a regular basis to check that each continues to attract the candidates that the organisation is seeking.

The candidate selection process should ensure that each individual is treated fairly, without discrimination or bias, and all selections should be made based on the candidate's ability to perform effectively in the role. Wilton (2022) summarises selection simply by saying that it is the process of selecting the most competent individual from the pool of candidates.

Selection

There are many options available when selecting candidates. Screening against previous work history and experience remains the most popular choice and is used extensively in CV screening and interviews (see Figure 4.1) (CIPD, 2022).

Organisations use this data to understand the skills, experiences and outcomes delivered by individuals as an indicator of their future performance. Despite its popularity, the subjectivity of the interview remains a concern due to bias and the potential for discrimination. Indeed, French and Rumbles (2010) suggest that making judgements on an individual's personal characteristics and suitability for future employment is inherently problematic and that many 'normal' selection methods contain significant flaws.

Virtual interviewing became essential in 2020 for most organisations due to the coronavirus pandemic. Managers are able to conduct more interviews in less time; they are easier to schedule and more flexible for both recruiters and candidates (Maurer, 2021). French and Rumbles (2010) suggest that reliability and validity are key determinants of what methods should be applied to select candidates. Reliability refers to retest stability. Would an individual taking a personality questionnaire at different times result in the same data? Consistency measures relate to the degree to whether the instrument measures what it intends, e.g., some IQ elements focus on vocabulary which might be related to education and background rather than intelligence. Validity refers to acceptance of the selection measure (i.e., the extent to which shoe size is relevant to performance on the job), the adequacy of the measure (the UK driving test does not test night driving) and its ability to predict future performance (ibid.).

The final stage in the resourcing of new staff is the onboarding process and this is discussed in the next chapter.

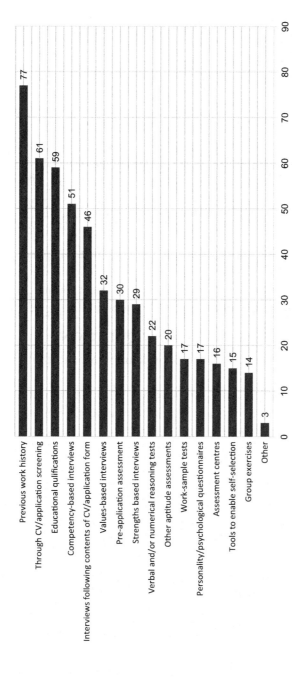

Figure 4.1 Most popular selection methods: CIPD Resourcing and Talent Planning Report (2022).

SUMMARY POINTS

- Talent planning and management is future orientated and focuses on resource planning and projecting staff requirements. The talent management strategy is compiled in response to the strategic goals of the organisation.
- Candidate attraction is an important part of the resources strategy and includes both employer branding and the employee value proposition. The employer brand should be based on an organisation's values. It includes the tangible and intangible rewards, and it is the way an organisation differentiates itself from its competitors.
- Job analysis provides a systematic assessment of the post. The job description and person specification follow from this process. Competency frameworks might also be used to support the selection of staff.
- Recruitment refers to finding and hiring the best candidates for the role in a timely and cost effective manner. Selection is the process of shortlisting candidates from the recruitment pool and selection should be made fairly, without discrimination or bias.

SELF-TEST QUESTIONS/REVIEW QUESTIONS

- Compare and contrast the EVPs for Bain, NASA and Unilever. Which appeals most to you and why?
- Review the Heineken case study above. What metrics is the organisation using to measure the effectiveness of the employer brand? What else might they measure?

STRATEGIC PLANNING IN PRACTICE

A case example

Reflect on your own organisation or on one in which you are familiar. What pillars would you choose to build the employer brand? What is your rationale?

REFLECTION

Reflect on your experience of recruitment and selection from the candidate perspective. How would you rate the experience from candidate attraction, to the employer value proposition, the job description, person specification, competency framework (if relevant) and the selection method.

References

Aon (2021). Available at: https://www.aon.com/unitedkingdom/media-room/articles/uk-benefits-and-trends-survey-2021-covid-19.jsp. (Accessed 3 August 2022).

Bain (2022). Available at https://www.bain.com/careers. (Accessed 31 August, 2022).

Chahal, H. and Kumari, A. (2013). Examining talent management using CG as proxy measure: A case study of State Bank of India. *Corporate Governance: The International Journal of Business in Society*, 13(2), pp.198–207. doi:10.1108/14720701311316670.

CIPD (2020) People profession 2030: A collective view of future trends. CIPD. 11 Nov. Available at: https://www.aon.com/unitedkingdom/media-room/articles/uk-benefits-and-trends-survey-2021-covid-19.jsp. (Accessed 2 August 2022).

CIPD (2021) Resourcing and talent planning. CIPD. Available at: https://www.cipd.co.uk/knowledge/strategy/resourcing#gref. (Accessed 3 October 2022). (Accessed 3 September 2022).

Dyson (2022) The Dyson degree. Available at: https://www.dyson.co.uk/newsroom/overview/features/october-2020/dyson-institute-degree-powers. (Accessed 1 September, 2022).

Edge Foundation. (2018–2022). *Skills Shortages in the UK Economy*. Available at: https://www.edge.co.uk/research/projects/skills-shortages-uk-economy/. (Accessed 3 September, 2022).

Edwards, M.R. (2010). (PDF) An integrative review of employer branding and OB theory. *ResearchGate*. Available at: https://www.researchgate.net/publication/211385429_An_integrative_review_of_employer_branding_and_OB_theory. (Accessed 30 September, 2022).

Erickson, R. (2009). Back to basics: The employee value proposition during tough economic times. Available at: www.bersin.com.

French, R. & Rumbles, S. (2010). Recruitment and selection. In G Rees and R French (eds.) *Leading, Managing and Developing People*. London: CIPD Publications, pp. 169–190.

GOV.UK. (2015). Equality guidance. Available at: https://www.gov.uk/guidance/equality-act-2010-guidance. (Accessed 15 September, 2022).

GOV.UK. (2019). Key facts you should know about the apprenticeship levy. Available at: https://www.gov.uk/government/news/key-facts-you-should-know-about-the-apprenticeship-levy. (Accessed 22 September, 2022).

Harasty, C. and Ostermeier, M. (2020). Population Ageing: Alternative measures of dependency and implications for the future of work. [online] International Labour Organization. Available at: https://www.ilo.org/employment/Whatwedo/Publications/working-papers/WCMS_747257/lang—en/index.htm. (Accessed 4 October, 2022).

Hein, P. (2015). What really matters to employees? [online] *Employee Benefit News*. Available at: https://www.benefitnews.com/opinion/what-really-matters-to-employees. (Accessed 27 September, 2022).

International Labour Organization. (2020). World employment and social outlook: Trends 2020. International Labour Organization. Available at: https://www.ilo.org/global/research/global-reports/weso/2020/WCMS_734455/lang—en/index.htm. (Accessed 4 October, 2022).

Kew, J. and Stredwick, J. (2016). *Human Resource Management in a Business Context*. 3rd edn. London: IPD.

Langer, M., König, C.J. and Krause, K. (2017). Examining digital interviews for personnel selection: Applicant reactions and interviewer ratings. *International Journal of Selection and Assessment, 25*(4), pp.371–382. https://doi.org/10.1111/ijsa.12191.

Leatherbarrow, C. and Fletcher, J. (2016). *Introduction to Human Resource Management: A Guide to HR in Practice*. 3rd ed. London: CIPD.

Maurer, R. (2021). The pros and cons of virtual and in-person interviews. [online] SHRM. Available at: https://www.shrm.org/resourcesandtools/hr-topics/talent-acquisition/pages/pros-and-cons-virtual-in-person-interviews.aspx. (Accessed 14 October, 2022).

Michaels, E., Handfield-Jones, H. and Axelrod, B. (2001). *The War for Talent*. Boston, MA: Harvard Business School Press.

Miller, T. (2019). Explanation in artificial intelligence: Insights from the social sciences. *Artificial Intelligence, 267*, pp.1–38.

NASA (2022) Available at: https://www.nasa.gov/careers. (Accessed, 31 August, 2022).

Nikolaou, I. (2021). What is the role of technology in recruitment and selection? *The Spanish Journal of Psychology, 24*(2). https://doi.org/10.1017/sjp.2021.6.

Silzer, R.F. and Dowell, B.E. (2010). *Strategy-driven Talent Management: A Leadership Imperative*. San Francisco: Jossey-Bass.

Unilever (2022). Available at: https://www.unilever.co.uk/. (Accessed 30 September, 2022).

United Nations (2019a). World population prospects 2019: Highlights | Multimedia library - United Nations department of economic and social affairs. United Nations. Available at: https://www.un.org/development/desa/publications/world-population-prospects-2019-highlights.html. (Accessed 4 October, 2022).

United Nations (2019b). World population prospects 2019: Highlights | Multimedia library - United Nations department of economic and social affairs. [online] United Nations. Available at: https://www.un.org/development/desa/publications/world-population-prospects-2019-highlights.html. (Accessed 7 October, 2022).

Wilton, N. (2022). *An Introduction to Human Resource Management*. 4th edn. London: Sage.

Woods, S.A., Ahmed, S., Nikolaou, I., Costa, A.C. and Anderson, N.R. (2019). Personnel selection in the digital age: A review of validity and applicant reactions, and future research challenges. *European Journal of Work and Organizational Psychology, 29*(1), pp.64–77.

Onboarding talent in different organisational contexts

Chapter 5

INTRODUCTION

The induction and onboarding experience has evolved considerably over the last few years. This chapter explores the meaning of onboarding, the process and why it is critical to employee retention and performance. The benefits of onboarding will be explored and good practices in an organisation context evaluated. An analysis of poor practice of onboarding will be undertaken with an assessment of the implications. The pre-boarding experience in hybrid organisations is examined, along with the challenges of remote onboarding. Finally, the chapter explores the value of capturing feedback to support the ongoing development of onboarding programmes in the short, medium and longer term.

ONBOARDING AS A CRITICAL RETENTION TOOL

Employers spend a considerable amount of time, money and energy on hiring the best candidates, and an effective onboarding process is critical to retention. Onboarding is probably the most important part of the retention strategy. Indeed, Petrilli et al. (2022) found in their research

DOI: 10.4324/9781003342984-6

that onboarding is an important part of the process that allows both the candidate and the company to get to know each other so that they are clear on expectations. The onboarding process can also support organisation socialisation. Induction is a critical element of staff retention. Much hard work goes into filling the vacancy or a new role, so it is essential that the organisation spends time making the new recruit feel welcome, helping them to settle in and giving them the platform to become productive members of the company (ACAS, 2015).

DEFINING ONBOARDING

Onboarding, also known as orientation or induction, is a process which helps new recruits to move from a position of organisational outsider to organisational insider. Onboarding or induction assists new members to adjust to their new surroundings and acquire the behaviours, attitudes and skills necessary to fulfil their new roles. It also supports new recruits to become effective members of the team. Onboarding is an integral part of employer branding and organisations must deliver on the proposition communicated at the attraction and recruitment stage. Not to do so will leave new starters discontent.

Induction or onboarding is the process of receiving and welcoming employees when they first join a company. A good first impression is very important and the new recruits should be provided with the information they need to quickly become productive members of the organisation. In some cases, the terms induction and onboarding are used interchangeably but for some the meanings are quite distinct. For example, Investors in People (2022) suggests that onboarding is the longer-term strategic and relationship approach to building high performance, whilst inductions are focused on more technical and administrative matters. Inductions in this case refer to form filling, practicalities and housekeeping, social contact such as meet and greet and legalities. It is a transactional process that happens at the beginning of the employment lifecycle. Onboarding begins at the pre-boarding stage, promoting a two-way process that results in more effective alignment of expectations between the employer and the employee. Chillakuri (2020) suggests that the onboarding process is an opportunity to introduce new hires to the values, goals, rules, responsibilities, procedures and organisation culture. An effective onboarding programme can also help reduce anxiety and uncertainty and provide clarity and understanding to new staff (Schroth, 2019).

In this chapter, we define onboarding as a long-term process which begins at the pre-boarding stage and may last for a year or so. It includes a number of activities to help the new recruit to settle into their new role as quickly as possible so that they are able to perform effectively. Onboarding includes a number of activities and is a shared responsibility between the people team, the line manager and the new recruit. To be effective, the process of onboarding should be measured at regular intervals and the feedback acted upon.

THE PROCESS OF ONBOARDING

The onboarding process varies across organisations and depends on the size of the company and the seniority of the employee (Chillakuri, 2020). It works most effectively when it is treated as a strategic intervention that will have a long-term impact on the career of employees. Krasman (2015) argues that onboarding is a strategic resource that requires planning and it should be incorporated into the larger business strategy as it has the potential to serve as a pillar for organisational growth. The onboarding programme starts before the employee joins the company and may last for 12 months or so. Indeed, Chillakuri (2020) argues that the employees' experience of an organisation starts from the day they attend for the interview, and therefore managers need to provide a realistic view of what the job entails. Certainly, the quicker that the new employee is integrated into the organisation the sooner they will be able to contribute as effective onboarding leads to increased job performance, job satisfaction and company loyalty.

Bouer (2010) developed the 4Cs model to support the design of the onboarding experience. The model works well in both a digital and hybrid working environment. In order of importance, the first activity is connection whereby the focus is on the creation of connections and interpersonal relationships aimed at creating a network of information that is essential to the successful performance of the new employee. Second is culture which is about helping the new recruit to understand the organisational norms and values. Too often the organisation takes for granted that these are immediately understood (Petrilli et al., 2022). Thirdly, the activity focuses on clarification whereby newcomers should be able to clarify their role and the expectations associated with it and, finally, compliance where newcomers are clear about the general rules of the organisation so that they become familiar with how it works.

Carucci (2018) concurs with the work of Bauer and highlights culture as an integral part of the onboarding process. Organisations must be intentional about helping new hires adapt to organisational values and norms, especially during that first year. Initial discussions of culture can be continued, perhaps at key intervals of three, six and nine months. Recruiting managers might engage new team members in conversations about the organisation's history and brand, how performance is measured and rewarded and how growth opportunities arise (ibid.).

It is essential that organisations design onboarding programmes in line with new hires expectations, values, attitudes and behaviours. The onboarding design should be consistent with the employer brand and should provide the new member of staff with a positive experience. In the age of digital disruption, if the onboarding process is still paper-based and begins on the joining day of the new employee, they will likely perceive the organisation lacks digital thinking (Deloitte, 2019). Companies need to implement structured and functional digital onboarding processes that allow newcomers to feel supported and guided, to understand their role and fit in the organisation.

ONBOARDING ACTIVITIES

Pre-boarding experience in hybrid organisations

Providing a structured pre-boarding plan will help new recruits to feel part of the organisation before they arrive. Details might include logins to email, portals and social media accounts so that new hires can familiarise themselves with communication systems. Asking the new recruit for a photo, short message and interests and hobbies will help with icebreakers, and the company might like to put an announcement on the intranet just prior to the new recruit starting. If the new team member is required to be onsite for their first day, it is good practice to provide a map, an idea regarding dress code and any other equipment they may require. An organisation might also provide welcome gifts such as pens, notebooks, water bottles, headphones etc.

CASE STUDY: MASTERCARD

New staff at Mastercard are sent a comprehensive welcome email before they start which includes links to company videos and access to a website where they can update their employment information, upload a photo for their badge, read about learning opportunities and complete paperwork for benefits enrollment, taxes and direct deposit (Mastercard, 2022).

COMPANY TOUR

In a hybrid organisation, it is very beneficial to invite the new starter to an event at a company office at some point in the first few weeks of starting in the new role. This might include a lunch out with the new team. This might be for a specific meeting or to meet colleagues. A company tour might be included. Employees expect the onsite days to be worth the commute and investment time so it is a good idea to plan office activities carefully in advance.

TRAINING EVENTS

Onboarding training might include a number of mandatory e-learning modules such as health and safety, equality, diversity and inclusivity and General Data Protection Regulations (GDPR). Specialist training might also be provided in sectors such as health, construction, education etc. Ensuring that training is undertaken in a timely manner is critical to ensure that the new recruit is appropriately prepared for their new role. It is a good idea to ensure that the new hire has some control over their development rather than respond only to compliance training. Chillakuri (2020) found that new hires are more engaged when they are able to influence and shape their own onboarding experience, for example, through personal development plans.

SOCIALISATION

It is important for new staff to be able to closely observe the actions and behaviour of their colleagues in order to understand organisational ways of working. Organisational socialisation is the process through which newcomers learn the requisite social and task knowledge in order to resolve role uncertainty and become 'organisational insiders' (Kowtha, 2018, p. 87). In a remote working situation, the digital onboarding process will need to consider how new team members will have an opportunity to interact with each other in order to understand organisational norms and to start building relationships, both formally and informally. A buddy, coach or mentor will provide newcomers with the opportunity to socialise with colleagues and this is an effective way of accelerating socialisation. Leatherbarrow and Fletcher (2018) suggest that employing a buddy in the first week will help answer some of the practical questions and deal with problems in an informal way. In an office, the new recruit might be invited to lunch. Telecom company O2 collaborate on ideas, ask questions and share feedback using social networks such as Yammer and Slack.

THE CULTURE HANDBOOK

Traditionally, companies would issue staff with a hard copy employee handbook that consisted of between 50 and 100 pages that cover every aspect of employment from recruitment to dismissal. The handbook provides consistency through detailed information about policies and procedures. It is a manual and a road map for employees clearly outlining the behaviours and work patterns and tends to be written from a compliance perspective.

Many organisations today provide staff with a culture guide, rather than an employee handbook. The culture guide is designed to highlight an organisation's culture and should be easy and enjoyable to read. A culture guide explains the history of the organisation, its mission and vision. It discusses how the organisation responds to problems and outlines communication norms. It will be informative, containing everything from how to survive your first day, to common policies and procedures, working with colleagues, working habits, compensation and benefits and organisation structure. Wording should be clear and simple.

CASE STUDY: MONEY AND PENSIONS SERVICE

The Money and Pensions Service (MaPS) is an arm's-length body sponsored by the Department for Work and Pensions, established at the beginning of 2019. It engages with HM Treasury on policy matters relating to financial capability and debt advice. The organisation launched their culture book in 2021 with the following introduction,

> this is our culture book, which sits alongside your contract of employment and follows on from our pre-induction welcome pack. It's a collection of what we hope are useful things about working here. That doesn't mean we don't have the serious people policies to protect you and us, but it's very rare they're needed, so we have focused on those aspects that help make this a great place to work.
>
> (Money and Pensions Service Culture Book, 2021)

THE CULTURE BOOK CONTAINS
THE FOLLOWING SECTIONS:

The culture of the organisation breathes through every section (See Table 5.1 below). For example, in the section 'your career experience', it states:

> We believe in creating an environment where people are treated as adults. To provide high quality and customer focused services, we need people who can innovate, take personal accountability and make great judgement calls. This means we aim to strike a balance between having policy that keeps us all safe, without creating an unnecessary rulebook for everything!

Table 5.1 Money and Pensions Service Culture Book Sections.

About Us	Your career	Family friendly	Keep us all safe	How things work around here	If things go wrong
Our People Our Strategy	Your career experience Career and learning Reward and recognition Helping you do your best work	Maternity, Surrogacy & adoption Paternity Shared parental leave	Data protection policy Health and safety policy Technology usage policy Whistle-blowing policy	The working day Time off If you're sick Well-being Getting stuff done	Resolution policy Disciplinary policy Equal opportunities policy

When reading this Culture Handbook, you will pick up on five important themes about how we want you to feel working here. We know some of it is aspirational and we're relying on everyone's input to make it a reality.

Our values define us

Strong values are the foundation of our success. They permeate every area of our work and define all our business relationships and the way we work with each other. We hire and promote the people who match our culture and values.

We trust you

We are keen to encourage freedom and autonomy rather than stifle it. This helps us to attract and retain the best people who flourish in our culture. So, you won't find a process or rules for everything – just some guidelines to help you think things through. We have hired you because you have great judgement.

You are unique

We want everyone to feel they can be themselves here – it means diversity, individuality and the freedom to be you! We don't want to treat everyone the same. Each of you will have a different role, different things that motivate you, different training needs and be at different stages of your career journey. We celebrate your uniqueness and try and avoid a 'one size fits all' approach.

Personal responsibility

We have a huge responsibility for achieving our vision, of everyone making the most of their money and pensions. We need people who can take personal responsibility for their contribution to this. When it comes to your performance at work, we want you to take ownership. Challenge yourself, challenge us, ask for feedback, stretch yourself, grab every opportunity you can. Don't wait to be asked and if there is something bugging you, speak up, we want to hear.

The way we communicate

We aim to be transparent and will share as much as we can. We believe that as we trust you, we'd rather put it out there and you can determine if it's of value to you or not. We want you to share what you're doing and how you feel about working here and there are lots of opportunities to do this. We encourage open and constructive debate and challenge. We want your help to create and suggest communication and social activities that you value – and we'll support them in any way we can.

Source: Reproduced here with kind permission from Jenny Liebenberg, Chief People Officer, Money and Pensions Service.

You may note that the information contained in the culture book is not dissimilar from that in the employee handbook but it is the way policies and practices are presented, the language used and the tone. In the Money and Pensions Service example, the focus is on trust and celebrating the diversity of individuals. It puts employees in charge of their career with the people department as the supporter and facilitator of the employee lifecycle.

STAKEHOLDERS

There will be a number of key stakeholders involved in the onboarding process. The first point of contact is likely to be the people professional who will arrange pre-boarding packs, security passes, passwords and initial briefings. The head of department and line manager of the new recruit will be important first points of contact on the first day. The head of department might only spend a few minutes with the new hire but this is important, welcoming the new recruit and providing a brief introduction to the team will be beneficial for the longer-term retention of the staff member. Line managers play an important role in the introduction of the new recruit to the rest of the team. Some organisations hold a formal corporate welcome, perhaps for a half or one day depending on whether the session is in person or remote. This might involve several senior members of staff introducing themselves and their departments. In remote inductions, these introductions are more likely to be available as short videos that new recruits can view at their convenience.

POOR ONBOARDING PRACTICES

Guy (2017) reports on global research from Webonboarding which revealed that businesses are failing to onboard new employees effectively. Almost four in ten (39 per cent) of employees surveyed said they had encountered problems when starting a new job. While almost half (42 per cent) said they didn't have a computer or laptop ready for them when they started, more than one in four (26 per cent) lacked a basic desk. Seventy-nine per cent agreed they would have settled into a new role a lot quicker had there been a better process and 15 per cent admitted they had turned down a job due to issues. The fundamental themes relative to businesses globally throughout the research were a lack of preparation, support and engagement. This impacts the ability of new staff to become productive members of the organisation, leading to frustration and disengagement.

Onboarding practices vary across organisations but also departments, countries, professional groups and industries (Jeske and Olson, 2022). Additionally, onboarding practices and processes can vary depending on the type of employment contract. Often, more formalised and structured onboarding is offered to permanent staff rather than temporary, contract and gig staff. Regardless of their status within the company all workers should receive an effective onboarding process. This is important so that non-permanent employees understand the values and behaviours of the organisation culture and how they should interact with colleagues. Honing effective relations at the start makes good business sense.

GETTING FEEDBACK

The costs and time of an effective onboarding programme can be significant but the real cost should be equated with the amount required to replace a new member of staff and start the recruitment process once again. It's a good idea to obtain feedback from new recruits about their experience across all levels of seniority. This is a good way to refine the programmes offered as quickly as possible if required. Some thought should be given to the onboarding lead. Jeske and Olsen (2022) found that large-scale onboarding events are often led by interns and junior staff who are likely to be the least experienced. Organisations should seek to measure the onboarding experience through both quantitative and qualitative measures. For example, 'how would you rate your trainer?' (on a 5–7 point Likert scale) and 'how can we improve your onboarding experience?' (see Table 5.2). Organisations might be reminded of their employer brand and

Table 5.2 Suggested Feedback Questions for New Starters

Pre-boarding experience	Prior to commencing my new role I felt welcomed by my team (measure 1–5, with 1 being low and 5 being high)
	My manager has been supportive of my transition into the organisation (measure 1–5, with 1 being low and 5 being high)
	I have been provided with the necessary equipment and logins/passwords to do my job (measure 1–5, with 1 being low and 5 being high)
Onboarding	I have a clear understanding of what my job entails (measure 1–5, with 1 being low and 5 being high)
	My role matches my expectations (derived from my interview and other role information) (measure 1–5, with 1 being low and 5 being high)
	I have received adequate training to get started in my role (measure 1–5, with 1 being low and 5 being high)
	I have the necessary equipment to perform effectively in my role (measure 1–5, with 1 being low and 5 being high)
Three-/sixth-month reviews	I am clear about what is expected of me (measure 1–5, with 1 being low and 5 being high)
	My line manager is supportive (measure 1–5, with 1 being low and 5 being high)
	I am aware of progression opportunities in the organisation (measure 1–5, with 1 being low and 5 being high)
	I would recommend this organisation to family and friends (measure 1–5, with 1 being low and 5 being high)
General feedback	What could we have done/do to improve your onboarding experience?

(Money and Pensions Service, 2021)

reflect on whether the onboarding experience is aligned. Focus groups to explore the experience of the new hire at 3-, 6- and 12-month evaluation reviews might also be undertaken. Line managers are well placed to gain informal feedback from their new recruits about their experience, and this is ongoing through regular meetings and reviews. All stakeholders should review the feedback in order to respond accordingly.

SUGGESTED FEEDBACK QUESTIONS TO NEW STARTERS

The value of the feedback obtained will likely be dependent on the confidence that the new recruit has in the confidentiality of the system used to collect the data. Careful thought should be given to the way in which feedback is sought and the technology used. Using a mix of formal and informal methods to collect data is likely to be most effective.

SUMMARY POINTS

- In this chapter, we discussed onboarding as a long-term process which begins at the pre-boarding stage and may last for a year or so. It includes a number of activities to help the new recruit to settle into their new role as quickly as possible so that they are able to perform effectively.

- Onboarding includes a number of activities and is a shared responsibility between the people team, the line manager and the new recruit. To be effective, the process of onboarding should be measured at regular intervals and feedback acted upon.

- The process of onboarding might be considered through the 4Cs model to structure the focus on connection, culture, clarification and compliance.

- Onboarding is a strategic tool which should be aligned to the business strategy.

- Onboarding activities will depend on whether the design of the programme is remote, in office or a mixture of both in a hybrid model. Activities might include a formal corporate event, meeting with the people team and line manager, lunch with colleagues, a company tour, allocation of a buddy and training events.

- Feedback is key to an effective onboarding process, and this should be collected throughout the onboarding programme both formally and informally.

SELF-TEST QUESTIONS/REVIEW QUESTIONS

- Review the Money and Pensions Service Culture Book example in this chapter. Evaluate the extent to which organisation culture can be understood through this book.

- Choose an organisation you are familiar with through your experience as an employee. If you don't yet have any work experience, undertake an interview with a family member or friend about their experience. Review Bauer's 4Cs model included in this chapter. To what extent does your experience align to this model?

A CASE EXAMPLE: NETFLIX

At Netflix, they give new employees bingo-style cards which get stamped each time they go for coffee or lunch with other employees. Once the card is filled, they get a prize. Evaluate the company rationale for including this activity as part of the onboarding programme.

REFLECTION

Reflect on your own experience of onboarding from an employee perspective (or that of a family or friend). Answer the feedback questions included in this chapter. What made it an effective onboarding experience for you? What recommendations would you make to your employer to improve the onboarding experience for future employees?

References

ACAS (2015). Starting staff: Induction. [online] Available at: https://www.acas.org.uk/sites/default/files/2021-03/Starting-staff-induction.pdf. (Accessed 31 August, 2022).

Bouer, T. (2010). Onboarding employees: Maximising success. SHRM. Available at: https://www.shrm.org/foundation/ourwork/initiatives/resources-from-past-initiatives/Documents/Onboarding%20New%20Employees.pdf (Accessed 12 August, 2022).

Carucci, R. (2018). To retain new hires, spend more time onboarding them. [online] *Harvard Business Review.* Available at: https://hbr.org/2018/12/to-retain-new-hires-spend-more-time-onboarding-them. (Accessed 13 August, 2022).

Chillakuri, B., (2020). Understanding generation Z expectations for effective onboarding. *Journal of Organizational Change Management,* [e-journal]. https://doi.org/10.1108/jocm-02-2020-0058.

Deloitte (2019). ConnectMe: Employee onboarding. [pdf] Available at: https://www2.deloitte.com/content/dam/Deloitte/us/Documents/human-capital/us-cons-connectme-onboarding.pdf. (Accessed 13 September, 2022).

Guy, M. (2017). Uncovered: Employees' worst onboarding experiences. [online] HRZone. Available at: https://www.hrzone.com/community/blogs/webonboarding/uncovered-employees-worst-onboarding-experiences. (Accessed 14 July 2022).

Investor in People (2022). Onboarding and induction. Available at: https://www.investorsinpeople.com/knowledge/onboarding-induction/. (Accessed 30 August, 2022).

Jeske, D. and Olson, D. (2022). Onboarding new hires: Recognising mutual learning opportunities. *Journal of Work-Applied Management, 14*(1), pp.63–76. https://doi.org/10.1108/JWAM-04-2021-0036.

Kowtha, N.R. (2018). Organizational socialization of newcomers: The role of professional socialization. *International Journal of Training and Development, 22*(2), pp.87–106.

Krasman, M. (2015). Three must-have onboarding elements for new and relocated employees. *Employment Relations Today, 42*(2), pp.9–14. https://doi.org/10.1002/ert.21493.

Leatherbarrow, C. and Fletcher, J., (2018). *Introduction to Human Resource Management: A Guide to HR Practice.* 4th edn. London: Kogan Page CIPD.

Mastercard (2022). Available at: https://mastercard.jobs/. (Accessed 20 September, 2022).

Money and Pensions Service (2021). *Money and Pensions Service Culture Book.* Interview (23 July 2022).

Petrilli, S. Galuppo, L. and Ripamonti, S.C. (2022). Digital onboarding: Facilitators and barriers to improve worker experience. *Sustainability, 14*(9), p.5684.

Schroth, H. (2019). Are you ready for Gen Z in the workplace? *California Management Review,* [e-journal] *61*(3). pp.5–18. https://doi:10.1177/0008125619841006.

Developing people in the contemporary workplace

Chapter 6

INTRODUCTION

Strategic people development is about the alignment of learning and development to organisational goals in order to ensure that business objectives are met. This chapter explores people development from the perspective of the individual, team and organisation. To begin with, this chapter provides a focus on employee development strategy formulation and how this is compiled. The rationale for people development is explored in relation to competitive advantage. Ways in which organisations can reskill and upskill the workforce are explored to fill skills gaps. A variety of people development interventions are explored including traditional learning (in-house programmes, coaching and mentoring) and digital learning. The opportunities that rapid technological developments offer are considered in relation to stakeholder interests.

STRATEGIC EMPLOYEE DEVELOPMENT

Employee development strategy has shifted considerably in recent years. Traditionally, development plans were compiled in relation to strategic objectives designed in static environments and training was employer led with an instructor delivering developmental activities in accordance with the plan. This classical approach to strategy formation leaves employee development responsive to predefined organisational strategy and the

DOI: 10.4324/9781003342984-7

skills, knowledge and behaviours identified as required. Because jobs were steady and routine and undertaken within predictable parameters, it was relatively straightforward to forecast training needs well in advance. During the coronavirus pandemic, organisations had to adapt quickly to the changes to retain their competitive advantage and rapid development of emergent learning was required to build new skills and knowledge, for example digital skills. The reskilling and upskilling of employees to manage within the context of remote working was a key challenge for learning and development professionals.

Even before the pandemic, the learning and development landscape was changing. Durai and Jose (2022) acknowledges four key trends in the context of learning. Firstly, because job design has moved from the steady and routine to unpredictable and non-routine work tasks, people now require creative thinking and problem-solving strategies and different ways of learning are required. Secondly, employees are working longer hours, have greater work demands, travel more and have more responsibility leaving little time for formal learning and development. Thirdly, organisational structures are flatter resulting in less opportunity for promotion and therefore organisationally driven development routes are far fewer. Fourthly, the increased use of advanced technology facilitates learning through technology which has enabled more flexible and self-directed forms of learning, e.g., through video conferencing, social media and discussion boards. Employees are able to develop both formally and informally and so learn through a mix of mediums and activities, some self-led and others organisationally directed. The final trend is recognition that employees now job hop between positions, organisations, sectors and even occupations requiring new learning and knowledge and the ability to learn quickly. Indeed, Durai and Jose (2022) argue that companies are now evaluating people on their ability to learn as organisations increasingly expect employees to manage multiple jobs.

DEVELOPING A LEARNING CULTURE

The most effective way of encouraging people to learn in organisations is to provide the mechanism and support for them to learn. The objective is to enhance the skills, knowledge and capability of employees to give the organisation a competitive advantage. Learning and development activity should be carefully aligned to the strategic objectives of the organisation but also balanced with the needs of staff. Senge (1990) described a learning organisation as one in which people continually expand their capacity to create the results they truly desire, where new and expansive patterns of thinking are nurtured, where collective aspiration is set free and where people are continually learning how to learn together. Pedler et al. (1997, p.3) describe an organisation as simply that 'which facilitates the learning of its members and continuously transforms itself'. Learning organisations make good business sense as they continuously focus on learning and a learning culture can be achieved 'when learning is recognised by top management, line managers and employees as an essential organisational process to which they are committed and in which they engage continuously' (Armstrong and Taylor, 2020, p.380). This commitment to employee learning and development is critical to high performance working (where work system processes and practices and policies enable employees to perform at their full potential) as a strong focus on continuous learning induces greater employee commitment, flexibility and overall improved quality.

LEARNING AT INDIVIDUAL, TEAM AND ORGANISATIONAL LEVEL

Wilton (2019) suggests that the benefits of learning and development can be understood at three levels, the individual, organisational and societal level. For the individual, the benefits of learning support skills and knowledge acquisition, enhanced employability, greater value to their current employer, improved job security and perhaps an increase in reward. At the societal level, learning and development impact on national economy and economic competitiveness and social and economic wellbeing. For organisations, learning and development improves the quality of employed labour, reduces labour turnover, reinforces organisational culture, enhances employee commitment, facilitates change and improves the employer brand (ibid.).

TERMINOLOGY

The terminology used in learning and development has evolved considerably and this is in somewhat a response to the changing business landscape, the volatile, uncertain, complex and ambiguous (VUCA) world and the speed of change. Terms such as education, training, development and learning are often used interchangeably, but there are important differences. Education is broad and is training for life. Training refers to work or specific tasks (and historically was considered as an intervention that is done unto you). Certainly, in the workplace there has been a move away from the training function to human resource development and now learning and development (Leatherbarrow and Fletcher, 2016). The focus of development is personal growth that supports skills and knowledge development for career progression. Learning too is focused on developing skills and knowledge, changing behaviour, supporting growth in our roles and our careers. Learning puts the individual in charge as we are responsible for what we learn and this is often related to our learning preferences and engagement in the activity.

LEARNING THEORY

People learn generally through their experience, through their social connection or through instruction. Learning also takes place through self-directive practice. The 70/20/10 model suggests that people will learn 70 per cent through their work experience, 20 percent through social learning and 10 per cent through formal training programmes (McCall et al., 1988). The framework originates from the research undertaken across four separate studies of over 200 executives from six major corporations. The research identified that most learning was gained on the job and through peers. Harding (2021) argues that there is actually no empirical evidence supporting the assumptions behind the 70:20:10 rule and it's unlikely to apply exactly in any one organisation. Harding (ibid.) also argues that the central assumption is misleading as the modes of learning are not independent. It is, however, a very popular approach to learning; although in practice its implementation is not always as a result of a planned approach. In any case, this model has been severely challenged in the wake of the coronavirus pandemic where all learning was disrupted and many online programmes introduced. However, the social aspect of the framework has proved to be particularly welcome in response to the surge of online learning and this is the 'glue' that integrates formal and experiential learning and fosters a conducive work environment (Johnson et al., 2018).

There are a number of learning theories that underpin approaches to learning and development (Harrison, 2009). Social learning theory is discussed in greater detail below but essentially it purports that effective learning occurs when people share expertise through a series of information sharing interactions. Experiential learning theory is undertaken through experience and reflection so that we become integral to our own development. Cognitive theory explores how individuals take in, store and retrieve information. It is how the brain learns through information processing. Behaviourist theory is based on punishments and rewards. Rewards increase the likelihood of behaviour being repeated whilst punishments decrease the likelihood of repetition. It is useful to understand our own preferences for learning so that we can maximise our chances of success when engaging in any learning and development activity.

THE LEARNING AND DEVELOPMENT POLICY

In an organisation, the primary purpose of learning and development is to improve the performance of employees which enables the organisation to achieve competitive advantage in the marketplace. Individuals, however, often consider learning and development opportunities to be an important part of their employee package (a non-financial reward) and vital for their career progression. Learning and development professionals develop learning and development policies that align to the needs of the business. Policies will likely include the organisation's approach to personal development planning, methods used to facilitate learning and development, formal and informal learning opportunities and resources, equality of opportunity in learning and development, internal and external provision, how to book formal training and how to enrol on qualifications. Additional details regarding expenses for travel, subsistence and hotels where appropriate and cancellation may also be included. The approach taken to evaluation and monitoring of all learning and development activity should also be included.

THE LEARNING AND DEVELOPMENT CYCLE

When exploring the various stages of identifying and responding to learning needs, it is useful to consider the learning and development cycle (Harrison, 2009). This provides a structured framework to the various phases of formal learning and development including identifying learning needs, setting learning objectives, planning the learning and development, implementing the learning and development, evaluating the intervention and then analysing and reviewing the evaluation (Figure 6.1).

Before developing any learning and development activity, it is necessary to identify learning needs. Boydell (1976) identified that training needs are identified from three possible levels: organisational, job or occupational and individual. I prefer to discuss learning rather than training needs (so that we focus on output rather than input) and at individual, team (or departmental) and organisation level. At the individual level, the most objective way is to start with a job analysis (as discussed in chapter 4). By identifying the competence gap, it will be possible to assess what the individual is able to do and what they should be doing. From a behavioural perspective, it is possible following this analysis to then determine what an individual is expected to do and what they actually do (Leatherbarrow and Fletcher,

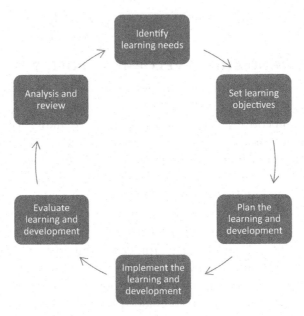

Figure 6.1 The learning and development cycle.

2016). In this approach, we are reflecting back to support the needs analysis and this should be balanced with looking forward by determining the organisational strategic objectives and how the needs of the role might be changing in response to internal and external change. For example, if we consider the role of the learning and development professional, does the role holder have the people analytics skills to be able to compile metrics to aid organisational decision making? Does the role holder have the required skills and knowledge to support the organisation in delivering on its commitment to sustainability issues through learning and development activities? Training needs are typically identified through performance reviews, mentoring and coaching, self-reflection, professional skills frameworks, assessment and development centres.

At a team or departmental level, discussions with heads of department will be critical for identifying learning needs. Learning and development interventions might be required at the team level to support organisational change, or perhaps the implementation of a new computer system that will be used by finance professionals. Alternatively, a team away day might be required to support team development or support the compilation of the strategic plan for the department.

At an organisation level, learning needs might be determined by an organisation wide skills audit arising from the strategic plan, staff attitude

Developing people in the contemporary workplace

survey or the organisation's focus on sustainability and equality, diversity and inclusivity objectives (these areas are covered elsewhere in this book). The main focus for all training needs analysis should be on balancing the analysis of a skills gap led approach with future skills analysis requirements.

DESIGNING LEARNING AND DEVELOPMENT INTERVENTIONS

After learning needs have been analysed, it is necessary to translate these into specific aims and objectives to inform learning interventions. Objectives should be SMART, in that they are specific, measurable, achievable, realistic and time related. The learner should be clear regarding what they will be able to do at the end of the learning intervention. For example, 'by the end of this session you will be able to discover techniques for introducing critical coaching aspects into your management style'.

There are a myriad of learning interventions that can be designed to support an identified need. Interventions might include:

Mentoring: designed to promote learning on the job and traditionally built on the relationship where an experienced worker supports a more junior member of staff. Reverse mentoring, also known as upward mentoring, is now more common too whereby the senior individual is the learner with a more junior member of staff providing expertise to support their development, for example in the use of social media. In either case, it is usual for both the mentor and mentee to benefit from the arrangement.

Coaching: may be undertaken through the daily practice of management or might be more formalised through the use of an external coach. Coaching usually consists of asking people questions to help them to think through what they are doing. This often supports a deeper level of learning through reflection.

Buddy system: tends to be a more informal system whereby someone with more experience assists perhaps someone new to the job or where someone needs to learn a new computer system. The buddy system is often used in onboarding programmes.

Shadowing: is where one colleague spends some time observing another colleague to get a sense of what they do and how they do it. The success of the arrangement depends on clear outcomes and time spent on helping the trainee to understand what is happening through a coaching arrangement.

In-house or external provision: from courses to conferences, seminars, qualifications and networking, there are many activities which might effectively respond to learning and development needs. Some organisations contract specialists and consultants to deliver training on their behalf.

Typically, in-house learning and development in the form of traditional courses is delivered by learning and development professionals.

SOCIAL AND COLLABORATIVE LEARNING

Social and collaborative learning might be described as learning in the flow of work. It works most effectively when learners are working together on a genuine project with an outcome that needs to be delivered. Hart (2014) argues that social learning is about people connecting, conversing, collaborating and learning from, and with, one another on a daily basis at work. Collaboration, on the other hand, is a philosophy of interaction and personal lifestyle where individuals are responsible for their actions, including learning, and they respect the abilities and contributions of their peers (Laal and Ghodsi, 2012). The CIPD (2021) found that more organisations are now using social and collaborative learning with 28 per cent of respondents in the 2021 Learning and Skills at Work Survey reporting that they are using this form of learning in comparison to 19 per cent in 2020. It is an important element of digital learning as it provides participants with the opportunity to maximise their learning through engagement with peers leading to a deeper level of learning. Indeed, finding opportunities for social collaboration in the hybrid working model is an important aspect of learning design.

However, Ambrus et al. (2021) neuroscience research suggests that in-person interactions are more effective than digital meetings as being face to face allows us to process more non-verbal clue data to support our brain in gaining knowledge about a person's characteristics through social collaboration. Where it is not possible to meet in person, it is important to counterbalance the deficit with more frequent and intentional interactions (Andretta, 2019). Collaborative learning provides a number of benefits and typically results in higher achievement and greater productivity, more caring, supportive and committed relationships and greater psychological health, social competence and self-esteem (Laal and Ghodsi, 2012).

SELF-DIRECTED LEARNING

Self-directed learning focuses on self-managed learning and might include personal development planning. Individuals are responsible for taking control of their own learning and development so that they analyse their own needs, set their own goals, prepare action plans, undertake development activities and then reflect on their progress. Loeng (2020) suggests that self-directed learning entails individuals taking the initiative and responsibility for their own learning so that each of us are able to set our own goals and define what is worth learning. The success of self-directed learning depends on our ability and willingness to reflect and engage in critical judgement. Dachner et al. (2019) argue that the problem with self-directed learning is that it suffers from interruptions and its success depends on the form of interaction, job type and time available to make the developmental intervention meaningful. Additionally, Dachner et al. (ibid.) argue that there is the possibility that unlike organisationally sponsored development activities, self-initiated learning sources (e.g., peers and websites) may provide incorrect or incomplete knowledge.

DIGITAL LEARNING

Web 2.0 technology is the second generation of the world wide web. It refers to the dynamic way in which individuals interact, collaborate and participate via the web providing user-control. Social media such as Facebook and Instagram can be used to support learning, providing just in time access to knowledge and information for both individual and organisational learning through blogs, vlogs and wikis (online applications that provide people with the opportunity to add, delete content in collaboration with others). Social media can support collaboration activities through the use of platforms such as Yammer and Slack. From a learning perspective, there are multiple possibilities for personalised development aligned to individual learning styles (Kompen, et al. 2019).

Game based learning often referred to as 'gamification' takes the concept of video games and applies it to learning. Learners are able to actively practise skills development and problem-solving in a structured immersive experience. Arguably, games-based learning makes learning more exciting, interactive and productive. As an example, Sally Beauty uses scenario-based games in eLearning modules designed for the company's beauty advisors. The associates lacked confidence in customer interactions regarding hair colour purchases and the company was keen to create a way for them to practise consultations in realistic scenarios. If a learner selects the wrong hair colour product, instant feedback is provided (Roundtable Learning, 2022).

Virtual reality (VR) in games-based learning is becoming increasingly popular in organisations and can be cost effective when used to train large numbers of people over time. For example, FedEx are using VR in its safety training. VR simulates actual warehouse operations and trains staff to load and unload trailers effectively and how to work in a warehouse environment (Forde, 2019). Games-based learning certainly presents a number of benefits but it is not an easy option and requires time and effort to implement effectively. As with any learning intervention, it is still necessary to define objectives which can be measured, ensure that the design focuses on the intended objectives, support learners in analysing their progress and ensure that any scenarios are directly transferable to the workplace and that the learner is able to do this. Digital badges (to reward learner achievements) is a common approach to engaging participants in game based learning. An IBM-led study reported that the use of digital badges had supported employee engagement with 87 per cent of staff saying that they were more engaged because of the digital badge programme (Leaser, 2019).

The CIPD (2021) categorise digital learning into three components. The first is formal digital learning where technology is delivered formally through courses and usually involves a fee; secondly, informal digital learning provides opportunities to support informal workplace learning, and thirdly, blended or supported learning which includes both formal and informal learning combined with other types of learning. Digital learning is now used by 57% of organisations (pre-pandemic figures 2020) compared with 29% in 2015 (ibid.). Digital learning is therefore used more highly now than trainer led training (36%). In a study by online and blended learning specialist Arden University, almost 60% of learning and development professionals said the pandemic had changed their organisations' attitudes to learning (Evans, 2020). The coronavirus pandemic has provided the catalyst for many organisations to invest in learning technologies to align learning and needs.

Walters (2022) acknowledges a number of benefits to digital learning including the accessibility of materials 24 hours a day, 7 days a week so that learners have complete flexibility over their study schedule. Additional resources such as recorded lectures and additional reading can be easily shared and learning can be designed to be more personalised as instructors learn additional methods for effective teaching incorporating a range of videos, podcasts, e-books and traditional virtual classroom based sessions. One of the biggest advantages is the ability for digital analysis so that the progress of learners can be tracked and interventions made to support engagement. In their 2021 survey of Learning and Skills at Work, the CIPD (CIPD, 2021) found that webinars were the most popular digital tool used for learning. Learning management systems (LMSs) were cited as the second most popular way of delivering education, learning, training and development. As well as providing accessible learning to users, these LMS systems apply software for the effective administration, documentation, tracking, reporting and automation of learning and development.

The BAE SYSTEMS case study below provides an example of how an organisation has adapted to a hybrid approach to learning and development. It introduces the strategic intent of the learning and development strategy. It highlights progression opportunities, both virtual and in person and it emphasises retention through career advancement and retraining. It segments training into mandatory requirements at organisational and functional level and highlights the talent pool for high performance workers that are keen to accelerate their development. It focuses on diversity and inclusivity and links to the resourcing strategy for internal mobility.

CASE STUDY – BAE

Learning and development: beginning your life-long learning journey

BAE Systems provides some of the world's most advanced, technology-led defence, aerospace and security solutions. The company employs a skilled workforce of 90,500 people in more than 40 countries. Working with customers and local partners, the organisation develops, engineers, manufactures and supports products and systems to deliver military capability, protect national security and people and keep critical information and infrastructure secure.

The learning and development strategy mission is detailed in the talent management framework.

Our mission is to build a strong pipeline of diverse, adaptable and inspirational talent that will lead and grow our future business. We believe that everyone has talent, and at the heart of our talent management approach our ambition is to be recognised as the leading employer in the defence and security sector for valuing diversity and inclusion.

Accelerated development will be offered to those who have the aspiration, ability and performance to fulfil leadership and technical roles that are critical to our future success. We will identify those employees who have high potential.

The company promotes its internal progression opportunities through its internal mobility policy and emphasises its commitment

> to support our colleagues reach their full potential and so you'll always find something new that will continue to inspire and provide an exciting and varied career that continues to play a crucial role in creating a secure tomorrow for generations to come.

BAE encourages retention through the opportunity to have multiple careers with the organisation and the opportunity to retrain or reskill through a formal programme or on demand virtual learning platform where tailored resources are aligned to each of the functions.

Learning resources are accessible at any time and from any device. Inclusive learning styles are incorporated through a variety of platforms such as videos, books, guides and structured virtual learning programmes through the digital learning platform, Spark.

THE BAE LEARNING PORTFOLIO INCLUDES THE FOLLOWING:

Core skills: the skills we all need to be effective in our roles and to support the business

Leadership learning: the skills required to lead and inspire high-performing teams

Functional learning: the technical knowledge and skills specific to your role and function

Business integrity training: the essential training we must all complete to ensure we operate to the highest standards of business conduct.

Each employee has a learning plan that is developed in partnership with a people manager. There are opportunities to get involved in projects beyond the remit of the employee in order to gain wider experience. Additionally, there are opportunities to get involved in community projects, STEM (science, technology, engineering and maths) initiatives and employee resource groups.

To ensure the company retains its talented people, BAE maintains future-focused critical skills by offering a blend of sponsorship, additional support in career development planning and a portfolio of high-potential development programmes.

Exploring organisation case examples is helpful for benchmarking. Learning and development professionals might participate in CIPD branch events, conferences, seminars, webinars and networking to continuously review their learning and development offer. This external evaluation can support the internal evaluation process.

EVALUATING LEARNING AND DEVELOPMENT

Evaluation of any learning and development intervention is a critical element and should be considered at the same time as designing the objectives of the activity. There are a number of recognised models of training evaluation with Kirkpatrick's (1994) model being the most popular. This model measures learning at four levels. The first is the reaction to the event, second is the learning from the event, third is the behaviour on the return to work, and the fourth is the impact on organisational performance.

Evaluation will provide an indication of where improvements might be made and will also provide the data for measuring return on investment (ROI) and return on expectation (ROE). ROI is a measurement used to assess the overall impact of learning activities on organisational performance and is calculated as:

Benefits from training ($£$) – costs of training

$$\frac{\text{Benefits from training (£) – costs of training}}{\text{COSTS OF TRAINING (£)}} \times 100$$

COSTS OF TRAINING ($£$)

Return on expectation is the measurement of whether the intervention met the planned expectations. It is a qualitative measure and works most effectively when ROE is agreed with all stakeholders at the planning stage of the activity.

Measuring learning and development activity is generally difficult as apart from the evaluation of the immediate activity, all other measures that might be undertaken at three-month, six-month and longer-term intervals are not directly aligned to the learning and development activity. Other factors such as line manager support, peer collaboration, opportunity to implement the learning etc. will impact the success of any intervention. Aside from this, some organisations do not always prioritise evaluation, and some learning and development professionals do not have the time or experience to undertake effective evaluation. Evaluation also suffers sometimes from lack of resources and misalignment of objectives to the activity.

After the evaluation has been undertaken, it should be analysed and actions taken to make improvements or amendments. Metrics and learning analytics are a fundamental aspect of the evaluation process, and this is discussed in Chapter 10.

SUMMARY POINTS

- Learning and development strategy should be aligned with the organisation's strategic objectives and encourage a learning culture in order to support the institution in achieving a competitive advantage.
- The learning and development cycle refers to a structured framework of learning and development which includes identifying learning needs, setting learning objectives, planning the learning activity, implementing learning and development, evaluating the intervention and then analysing and reviewing the data obtained.

- Learning and development needs should be analysed at the individual, team and organisation level. They should take account of job analysis looking back and organisational strategic objectives looking forward.
- There are many learning and development interventions that might be explored in relation to developmental requirements. These include mentoring, coaching, buddy systems, shadowing, in-house and external provision. In a hybrid workplace, social and collaborative, self-directed and digital learning have grown in popularity.
- Evaluating learning is a critical part of any learning and development intervention and might be analysed in terms of return on investment and return on expectation.

SELF-TEST QUESTIONS/REVIEW QUESTIONS

- Review the training cycle model discussed in this chapter. To what extent is it necessary to follow this structure when exploring individual, team and organisation learning and development needs?
- What is meant by self-directed learning? Explore the advantages and disadvantages of self-directed learning from your own perspective. How can self-directed learning be used most effectively in an organisation context?

A CASE EXAMPLE: BAE SYSTEMS

Review the BAE Systems organisation case study example discussed in this chapter. What training needs analysis do you think the organisation engages in to support the delivery of the learning and development strategy? How can the organisation ensure that its virtual learning programmes delivered on its digital learning platform, Spark, are not an isolating experience?

REFLECTION

Reflect on your own experience of digital learning. Have you attended a webinar or course online? How much of the session do you remember? Evaluate the programme for its strengths and limitations. What might be improved and how?

References

Ambrus, G.G., Eick, C.M., Kaiser, D. and Kovács, G. (2021). *Journal of Neuroscience*, 30 June, *41*(26), pp.5687–5698. https://doi.org/10.1523/JNEUROSCI.2466-20 .2021

Andretta, B. (2019). The brain science of creating high-performing teams. [online] *Training Industry*. Available at: https://trainingindustry.com/articles/performance -management/the-brain-science-of-creating-high-performing-teams/. (Accessed 13 August, 2022).

Armstrong, M. and Taylor, S. (2020). *Armstrong's Handbook of Human Resource Management Practice.* 15th edn. London: Kogan Page.

Boydell, T.H. (1976). *The Identification of Training Needs.* London: British Association for Commercial and Industrial Education.

CIPD (2021). Digital learning. CIPD. 8 June. Available at: https://www.cipd.co.uk /knowledge/fundamentals/people/development/digital-learning-factsheet#gref. (Accessed 4 July 2022).

CIPD (2021). Learning and skills at work survey. Report. CIPD. May. Available at https://www.cipd.co.uk/Images/learning-skills-work-report-2021-1_tcm18-95433 .pdf (Accessed 13 October, 2022).

CIPD. (2022). *Qualifications that connect.* [online] Available at: https://www.cipd.co.uk/ learn/training/qualifications.

Dachner, A., Ellingson, J.E., Noe, R.A. and Saxton, B. (2019). The future of employee development. John Carroll University. Available at: https://core.ac.uk/download/pdf /289197727.pdf. (Accessed 13 October, 2022).

Durai, A.P. and Jose, J. (2022). The shifting corporate strategy of learning and development in the post-pandemic era. *Journal of Positive School Psychology. [online].* http://journalppw.com, 6(4), 7005–7010.

Evans, C. (2020). The future of learning: Online training in a post Covid world. Training Zone. 16 December. Available at: https://www.trainingzone.co.uk/deliver /training/the-future-of-learning-online-training-in-a-post-covid-world (Accessed 2 August, 2022).

Forde, M. (2019). FedEx Ground using virtual reality to train, retain workers. Supply Chain Dive. Available at: https://www.supplychaindive.com/news/fedex-ground -using-virtual-reality-train-retain-workers/567235/ (Accessed 15 October, 2022).

Harding, R. (2021). Debate: The 70:20:10 'rule' in learning and development: The mistake of listening to sirens and how to safely navigate around them. *Public Money & Management,* [e-journal] pp.1–2. http://doi:10.1080/09540962.2021.1951517.

Harrison, R. (2009). *Learning and Development.* 5th edn. London, CIPD.

Hart, J. (2014). *Social Learning Handbook 2014.* London: Centre for Learning & Performance Technologies.

Johnson, S.J., Blackman, D.A., Buick, F. (2018). The 70:20:10 framework and the transfer of learning. *Human Resource Development Quarterly,* pp.1–20. https://doi.org /10.1002/hrdq.21330.

Kirkpatrick, D.L. (1994). *Evaluating Training Program: The Four Levels.* San Francisco: Berret-Koehler Publishers, Inc.

Kompen, R.T., Edirisingha, P., Canaleta, X. Alsima, A. and Monguet, J. (2019). Personal learning Environments based on Web 2.0 services in higher education. Telematics and Informatics, 38(May 2019), pp.194–206.

Laal, M. and Ghodsi, S.M. (2012). Benefits of collaborative learning. *Procedia: Social and Behavioral Sciences,* [e-journal] *31*, pp.486–490. https://doi.org/10.1016/j.sbspro.2011 .12.091.

Leaser, D. (2019). Do digital badges really provide value to businesses? 18 June. Available at: https://www.ibm.com/blogs/ibm-training/do-digital-badges-really -provide-value-to-businesses/ (Accessed 13 July, 2022).

Leatherbarrow, C. and Fletcher, J. (2016). *Introduction to Human Resource Management: A Guide to HR in Practice.* 3rd edn. London: CIPD.

Loeng, S. (2020). Self-Directed learning: A core concept in adult education. *Education Research International,* 2020(3816132), pp.1–12. https://doi:10.1155/2020/3816132.

McCall, M.W., Jr., Lombardo, M.M. and Morrison, A.M. (1988). *The Lessons of Experience: How Successful Executives Develop on the Job.* Lexington, MA: Lexington Books.

Pedler, M., Burgogyne, J. and Boydell, T. (1997). *The Learning Company: A Strategy for Sustainable Development.* 2nd edn. London: McGraw-Hill.

Roundtable Learning (2022). Available at: https://roundtablelearning.com/case_study/sally-beauty-case-study/. (Accessed 13 September, 2022).

Senge, P. (1990). *The Fifth Discipline: The Art and Practice of the Learning Organization*. New York: Random House Business Books.

Walters, H. (2022). The top 10 benefits of digital learning. [online] *eLearning Industry*. Available at: https://elearningindustry.com/the-top-benefits-of-digital-learning. (Accessed 13 August, 2022).

Wilton, N. (2019). *An Introduction to Human Resource Management*. 4th edn. London: Sage.

Rewarding talent in the virtual, hybrid and traditional workplace

Chapter 7

INTRODUCTION

Reward is an integral part of attracting and retaining talent. The reward strategy is vital in ensuring that the employer's values are communicated and conveyed through its employees. This chapter provides an introduction to planning, implementing and evaluating reward systems in a range of organisational contexts. Ways of rewarding individual, team and organisational performance in a fair, reasonable and equitable way are explored along with gender and ethnicity pay gaps. An exploration of the guiding principles and reward philosophy is undertaken along with market intelligence in pay decisions. Base pay and variable pay are considered and a suite of incentive schemes designed for the contemporary organisation explored. Regional pay model challenges are noted in relation to contractual and fairness dimensions. The chapter reviews hybrid dilemmas such as how to balance the needs and wants of employees working anywhere.

DEFINING REWARD

Reward management is defined by Armstrong (2010: p.267) as 'the strategies, policies and processes required to ensure that the value of people

DOI: 10.4324/9781003342984-8

and the contribution they make to achieving organisation, departmental and team goals is recognised and rewarded'. Reward is generally understood as the total amount of financial and non-financial compensation or total remuneration provided to an employee in return for labour or service rendered at work. The CIPD (2021a) suggest that pay may be divided into two categories, base (or fixed pay) which is a guaranteed cash wage or salary paid to employees for their work for a contracted time period (this may include location allowances and other associated guaranteed payments) and, secondly, variable pay which is not guaranteed and may include bonus, incentives and overtime payments.

Reward, which is sometimes described as compensation or remuneration, is possibly the most critical contract term in paid work (Anku et al., 2018). Compensation may be taken to mean just pay (both fixed and variable) whilst remuneration and reward might refer to the wider benefits package (CIPD, 2022). Reward is an area of specialist knowledge in the CIPD HR profession map and focuses on designing and implementing strategies that ensure workers are rewarded in line with the organisational context and culture, relative to the external market environment (CIPD, 2021b).

TOTAL REWARD

The CIPD (2022) suggest that reward generally covers all financial provisions made to employees, including cash pay and the wider benefits package (such as pensions or private medical insurance). It can also include wider provisions for employees, with the term 'total reward' sometimes used to encompass compensation and benefits. The notion of total reward is used to cover all aspects of work that are valued by people across the employee lifecycle. Examples might include flexible benefits, access to professional and career development, meaningful work, freedom and autonomy, opportunity for personal growth, being treated fairly, recognition of achievements, transparency in reward processes and outcomes, being able to raise matters of concern, being involved in decisions that affect the way work is done, flexible working options and supportive line managers. Total rewards will differ across organisations but Armstrong and Taylor (2020) suggest that both intrinsic and extrinsic factors will be prevalent in a total rewards package. For example, intrinsic factors might include quality of work, work and life balance, alignment of personal and organisation values, an enabling environment and growth opportunities. Extrinsic factors are tangible and might include professional memberships, retail discounts, health and welfare, performance share options, team awards etc.

Taylor (2010, p352) argues that "payment is a good deal less powerful as a positive motivator than intrinsic rewards (the pleasures people gain from doing the job itself) and raising pay only buys short term job satisfaction". Any underlying problems which are making employees unhappy will not, therefore, be changed in the longer term with the offer of additional money. Happy employees are unlikely to leave only for money.

Blending financial and non-financial elements of reward will provide a long-lasting impact on job satisfaction and performance and can be communicated in the employee value proposition with the aim of sourcing skilled staff. A total reward package can help to attract, retain and motivate staff and if designed effectively it can meet both employee and organisational priorities and help the organisation enhance its reputation so that it becomes an employer of choice. However, such a package can be expensive and needs to be tailored to the needs and desires of staff.

The CIPD (2022) argues that for some staff, the options and value of the reward package are confusing and organisations need to focus further on communicating the value of reward to staff. Brown and Hewitt (2014) concur, proposing that organisations need to move away from generic total reward strategies with a 'chocolate box of flexible benefits' to a smart rewards approach characterised by a simpler, clear and more flexible focus on a few core values and reward principles that are evidence based with clear measures of success and a strong emphasis on engaging all employees. Sylvester (2011) agrees and suggests that rather than simply confusing employees with offering too much, it is better that organisations focus on some core benefits which can really drive value for the employee and in turn the employer (Sylvester, 2011). A stronger focus on communication and delivery is required so that there is clear alignment between what employees are seeking and what employers are offering. The NHS in the UK has implemented Total Reward Statements for their staff to help them to understand and appreciate their overall reward package including the value of their pension benefits. Rather than focusing on the benefits that an organisation might offer to staff, the starting point should be the business strategy so that the reward strategy is aligned to the strategic objectives of the company (NHS, 2021).

DESIGNING THE REWARD STRATEGY

The starting point for the reward strategy is to consider the rewards philosophy which should be consistent with the organisation's culture and values. Making the reward philosophy explicit will support the communication of the rewards strategy and will make it easier to share with managers, employees, shareholders.

Strategic reward is now at the very centre of any people management strategy as it has long since been recognised that employees provide organisations with a sustained competitive advantage. Taking a strategic approach to reward is a concept emphasised by Lawler back in 1990s (Lawler, 1990) who argued that strategic pay should be person centred (rather than job centred), based on the market value of skills and knowledge, benchmarked externally, non-hierarchical emphasising employability and performance rather than loyalty and entitlement (Lawler, 2000). Reward strategy is a statement of intent (Armstrong and Brown, 2019) which is essential to the long-term viability of companies particularly in challenging economic times (Nyandoro and Goremusandu, 2016). The reward strategy should be horizontally aligned to all other HR policies. The case study below provides an example of how to align the reward strategy to the business objectives.

CASE STUDY:

Gemserv is a specialist market design, governance and assurance service provider within the utilities and environment sectors. Based in the UK, the company employs over 120 staff. Gemserv's prime objective in reviewing its reward and benefits strategy was to help attract, engage and retain key staff. Gemserv wanted to encourage and reward performance linking it to individual long-term career and corporate growth aspirations. The company set out to achieve this by creating an 'Employee Deal' that aligned contribution and performance and individual and team performance incentives to deliver long-term growth aspirations (Lardner, 2015). This is not something that can be achieved short term. Strategic reward focuses on a long-term organisation approach that balances the needs of both the organisation and its employees (Gemserv, 2022).

People will behave based on what they perceive will lead to rewards and therefore reward systems must be designed in alignment with what the organisation values. Dunn–Coleman (2020) suggests that when designing a reward strategy the focus should start with what behaviours the organisation intends to encourage, for example, innovation and teamwork. Reward and culture are closely aligned. The case study below provides an example of how an organisation designed its reward strategy in alignment to its commitment to equality, diversity and inclusivity.

CASE EXAMPLE: IFS

IFS is a global software organisation employing over 5,000 staff in more than 50 countries worldwide (IFS, 2022). Using a total reward approach, the company aims to ensure that everyone is paid fairly for their contribution to the organisation's success which helps to foster a strong team spirit and positive culture.

Benefits include a bonus plan designed to guide employee effort to a common objective: maximising group cash earnings before interest, taxes, depreciation, and amortisation (EBITDA) and enabling everyone to share in the success. The company is agile in the way it rewards staff. The company has a flexible hybrid working model in place. This approach has helped IFS to unify its organisational culture across different geographical borders and across different working patterns, including hybrid and remote working. The organisation's total reward approach aligns to its focus on diversity, equality and inclusivity (DE&I) strategy (Coleman, 2022).

Following an assessment of desired behaviours, the next phase in designing a reward strategy is to explore how the behaviours align to the extrinsic rewards (pay, benefits etc.) and intrinsic rewards (recognition, personal development). This process will also support the gap analysis, for example where a reward element is not in place to support a particular behaviour. Organisations need to evaluate whether they have the right people to deliver the organisation's strategic objectives in both the short and longer term. Depending on the findings, organisations will either need to focus on resourcing or retention. A benchmarking exercise with competitors in the sector will provide an insight into what reward packages other organisations are offering. This insight needs to be balanced with affordability, however. Leatherbarrow and Fletcher (2018) suggest that employers will also need to take account of government policies on pay and trade union demands.

As indicated above, it is important that employees understand the value of the benefits on offer and careful thought must be given to how the package is communicated. Consideration of how employees will be able to progress in the organisation based on performance, values, behaviours and skills is required at this stage. It is important to explore how the effectiveness of the reward strategy will be measured in terms of encouraging the intended behaviours. Clear metrics are necessary to support this process and qualitative and quantitative data can support the evaluation process through staff surveys, exit interviews, Glassdoor reviews and pulse surveys (see Chapter 12). The reward strategy should be regularly reviewed in relation to feedback received and action taken where required.

REWARD AT INDIVIDUAL, TEAM AND ORGANISATION LEVEL

The way in which rewards are allocated will influence employee behaviour. Whether it be individual input, team effort or collective attention, the aim of reward at any level will be focussed on the achievement of results to meet the organisational strategic objectives. The case study example below provides an insight into how individual reward packages might be designed in line with strategic goals incorporating fixed and variable pay, a wider benefits package and an organisation based bonus scheme.

CASE STUDY: SHOOSMITHS

Shoosmiths is a law firm with over 1,500 employees in over 14 locations with a £181 million turnover (Shoosmiths, 2022). The company won the Law Firm of the Year award from the Legal Business Awards in 2022. The company has launched its first formal employee bonus scheme as part of its reward strategy review. The bonus scheme is based on non-financial strategic goals and financial targets paying the same percentage bonus to all employees in order to promote teamwork and collaboration. The bonus will be paid on criteria including the meeting of profit targets, goals associated with client feedback and helping to meet the firm's carbon emissions targets through reduced travel. The company has a target to reduce greenhouse gas emissions by 50 per cent across the value chain by 2030. The reward package has been designed to include a competitive salary (which reflects the employee's role and contribution), a collegiate bonus scheme, recognition rewards and a range of benefits from which employees can choose to reflect their personal priorities).

There is an increasing focus on collaboration in organisations, particularly those operating in a hybrid working model. Team rewards can encourage a group to achieve a collective goal and celebration of results may increase team morale. Team reward has grown in popularity as a consequence of the way work is organised within organisations and are generally designed as incentives to improve performance. For example, it is common for senior management teams to be rewarded for meeting key performance indicators. Technological developments have changed the way work is organised with increased flexibility and agility aiding communication and filesharing. There are now many interdependencies between job roles which encourages team-based work.

Gu et al. (2022) argue that smaller group rewards tend to be more motivating than large organisational profit sharing as individuals are able to identify further with their contribution to the group. To be effective, team-based rewards must be communicated effectively through a team-based reward policy. In smaller groups, team members may be more aware of individual contributions. In larger groups, it may be possible for some members of the team to be less effective than others without consequence. In any team-based reward, there is the potential for a perception of inequity in the distribution of reward, however.

CASE STUDY EXAMPLE: BAE

Some years ago, when I was working in organisation development at BAE SYSTEMS a Christmas bonus was offered to all employees if the passenger aircraft were refitted as a freighter and delivered on time to the client within each 12-week agreed period during the year. The bonus was offered to every member of the staff in the division, both office and hanger based. There was a sense of inequity from some of the technical staff working on the shop floor as office-based workers were not deemed as deserving of the reward as they were not directly involved in the project. Office workers were considered passive bystanders!

FAIR, REASONABLE AND EQUITABLE

Adams's (1963) equity theory (discussed below) is the most widely used theory to explain fairness in organisations. At its core, the theory suggests that the distribution of rewards should be based on the individual's contribution. Justice in reward relates to how equitable or fair employees perceive a reward to be. Employees will be concerned with two key areas, firstly the process of how rewards are made (procedural justice) and how the rewards are allocated (distributive justice) (Leatherbarrow and Fletcher, 2018). Involving staff in reward-based decision-making, particularly in relation to benefits will support a climate of equity.

In the UK, employers must meet legal requirements on equal pay and the national minimum wage which applies to all workers 16 and over. The National Minimum Wage is the minimum pay per hour almost all workers are entitled to. The National Living Wage is higher than the National Minimum Wage and workers get it if they're over 23 (Gov.UK, 2022). While not a legal requirement almost 9,000 organisations have signed up for the National Living Wage (CIPD, 2022). Equal pay is an aspect of sex discrimination law which gives the right for men and women to be paid the same for the same, or equivalent work. Despite the legislation, there remains significant gender pay differences, and larger employers are now required to report on the size of the gender pay gap in their organisations.

PAY GAP REPORTS

The Gender Pay Gap Reporting Regulations were introduced in 2017 and make it a legal obligation for employers to take action to identify and publish any gender pay gaps within their organisation. Organisations with 250 or more employees in England, Scotland and Wales must publish their gender pay gap figures annually. These provisions are not yet in force in Northern Ireland (CIPD, 2022). The gender pay gap is an equality measure that shows the difference in average earnings between women and men (GOV.UK, 2016). Although the gender pay gap in the UK has decreased over the last few decades, it continues to be large and significant. According to the ONS (2021), among full-time employees the gender pay gap in April 2021 was 7.9 per cent. There remains a large difference in gender pay between employees aged 40 years and over (12 per cent) and those aged below 40 (3 per cent). The gender pay gap is higher in every English region than in Wales, Scotland and Northern Ireland. Any gender pay gap is likely to be the result of both internal and external factors that should be analysed and communicated to all stakeholders. According to Dias et al. (2020), UK women across all education levels face a so-called child penalty in wages of around 30 per cent with respect to men by the time their oldest child reaches age 18. These earning gaps are by definition the combined effect of the gap in employment rates, the gap in hours of work, and the gap in hourly wage rates between women and men (ibid.).

Although at the time of writing, reporting of the ethnicity pay gap is not mandatory it is likely that this will be implemented in the UK in the near future. PWC (2022) reports that only 67 per cent of employers are currently collecting ethnicity data which has implications for the reliability of any ethnicity pay gap reporting. An organisation that has low ethnicity disclosure rates will struggle to gain a true picture of its ethnicity pay gap based on this limited sample of employees. For example, in 2021, Aviva voluntarily published its ethnicity pay gap in order to be transparent and work towards an inclusive workforce (Aviva, 2022). The pay gap figures are based on the 72 per cent of the UK workforce that informed the company of their ethnicity. Based on the current disclosure rate, Aviva confirmed that 8 per cent of its workforce is from an ethnically diverse background. In its analysis, Aviva advised that it disaggregated its ethnically diverse data set and calculated pay and bonus gaps in relation to the following ethnic groups: Black, Asian, Mixed/Multiple Ethnicity and Other. Due to the small population size, Aviva aggregated the data for reporting purposes.

Implementing initiatives to support the disclosure of ethnicity will assist organisations in analysing ethnicity pay gaps but this will require clear communication and transparency so that individuals understand the reasons why this is necessary and how personal data will be used. The CIPD (2022c) in their report on ethnicity pay reporting recommend that employers publish annual ethnicity reports in relation to six key principles. These include aligning ethnicity pay reporting with gender pay reporting, but recognising the differences, remembering ethnicity representation is as important as, and strongly linked to ethnicity pay gaps, recognising the value of simplicity and clarity, focusing on action, starting and improving (reporting) and combining comparability in data with tailoring of analysis and actions. In its future of reward report, PWC (2020) reports that 10 per cent of employers have reported their ethnicity pay gap and 50 per cent plan to do so in the next three years.

HYBRID WORKING AND REWARD

Traditional employee reward structures are under review following the pandemic and the move to hybrid working. Benefits such as free lunches, snacks, parking and onsite gyms are less likely to be attractive as they will only be relevant to a portion of the workforce. Regional pay variations are another area for consideration. Whilst organisations that are based in one location will likely not have regional pay variations in place, increasingly this is something that will need to be explored as people are being recruited from a wider geographical base for hybrid working models. Staff may feel that it is unfair for colleagues living in locations where the cost of living is cheaper to be remunerated in the same way as those living in expensive cities. Organisations may need to pay a premium for skills that are in high demand. People working mainly from home may consider that they should receive an allowance for additional heating and electricity costs. PWC (2020) notes that organisations that have a regional pay model differentiating high- and low-cost work locations are likely to shift towards national pay ranges with more flexibility in the future to include allowances and expenses for office set-up and travel.

PWC (2020) found that in a hybrid working model, organisations are beginning to move to greater use of profit share and team and project bonuses. There is a growing focus on peer-to-peer recognition linked to technology and more frequent check-ins between line managers and their staff with a focus on well-being and development. Peer recognition is the expression of appreciation between co-workers. Recognition is a powerful tool, and increasingly organisations are using dedicated employee recognition platforms to promote peer-to-peer recognition. This allows all staff to recognise the contributions of colleagues. Managing in a hybrid working model will require different skills with a strong focus on mental health and well-being. Line managers will need to be appropriately trained and supported to understand their roles effectively.

Responding to individual needs and desires in reward is complex. Formulating an individualised offer through a reward passport is one way to support reward in a hybrid working arrangement. This allows individuals to draw down spend for things such as well-being, training and travel for example. The passport provides an agile approach to reward that is customised to fit individual employee needs putting individuals in control of their reward package. The following case example provides an insight into how the reward passport might be designed.

CASE STUDY: DIGITAL DETOX

Digital design agency Digital Detox employs a team of 50 engineers, creatives and strategists (Digitaldetox, 2022). It has a flexible benefits package in place to support the new way of working and the changing work culture. The flexible benefits pot is worth £2,000 per employee which they can spend however they choose. The offer aligns to the three-pillar approach of people, planet and technology, and benefits fall under the headings of flexible and financial benefits, learning and development, mental health, employee welfare, health and wellness and culture.

The benefits package at Digital Detox allows staff to take control of their benefits package so that they are able to tailor it to their own circumstances. Organisations that take an individualised approach to reward recognise the individual needs and preferences of the workforce.

SUMMARY POINTS

- To be effective, reward management should be strategically aligned to the business objectives, the culture of the organisation and the desired behaviours sought, for example, innovation or teamwork.
- Reward refers to financial and non-financial benefits. Financial benefits include base (wage or salary) and variable pay (bonuses and incentives). Non-financial benefits include recognition, development opportunities, discount schemes and the ability to buy additional holiday.
- Reward must be fair, reasonable and equitable in relation to both process and distribution. Legal requirements are in place in the UK in relation to equal pay and the national minimum wage. Gender pay gap reporting regulations are in place for organisations with over 250 employees making it an obligation for employers to identify and

publish pay gaps. Ethnicity pay gap regulations are not yet mandatory but some employers have published their data. The National Living Wage is a rate that is objectively defined in relation to the cost of living for those aged over 23. It is a voluntary rate paid by employers.

- Reward strategy will need to be reviewed in relation to hybrid work models. Regional variances may become less appropriate and office-based rewards such as onsite gyms and free lunches will be of benefit only to a percentage of the workforce. Individual benefits will need to be customised to employee needs and preferences.

SELF-TEST QUESTIONS/REVIEW QUESTIONS

- Explore the factors that organisations should consider when designing a reward strategy for a hybrid workforce. How can organisations balance the needs of employees working anywhere?
- What is meant by financial and non-financial rewards? Explore the advantages and disadvantages of a total reward package. How can organisations design reward strategies that meet organisation, team and individual preferences?

A CASE EXAMPLE: SHOOSMITHS

Review the Shoosmiths law firm case study in this chapter. To what extent does the reward strategy align with the strategic goals of the organisation? How does the reward strategy encourage team collaboration whilst balancing individual reward preferences?

REFLECTION

Reflect on your own work experience and rewards that you received in relation to financial and non-financial benefits (or perhaps interview a family member or friend about their experience). To what extent did the reward package encourage team collaboration? How much control did you have over the design of your benefits package? How well did the organisation communicate to you the value of the rewards on offer?

References

Adams, J.S. (1963). Towards an understanding of inequity. *The Journal of Abnormal and Social Psychology*, 67(5), p.422. https://psycnet.apa.org/doi/10.1037/h0040968.

Anku, J.S., Amewugah, B.K. and Glover, M.K. (2018). Concept of reward management, reward system and corporate efficiency. *International Journal of Economics, Commerce and Management*, 6(2), pp.621–637.

Armstrong, M. and Brown, D. (2019). Strategic human resource management: Back to the future? Institute for employment Studies. [online] Available at: https://www.employment-studies.co.uk/system/files/resources/files/517_Strategic-Human-Resource-Management-Back-to-the-future-IES-CIPD-2019.pdf.

Armstrong, M. and Taylor, S. (2020). *Armstrong's Handbook of Human Resource Management Practice*. 15th edn. London: Kogan Page.

Armstrong, M. (2010). *Armstrong's Essential Human Resource Management Practice: A Guide to People Management*. London: Kogan Page.

Aviva (2022). UK pay gap report 2021. Available at: https://www.aviva.com/about-us/uk-pay-gap-report/. (Accessed 3 July, 2022).

Brown, D. and Hewitt, A. (2014). The future of reward management: From total reward strategies to smart rewards. *Compensation & Benefits Review, 46*(3), pp.147–151.

CIPD (2021a). Reward: An introduction. CIPD, 31 March. Available at https://www.cipd.co.uk/knowledge/fundamentals/people/pay/reward-factsheet#gref. (Accessed 12 July, 2022).

CIPD (2021b). Explore profession map. Available at: https://peopleprofession.cipd.org/profession-map#gref. (Accessed 12 August, 2022).

CIPD (2022a). Reward management survey. CIPD, 13 April. Available at: https://www.cipd.co.uk/knowledge/strategy/reward/surveys#gref. (Accessed 13 August, 2022).

CIPD (2022b). Ethnicity pay gap reporting: A guide for UK employers. CIPD. 4 Jan. Available at: https://www.cipd.co.uk/knowledge/fundamentals/relations/diversity/ethnicity-pay-reporting-guide#gref. (Accessed 3 July, 2022).

CIPD. (2022c). Ethnicity pay reporting: A guide for UK employers. [online] CIPD. Available at: https://www.cipd.co.uk/knowledge/fundamentals/relations/diversity/ethnicity-pay-reporting-guide (Accessed 14 July, 2022).

CIPD. (2022d). Statutory rates. [online] CIPD. Available at: https://www.cipd.co.uk/knowledge/fundamentals/emp-law/about/statutory-rates#:~:text=National%20Living%20Wage%20and%20National%20Minimum%20Wage%20From. (Accessed 16 August, 2022).

Coleman, A. (2022). IFS uses total reward approach to unify global culture. [online] Employee Benefits. Available at: https://employeebenefits.co.uk/ifs-uses-total-reward-approach-to-unify-global-culture/. (Accessed 13 June, 2022).

Dias, C.M., Joyce, R. and Parodi, F. (2020). The gender pay gap in the UK: Children and experience in work. *Oxford Review of Economic Policy*, [online] *36*(4), pp.855–881. https://doi.org/10.1093/oxrep/graa053.

Digitaldetox (2022). Available at : https://www.digitaldetox.com/ (Accessed 22/01/2023).

Dunn-Coleman, A. (2020). Five ways your reward strategy can support your organisation's purpose, values and culture. [online] Rewards & Employer Benefits Association. Available at: https://reba.global/resource/five-ways-your-reward-strategy-can-support-your-organisation-s-purpose-values-and-culture.html. (Accessed 13 July, 2022).

Gemserv (2022). Available at: https://gemserv.com/ (Accessed 13 July, 2022).

GOV.UK (2016). UK gender pay gap. 17 November. Available at: https://www.gov.uk/government/news/uk-gender-pay-gap. (Accessed 30 August, 2022).

Gov.UK (2022). The national minimum wage in 2022. [online] Gov.UK. Available at: https://www.gov.uk/government/publications/the-national-minimum-wage-in-2022.

Gu, M., Li Tan, J.H., Amin, M., Mostafiz, M.I. and Yeoh, K.K. (2022). Revisiting the moderating role of culture between job characteristics and job satisfaction: A multilevel analysis of 33 countries. *Employee Relations, 44*(1), pp.70–93. https://doi.org/10.1108/ER-03-2020-0099.

IFS (2022). Available at: https://www.ifs.com/ (Accessed 14 July, 2022).

Lardner, S. (2015). Effective reward ensures effective engagement. *Strategic HR Review*. Available at: https://www.emerald.com/insight/content/doi/10.1108/SHR-06-2015-0050/full/html.

Lawler III, E.E. (1990). *Strategic Pay: Aligning Organizational Strategies and Pay Systems*. San Francisco: Jossey-Bass Publishers.

Lawler, E.E. (2000). Pay strategy: New thinking for the new millennium. *Compensation & Benefits Review, 32*(1), 7–12. https://doi.org/10.1177/088636870003200102

Leatherbarrow, C. and Fletcher, J. (2018). *Introduction to Human Resource Management: A Guide to HR Practice.* 4th edn. London: Kogan Page CIPD.

NHS (2021). Total reward statements. 26 April. Available at: https://www.nhsemployers.org/articles/total-reward-statements. (Accessed 14 August, 2022).

Nyandoro, Z.F. and Goremusandu, T. (2016). Employees' evaluation of the relationship between reward management and organisational strategy: A case study of Zimbabwe national family planning council (ZNFPC). *International Journal of Research in Business Management, 4*(7), pp.51–64.

Office for National Statistics (2021). Gender pay gap in the UK:2021. [online] Office for National Statistics. Available at: https://www.ons.gov.uk/employmentandlabourmarket/peopleinwork/earningsandworkinghours/bulletins/genderpaygapintheuk/2021. (Accessed 14 July, 2022).

PWC (2020). The future of reward. Available at: https://www.pwc.co.uk/services/human-resource-services/rewarding-your-people/future-of-reward.html. (Accessed 1 July, 2022).

PWC (2022). Ethnicity pay gap reporting: Preparing for the future. [online] PwC. Available at: https://www.pwc.co.uk/services/legal/insights/ethnicity-pay-gap-reporting.html. (Accessed 13 July, 2022).

Shoosmiths (2022). Available at: https://www.shoosmiths.co.uk/. (Accessed 14 August, 2022).

Sylvester, J. (2011). What is total reward? *Training Zone.* 15th March. Available at: https://www.hrzone.com/community-voice/blogs/johnsylvester/what-is-total-reward. (Accessed 13 July 2022).

Taylor, S. (2010). *Resourcing and Talent Management.* 5th edn. London. CIPD.

Strategic employment relations

A progressive approach

Chapter 8

INTRODUCTION

This chapter provides readers with an understanding of strategic employment relations issues, which take into account the local, national and international environment. Specifically, it will explore perspectives on employment relations and their application within different organisational contexts in relation to national and international influences across different working models. It will explore how people professionals can work with stakeholders to develop effective work cultures that are capable of rapid change through a bend and flex approach. The chapter will also assess how organisations work with trade unions and other formal groups to enhance organisational effectiveness. Using a variety of case examples, a range of strategies will be reviewed along with the move away from collectivism to individualism and the employee voice. This chapter encourages an analysis of how a strategic approach to employee relations can maximise the effectiveness of hybrid working models with trust, communication, transparency and effective leadership at the core of high-performing organisations.

CONTEXTUALISING STRATEGIC EMPLOYMENT RELATIONS

At the time of writing, the global economy is facing significant challenges with the impact of the Russian invasion of Ukraine, the cost of living

DOI: 10.4324/9781003342984-9

crisis caused by global inflation pressures and the slowdown in China. The IMF (2022) predicts that global growth will remain unchanged in 2022 at 3.2 per cent and will slow to 2.7 per cent. More than a third of the global economy is predicted to contract in 2022 or 2023. Increasing price pressures remain the most immediate threat to current and future prosperity by squeezing real incomes. PWC (2022) reports that the growth outlook for the UK has deteriorated and the GDP growth is predicted to average 3.1–3.6 per cent followed by two years of slow or even negative GDP growth. It is likely that the UK will enter recession by the end of the year largely due to inflation increases impacting all demographic groups. The CIPD Collective Employee Voice (CIPD, 2022a) report found that twice as many employers (42 per cent) agreed than disagreed that employers can expect to face increasing levels of industrial action over the next 12 months. Indeed, at the present time, there is news of strikes across the UK including Royal Mail, British Airways, Network Rail and Ryanair.

What impact does this have on employment relations? External market conditions can impact the employment relationships in a number of ways. In a loose labour market, there is plentiful talent, meaning that an employer is able to recruit a well-qualified workforce at a reasonable rate. In a tight labour market, there are fewer candidates available which can lead to recruitment challenges for employers and the possibility that organisations will need to pay higher salaries to attract the right people. In February 2022, the CIPD reported that employers are set to award record pay rises in the face of tough recruitment conditions but even with these pay increases, most people are set to see their real wages fall against the backdrop of high inflation (CIPD, 2022b). Thousands of workers are striking and requesting pay deals that keep up with the rise of inflation (which is 9 per cent at the time of writing). This may or may not add to existing inflationary pressures depending on whether higher productivity offsets higher labour costs. The challenging geopolitical and economic climate coupled with the move to a hybrid working model for many organisations demands that organisations invest time in reviewing their employment relations strategies to ensure that they are effective in developing a culture of trust and respect, engaging in two-way communication, focusing on inclusivity and effective leadership which are essential to strong employment relations and the retention of staff.

DEFINING EMPLOYMENT RELATIONS

Dibben et al. (2011, p.7) argue that employment relations represent both the study of the employment relationship within the individual firm and the regulation of employment in the wider social context. The CIPD (2022c) describes employee relations as the relationship between employers and employees noting that in the world of work today the interpretation relates to both individual and collective workplace relationships. This reflects the increasing individualisation of the employment relationship following the rise of individual workplace rights. How the employment relationship is managed is a key factor in people management and will impact on the success of the organisation. The employment relationship is dynamic and governed by a contract of employment. To be effective, the employment relationship needs to balance employer and employee expectations so that the needs of both are satisfied.

THE PSYCHOLOGICAL CONTRACT

Leatherbarrow and Fletcher (2016) identify both formal and informal aspects to the employer/employee relationship noting that both parties have rights, obligations and expectations. The formal side is regulated through the provisions of the contract of employment and UK legislation provides the standard for conduct of the relationship. The contract consists of an exchange involving work performance and pay. The informal side of the employment relationship is governed by what is known as the psychological contract. Schein (1980) first discussed the concept of the psychological contract and said that the contract implies an unwritten set of expectations operating at all times between every member of an organisation. Farnham (2015) argues that there is no definitive definition of the psychological contract but suggests that it relates to the set of beliefs that individuals hold regarding promises made and accepted. Armstrong (2010) purports that from an employee perspective the psychological contract includes aspects that relate to fairness in treatment, employment security, an opportunity to develop skills and trust in management and confidence that the organisation will keep their promises. From an employer's perspective, Armstrong (ibid.) suggests that the psychological contract covers areas such as competence, compliance, organisational commitment and loyalty. The psychological contract forms the basis of a positive relationship between the employer and the employee and refers to an employee's subjective beliefs, agreed understandings of promises and obligations made between respective parties in relation to work, pay, loyalty, trust, fairness, commitment, flexibility, security and career advancement (Farnham, 2015).

A negative psychological contract is likely to result in reduced performance. Any sense of inequity will impact satisfaction including a discrepancy between obligations perceived and received and this situation is identified by Rousseau (1995) as violation caused by disruption. Any breach of the psychological contract is likely to be based on the perception of the employee as to how they have been treated. This highlights the need for effective communication and transparency to enhance mutual understanding between employees and their managers in order to support the building of high levels of trust.

EMPLOYMENT RELATIONS STRATEGY

Strategic employment relations relate to the framework from which policy decisions are made. The employment philosophy of an organisation is determined through the relationship that management seeks with employees and, where recognised, trade unions. Employment relations philosophy is delivered through the employment relations policy which is developed in relation to the climate of trust and cooperation that the organisation promotes.

There are two key frames of reference widely discussed as models for distinguishing alternating perspectives in the employer–employee relationship. The frameworks were introduced by Fox (1974), a British sociologist. He first distinguished the unitary and pluralist approach and later added a third, the Marxist or radical frame of reference.

EMPLOYMENT RELATIONS FRAMES OF REFERENCE

The unitarist perspective assumes that everyone in the organisation is working towards similar goals and objectives. It sees conflict as negative and disruptive and, if at all possible, to be avoided. The assumption is that people are loyal and trade unions, if recognised, work as a quality check rather than an adversary. Reward systems are designed to motivate and inspire staff and are aligned to the achievement of organisation objectives.

The pluralist approach makes the assumption that conflict is inevitable as there will always be diverse groups with a range of differing views, objectives, rules and loyalties. In this perspective, diverse groups may include trade unions, shareholders, employees, management and other stakeholders. The focus is on managing by consent rather than by right with conflict seen as encouraging innovation and change.

The Marxist or radical approach is based on the assumption that conflict is a fundamental aspect of the employment relationship. Drawing on the ideas of Karl Marx (who argued that capitalist systems of production are inherently exploitative), it argues that there is an innate power imbalance in the relationship where workers need to work for a decent standard of living and an employer has the power to replace workers as and when required. This perspective is rather dated but is still seen occasionally.

Farnham (2015) suggests that there are two main approaches to developing effective relationships with employees in order to achieve organisational goals. The first is the traditional approach which is rooted in collectivism and a pluralist frame of reference. In this model, based on collective agreements between trade unions, communication is by way of joint consultation and representative methods of communicating. This compares with the HRM approach which is rooted in individualism and a unitary frame of reference. In this approach, the common interest of management and employees is emphasised, and objectives are met through individual employee commitment to organisational goals and business plans. Farnham (ibid.) also mentions the partnership approach but suggests that this is less common and rooted in mutuality between employer and the union. Armstrong and Taylor (2020) suggest, however, that in the partnership approach, the organisation involves employees in the drawing up and execution of organisational policies but management retains the overall right to manage.

In addition to the approaches mentioned above, Armstrong and Taylor (2020) discuss the adversarial approach, noting that it is now dated and less common but it is where the organisation decides what it wants to do with the expectation that individuals will comply (with the only alternative being a refusal to cooperate). Armstrong and Taylor (ibid.) also note that power sharing, although rare, can be seen in organisations where employees are involved in both day to day and strategic decision-making.

EMPLOYEE INVOLVEMENT, COLLECTIVISM AND EMPLOYEE VOICE

The workplace has changed considerably since the 1970s and early 1980s when trade unions represented the workforce and spoke for employees collectively (39 per cent of the workforce were in a union in 1989 compared to 23.7% in 2020). There is now a greater focus on individualism and the employment relationship has changed. Organisations invest in developing a positive climate of employee relations through employee involvement, commitment and engagement. CIPD research in 2022 (CIPD, 2022a) shows that, among those employers with representative arrangements for informing and consulting with staff, 40 per cent reported both union and non-union representation, 39 per cent just non-union representation and 18 per cent cited union representation only. Trade unions do continue to hold an influential voice, particularly in the public sector and they campaign for employment rights and improvement in working conditions. They also support members at tribunal cases in claims for unfair dismissal, discrimination cases etc.

COLLECTIVISM

Collectivism refers to the prioritisation of the group over the individual. Where trade unions or staff associations are recognised by organisations, collective bargaining is the means used to negotiate and address conflict in areas such as terms and conditions of employment, changes to working hours, redundancies and pay. The Trade Union Congress define collective bargaining as 'the official process by which trade unions negotiate with employers, on behalf of their members' (TUC, 2022). Collective bargaining is only possible where an employer recognises a trade union and between them they decide on the scope of negotiations. Most collective bargaining arrangements in the UK are voluntary. Good employers recognise the benefits that come from voluntary union recognition, such as being able to negotiate wages and other terms and conditions collectively for large groups of workers at the same time.

Industrial action can happen when a dispute between workers and employers is not resolved through negotiation and is designed to put pressure on employers to accept the demands relating to pay and conditions that the workers are seeking. A strike (where a group of employees withhold their labour in support of their demands against their employer) is bad news for all concerned. The loss of production will have consequences for the organisation, workers will lose pay when they are not working and the strike will impact customers and other stakeholders. The case example below provides an insight into the detrimental impact of strike action in relation to Royal Mail in the UK.

CASE STUDY: ROYAL MAIL

This is an extract from the *Guardian* newspaper article: 'Royal Mail workers strike over pay and conditions' (*The Guardian*, Thu 13 Oct 2022 09.27 BST)

> Postal workers have launched a 24-hour strike in a long-running dispute over pay and conditions, with industrial action planned for the coming weeks. The Communication Workers Union (CWU) said its 115,000 members across the UK were taking action on Thursday, describing it as the largest strike in a year. The move comes amid industrial unrest across several industries, including rail. Picket lines have been mounted outside Royal Mail offices on the sixth day of action in recent months. The union accuses the company of planning structural changes, which would in effect transform employees in secure, well-paid jobs into a 'casualised, financially precarious workforce overnight'. The CWU said the plans included delaying the arrival of post to the public by three hours, cuts in workers' sick pay and inferior terms for new employees. The union has

announced 19 days of strike action in the build-up to the busy Christmas period. A Royal Mail spokesperson said: 'Three weeks ago, Royal Mail invited the CWU to enter talks through ACAS to find a resolution to our change and pay dispute. We have not reached an agreement with the CWU on this request'.

EMPLOYEE VOICE AND EMPLOYEE INVOLVEMENT

The extent to which employees have a voice in the workforce is integral to the strategic management of an effective employment relationship. Employee voice refers to the degree to which employees are able to make a contribution to key decisions which can empower staff to engage directly and indirectly in decision-making (Boxall and Purcell 2003:162). There are both formal and informal mechanisms for voice participation in information, communication and consultation between employers and employees. In a pluralist organisation, there are likely to be processes for the collective voice through trade unions. In individualistic organisations, opportunities might be available for employees to have a voice through team meetings, management briefings and organisation wide innovation and problem solving groups. There are many different interpretations across different organisations and a variety of opportunities for how employees can get involved. Employee voice is integral to employee engagement and organisations can benefit from increased efficiencies and collaborations. A culture where employee voice is promoted will build trust and confidence through an inclusive working environment (CIPD, 2021).

Employee involvement provides the mechanism for employees to engage in regular workforce meetings with senior management. Consultations might take place through a representative forum such as a works council or a joint consultative mechanism where employee representative views are sought prior to decision-making. ACAS (2020) argues that mechanisms for involving staff should not be limited to discussing mundane issues. To ensure that cultural change is embedded into institutions in the longer-term, employers need 'robust voice mechanisms' and 'a willingness to work towards mutual interests', while 'acknowledging different starting positions'. This will require organisations to be open to some loss of control. The Virgin Media case study below provides an insight into how employee voice can be formalised and structured.

CASE STUDY: EMPLOYEE VOICE: VIRGIN MEDIA

Virgin media is a British telecommunications company employing around 14,000 staff (Virginmedia, 2022). Previously employee voice was an informal affair but to take it seriously the company implemented a formal structured process. A national employee voice lead was appointed and 360 voice representatives across the organisation were elected by employees for a four-year term. Local voice forums represent teams in areas of more than 2,000 people. Divisional voice forums (DVF) represent the 11 different business divisions (so 11 forums) to discuss matters affecting each particular division.

One representative in each division is elected as the division lead who runs the DVF. A business lead (the director of the division) and people lead (HR representative), together with the division lead, make up the division leadership team and attend the DVF meetings.

The 360 voice reps have job descriptions for their voice roles and are provided with allocated time to voice. The voice programmes have achieved a number of wins for employees, including overhauling the bonus scheme (Sharp, 2018).

BUILDING TRUST

Building trust takes time and generally requires us to accept a degree of uncertainty and to take risks in order to trust the other party. It is about a willingness to make oneself vulnerable in the face of uncertainty or insecurity (Hope-Hailey et al., 2012). The CIPD outlook survey in 2011 found that trust in an organisation increases the willingness of employees to recommend it to others and enhances job satisfaction in addition to reducing the likelihood that staff will leave (CIPD, 2011). Trust in an organisation is dependent on relations with line managers as well as the senior leadership team. Hope-Hailey et al. (2012) argue that organisations with high trust are those where staff feel their trust is reciprocated and that they are themselves trusted by their managers. For leaders to be trusted, they need to demonstrate ability (competence), benevolence (having concern for others), integrity (set of principles) and predictability (regular behaviour). Leadership trust may motivate employees to work efficiently and increase commitment to the organisation but it does require long-term mutual interaction between leaders and employees. When staff consider their leaders to be trustworthy, it is more likely that a stable relationship will be formed. Indeed, Seok-Young (2018) found that trust and organisational justice, increases employee collective identity and accountability to prioritise group or organisation interests over individual ones.

New hybrid working models provide an opportunity to create a workplace contract that brings together the essential contributors to workplace productivity, namely well-being and good employment relations.

Barber (2020) suggests that this necessitates some explicit promises in the core elements of the psychological contract including respect, compassion, fairness and trust. Barber (ibid.) suggests that in putting this new contract together we need to explore the following questions:

1. How do we create a fair balance between flexibility and fairness?
2. How do we review and revitalise voice mechanisms to build fairer, more inclusive workplaces?
3. Can we make flexible work arrangements the norm?
4. How do we balance the needs of employee well-being and business productivity?
5. Can we accept that short and long-term conflict will emerge; prepare for it and see it a creative force for positive change?

A NEW ERA FOR EMPLOYMENT RELATIONS

Managing hybrid working effectively from an employment relations perspective is a challenge. Hybrid working will not be accessible to all and therefore it is likely that for many organisations the workforce will be hybrid, with some staff working remotely all of the time, whilst others are in the place of work all the time and for others there may be the hybrid option. Being inclusive should be at the centre of employment relations. Focusing on how people would like to work and how they need to work and how technology can facilitate different working models. Effective communication is integral to positive employment relations. Organisations should revisit their communication strategy to ensure that it is tailored to the hybrid working environment. Effective communication is proactive, polite, imaginative, innovative, creative, constructive, professional, progressive, energetic, enabling, transparent and technology friendly (Venkatashiva and Gupta, 2020).

In a hybrid working environment communication and collaboration are key. Although the business infrastructure and processes need to be more flexible and individualised a central management system will support communication and aid continuity across the business. The CIPD (2021) argues that effective hybrid working is facilitated by strong communication and employees need to have the information they need in a timely way to ensure that they are able to undertake the work. Certainly, effective communication channels need to be balanced with well-being strategies so that people are able to balance their work and life effectively. If organisations are able to get this right, they will be effectively positioned for more harmonious relations with their staff.

SUMMARY POINTS

- Employment relations refers to the relationship between employer and employee. The formal side of the relationship is governed by the contract of employment and the informal side is influenced by the psychological contract. To be effective, the employment relationship must balance the needs of both employer and employee so that both needs are satisfied.
- Unitarist and pluralistic frames of reference influence the organisation's approach to employment relations strategy and policy. Despite a growing trend towards individualism, trade unions continue to hold a powerful voice negotiating wages and other terms and conditions.
- Collectivism refers to the way trade unions and staff associations negotiate and address conflict in areas such as pay and terms and conditions with employers.
- The employee voice denotes the degree to which employees are able to make a contribution to key decisions which can empower staff to engage directly and indirectly in decision-making.
- Building trust takes time and is an essential part of the psychological contract. In a hybrid workforce, organisations will need to work hard to ensure that they build a climate of reciprocal trust between managers and their employees. Inclusivity is key to hybrid working and effective employer and employee relations.
- A robust internal communication programme is necessary so that staff have sufficient information in a timely manner to undertake their work efficiently.

SELF-TEST QUESTIONS/REVIEW QUESTIONS

- To what extent does the psychological contract influence positive employer and employee relations in a hybrid working model?
- What considerations should a HR professional consider when designing an employment relations policy?

A CASE EXAMPLE: THE ROYAL MAIL

Review the Royal Mail case study in this chapter. Assess the impact of the strike for all stakeholders that may be affected. What strategies do you consider that the employer might have engaged in to prevent the strike action?

REFLECTION

Reflect on your own work experience and the extent to which you felt/feel able to have a voice in your organisation, either collectively through a trade union or individually through team meetings, consultation groups etc. (you may prefer to interview a family member or friend about their experience). Assuming you had an opportunity to take part in two-way dialogue, to what extent did you engage in the opportunities for giving feedback? What else might you have done? What else might the organisation have done? What issues did you discuss? Were they mundane or strategic? If you did not have any opportunity to engage with the organisation, what recommendations would you make based on what we have discussed in this chapter?

References

ACAS. (2020). Dealing with workplace problems. [online] ACAS. Available at: https://www.acas.org.uk/dealing-with-workplace-problems. (Accessed 13 August, 2022).

Armstrong, M. (2010). *Armstrong's Essential Human Resource Management Practice: A Guide to People Management*. London: Kogan Page.

Armstrong, M. and Taylor, S. (2020). *Armstrong's Handbook of Human Resource Management Practice*. 15th edn. London: Kogan Page.

Barber, B. (2020). *Building Back: Making Working Lives Better*. ACAS. 23 July. Available at: https://www.acas.org.uk/building-back-making-working-lives-better-html. (Accessed 2 July 2022).

Boxall, P. and Purcell, J. (2003). *Strategy and Human Resource Management*. Basingstoke: Palgrave Macmillan.

CIPD (2011). Annual review 2001–2012. Available at: https://www.cipd.co.uk/Images/annual-review_2011-12_tcm18-11768.pdf. (Accessed 14 August, 2022).

CIPD. (2021). Empowering employee voice. [online] CIPD. Available at: https://www.cipd.co.uk/knowledge/work/future-voice/employee-voice-guide. (Accessed 13 September, 2022).

CIPD (2022a). Collective employee voice. CIPD. 12 July. Available at: https://www.cipd.co.uk/knowledge/fundamentals/relations/employees/collective-employee-voice (Accessed 30 September, 2022).

CIPD (2022b). Employers set to award record pay rises in 2022 in the face of tough recruitment conditions, new CIPD research finds. CIPD. 14 Feb. Available at: https://www.cipd.co.uk/about/media/press/140222record-pay-rises-tough-recruitment#gref. (Accessed 13 August, 2022).

CIPD (2022c). Employee relations: An introduction. CIPD. 29 July. Available at: https://www.cipd.co.uk/knowledge/fundamentals/relations/employees/factsheet#gref (Accessed 3 August, 2022).

Dibben, P., Wood, G. and Klerck, G. (2011). *Employment Relations: A Critical and International Approach*. London: CIPD Publications.

Farnham, D. (2015). *Human Resource Management in Context: Insights, Strategy and Solutions*. 4th ed. London: CIPD.

Fox, A. (1974). Beyond contract: Work, power and trust relations. [online] *Internet Archive*. London: Faber. Available at: https://archive.org/details/beyondcontractwo0000foxa.

Guardian. (2022). Royal Mail workers strike over pay and conditions. *The Guardian*. [online] 13 Oct. 2022. Available at: https://www.theguardian.com/business/2022/oct/13/royal-mail-workers-strike-pay-conditions-union. (Accessed 14 October, 2022).

Hope-Hailey, V., Dietz, G. and Searle, R. (2012). *Where Has all the Trust Gone?* London: CIPD. Available at: http://www.cipd.co.uk/hr-resources/research/where-trust-gone.aspx (Accessed 1 September, 2022).

IMF. (2022). Latest global growth forecasts show challenges facing economies. [online] IMF. Available at: https://www.imf.org/en/Blogs/Articles/2022/10/19/latest-global -growth-forecasts-show-challenges-facing-economies#:~:text=October%2019%2C %202022%20The%20IMF%E2%80%99s%20World%20Economic%20Outlook. (Accessed 1 August, 2022).

Leatherbarrow, C. and Fletcher, J. (2016). *Introduction to Human Resource Management: A Guide to HR in Practice.* 3rd ed. London: CIPD.

PwC (2022). UK economic outlook. [online] PwC. Available at: https://www.pwc.co .uk/services/economics/insights/uk-economic-outlook.html.

Rousseau, D. (1995). *Psychological Contracts in Organizations: Understanding Written and Unwritten Agreements.* London: Sage publications.

Schein, E. (1980). *Organizational Psychology.* 3rd ed. London: Prentice Hall. *Organizational Psychology*, first published 1965, second edition 1970, third edition 1980.

Sharp, R. (2018). Case study: Virgin Media's employee voice structure. Available at: https://www.hrmagazine.co.uk/content/features/case-study-virgin-media-s -employee-voice-structure. (Accessed 13 June, 2022).

Seok-Young Oh (2018). Effects of organizational learning on performance: The moderating roles of trust in leaders and organizational justice. *Journal of Knowledge Management.* Available at: https://doi.org/10.1108/JKM-02-2018-0087. (Accessed 3 October, 2022).

TUC (2022). Available at: https://www.tuc.org.uk/. (Accessed 13 October, 2022).

Venkatashiva Reddy, B. and Gupta, A. (2020). Importance of effective communication during COVID-19 infodemic. *Journal of Family Medicine and Primary Care*, [online] 9(8), p.3793. https://doi:10.4103/jfmpc.jfmpc_719_20.

Virginmedia (2022). Available at: https://www.virginmedia.com/corporate.

Embracing technological developments in the people profession

Chapter 9

INTRODUCTION

This chapter will examine the benefits and challenges that emerging technologies create for people professionals. It will introduce artificial intelligence (AI) and machine learning, automation and virtual reality and how each can be used in the workplace. Through a variety of case study examples, we explore how technological developments are being used to improve hiring and onboarding, supporting the management of employee performance and reward, aiding career development and improving well-being. The chapter explores the benefits of reducing the time we spend on mundane and routine tasks such as initial screening of applications, allowing the people team to focus on more innovative and strategic activities. The chapter will also highlight the reluctance of some people in welcoming accelerations in Industry 4.0 and 5G technology and how HR can respond to these challenges.

DOI: 10.4324/9781003342984-10

NEW OPPORTUNITIES

The fourth industrial revolution includes a broad range of AI, robotics and machine learning technologies which together have the potential to transform the HR profession. Indeed, digitalisation in the workplace and other disruptive technology platforms are already impacting people practices at every stage of the employee lifecycle. AI and machine learning present opportunities for strategic planning, efficiencies and enhancing the employee experience through people resource planning, employee attraction, selection and retention, learning and development, remuneration and benefits along with career planning amongst others (Deloitte, 2018). HR technology has been evolving on a continuum, from the collection of basic data through human resource information systems (HRISs) that provide the opportunity to capture, store, manipulate, retrieve, analyse and distribute information (Kavanagh et al., 2015), to the opportunities presented by artificial intelligence in today's workplace which we will discuss below. The digital revolution has transformed the ability of both HR professionals and line managers to make strategic workforce decisions through statistical and predictive analysis (Fernandez and Gallardo, 2020). The rapid development of new technology provides people professionals with the opportunity to reduce the time spent on mundane repetitive administration tasks in order to maximise the value and potential of the people team in supporting the organisation in achieving and maintaining competitive advantage. In order to achieve this, however, people teams will need to invest in and embrace new technology and the ability to do this will differ across sectors and organisations according to their size and budget.

ALIGNING HR AND TECHNOLOGY

The CIPD HR Profession Map defines six core areas of knowledge required to drive change, create value and make a positive impact in the world of work. Technology and people form one of these core areas. The CIPD encourages people professionals to understand the impact of technology on people at work, knowing how it can improve the agility and productivity of the workforce and organisations and how it can enable more collaborative working (CIPD, 2021). The KPMG report on the future of HR concurs, arguing that HR needs to make a critical shift from a process-centric function to a worker-centric function with a deep understanding of the wants, needs and drivers of different employee groups. Enabling technology is one of the key elements that KPMG argues HR professionals should be focusing on (others include culture, employee experience and engagement, workforce analytics, workforce shaping and HR organisation of the future) to achieve this work-centric focus (KPMG, 2020).

Sivathanu and Pillai (2018) contend that the role of HR is to support organisational growth but most HR departments across different organisations seem to focus only on an operational role owing to highly inefficient processes that are worsened by inadequate or obsolete technology infrastructure. Nankervis et al. (2019) agree, suggesting that many HR professionals are not well equipped in terms of their attitudes, capabilities and competencies. They argue that new theories and models and further focus on more innovative systems and processes are required including updating higher education programmes to bridge the gap in professional skills. KPMG (2020) takes a more pragmatic approach, suggesting that the HR function should prioritise investment in technology arguing that automated technologies are set to become part of the modern workforce. HR will be expected to anticipate and plan for change associated with the employee lifecycle and organisation culture (ibid.). Investing in future focused technology will equip the HR team with the infrastructure to manage change effectively in the longer term. Implementing new technology will demand new professional skills and HR professionals will need to focus on digital skills acquisition to exploit fully the opportunities available. The case study below provides an insight into the potential offered by AI at the candidate attraction stage of recruitment.

CASE STUDY: IBM

AI candidate engagement at IBM

IBM is a multinational technology corporation with operations in 171 countries (IBM, 2022). IBM's goal was to create a meaningful experience that engages job seekers from the first interaction, while at the same time developing a shared understanding of their suitability for roles that match their skills. The AI solution IBM developed to address this challenge is called Watson Candidate Assistant (WCA). WCA has changed the way job seekers engage with IBM. Previously, candidates and employers would meet for the first time at the job interview, after learning about the opportunity from an online job board or career website. By leveraging AI, candidates and employers can now have real-time interaction via a chatbot (a computer program designed to simulate conversation with human users over the internet; see below for a fuller account), resulting in a more personalised application process for job seekers. The richer information applicants receive leads to a stronger fit of job applicants for roles. These chatbots learn through each interaction they engage in. Videos can also be embedded into the process to give a more realistic preview of what it's like to work at IBM. Implementing these capabilities in the organisation has resulted in an increased flow of high-potential candidates. In a trial study where WCA was compared to a traditional static website, the conversion from exploring the company to application was 36 per cent, compared with 12 per cent for the traditional static website. IBM receives about 7,000 resumes per day and implementing WCA has reduced the time it takes to hire whilst improving the match of candidates to jobs (Guenole and Feinzig, 2018).

INTRODUCING ARTIFICIAL INTELLIGENCE

Kew and Stredwick (2016, p.351) define artificial intelligence as the science and engineering of making intelligent machines, especially intelligent computer programs. It relates to the similar task of using computers to understand human intelligence. GOV.UK (2019) suggests that AI refers to the use of digital technology to create systems capable of autonomously performing tasks commonly thought to require human intelligence. Charlwood and Guenole (2022) argue that AI is a new and revolutionary general purpose technology that will transform the world of work. AI generally refers to an artificial creation of human-like intelligence that can learn, reason, plan, perceive or process natural language. AI is an umbrella term which encompasses machine learning and cognitive computing. It deals with the branch of computer science that deals with simulation of intelligent behaviour in computers. According to Dattner et al. (2019), AI can also provide the basis for competitive advantage through improvements in the efficiencies and fairness of how people are managed.

Guenole and Feinzig (2018) put together a business case for using AI in IBM. They suggest that AI is being used in HR for five key reasons. Firstly, to solve pressing business challenges through the insights that AI provides. Secondly to attract and develop new skills to respond quickly to opportunities in order to stay ahead of the competition. Thirdly, to improve the employee experience through the personalisation of work tailored to individual preferences and needs. Fourthly, to provide strong decision support at speed in relation to changing requirements as AI can support leaders in analysing vast amounts of information at the point when it is needed. Finally, AI can assist people professionals in managing budgets as efficiently as possible so that they are able to invest in higher value and more complex problem-solving. IBM reported that in a single year its cost savings due to implementing AI in human resources exceeded $100 million (Guenole & Feinzig, 2018).

Indeed, using AI to perform mundane and repetitive administrative duties in the HR function releases people professionals so that they are able to focus on strategic planning and adding value to the business. Charlwood and Guenole (2022) acknowledge that AI has the potential to support businesses in identifying applicant pools of people with the knowledge, skills, abilities and attitudes that the business needs whilst simultaneously making cost-effective decisions about who to recruit from candidate pools. They go on to say that whilst existing applicant management systems can partially automate selection by filtering out applications without keywords relevant to the post, AI has the potential to seek out and advertise posts to new applicant pools (the work that recruitment consultants currently do but on a greater scale and more cost effectively after the initial investment).

In addition to the efficiencies in cost and time and the opportunity for HR professionals to focus on strategic planning, Rathi (2018) argues that AI has the potential to prevent discrimination and promote diversity by reducing unconscious favouritism in job descriptions and selection processes. Guenole and Feinzig (2018) agree, finding that AI can dramatically improve the efficiency and fairness of how people are managed (ibid.). By planning algorithms effectively, AI applications can be used to analyse job descriptions to spot gender bias or language which would detract strong applicants.

AI first identifies the pattern and then makes predictions within the schema, allocating new cases based on existing categories. Initially, it requires a substantial amount of data and considerable effort to assist AI in making a successful first prediction. The cost of subsequent predictions is much less, however (Agrawal et al., 2018). Lebovitz et al. (2021) note that a complicating factor is the ability of AI to classify scenarios it has not yet encountered, for example, a candidate with a speech impediment in an automated video interview.

DEFINING TECHNOLOGICAL TERMINOLOGY

When discussing AI, a number of terms are used, sometimes interchangeably. The common terms used in this chapter are explained below.

Machine learning

Machine learning is a subset of AI. It focuses on teaching computers to learn from data. Mahesh (2018) explains that machine learning (ML) is used to teach machines how to handle data more efficiently. Tripathi et al. (2021 p.4882) suggest that 'machine learning allows computers to imitate human intellect and absorb vast amounts of data in order to swiftly spot patterns and insights'. The Office for AI describes machine learning as a subset of AI where digital systems autonomously improve their performance at undertaking a specific task or tasks over time as the system learns through experience (GOV.UK, 2019). AI and machine learning are terms that are used interchangeably but they are not the same. AI breaks down and then transforms data into a format that is usable. It achieves this through simulation and intelligent thinking. Machine learning is an advanced form of AI, identifying patterns and learning over time so that it can solve problems and make predictions.

Virtual reality

Virtual reality (VR) is a computer-based system that uses software to create a simulated environment. Using interactive controls, it is possible for individuals to enter a virtual or digital world. VR has been widely used in gaming for some time and is now increasingly being used in work-based learning. Virtual reality is used to provide a safe and effective realistic environment for doctors, nurses and paramedics to respond to multiple scenarios, for example working in a high-stress environment.

Automation

Automation refers to the creation of technologies that are applied to processes and systems so that they occur without human intervention and will run independently. For example, automation of the payroll in many organisations has enabled employee data to be verified, timesheets to be validated, earnings, reimbursements and deductions to be calculated with appropriate software. This reduces errors, ensures greater efficiency, reduces costs and offers scalability.

TECHNOLOGY THROUGH THE EMPLOYEE LIFECYCLE

From candidate attraction to the alumni stage, technology is having a significant impact on every aspect of the employee lifecycle. A chatbot can answer many of the questions that new recruits might have (such as how to connect to the office WIFI, how to set up an email account etc.). A chatbot is a strong way of addressing questions whilst retaining a sense of interaction. The bot can be continuously tweaked to allow for new queries that arise.

Chatbots can automate routine processes that are time consuming whilst simultaneously providing more access to HR for employees. They can provide instant and accurate responses to common queries with more complex issues being escalated to people professionals. Bots can support employees quickly with tailor-made support.

Bain and Co use artificial intelligence to explore social media data to learn where traffic is coming from in order to improve the flow of candidates. Additionally, AI and machine learning are used for candidate sourcing and screening where natural language understanding (a subfield of AI where machines process and understand human language so that they can perform repetitive tasks) and algorithmic selection tools (a number of programmed steps to be followed) are used on resumes. Unilever found that using AI in candidate screening has improved hiring accuracy by 75 per cent (Booth, 2019).

Natural language processing can be used on job descriptions to reduce bias (so long as the algorithm is carefully designed). It is even used in video interview assessments where it is possible to turn a video into data using facial movements, intonation and word choice to support the selection process (Heric, 2018).

Natural language processing can be useful for document generation whereby organisations can generate offer letters, contracts and other vital documents for employees. A human will still be needed to validate the output and ensure that documentation is appropriately signed, however.

Interviews might now include automated techniques and customised testing instead of a generic approach to selection which enables more informed predictions of on-the-job performance. Faster data network connections (4G/5G generations of mobile networking) are enabling remote video-based interview discussions in real time, which reduces the time it takes to get someone into post considerably (Sivathanu and Pillai,

2018). AI chatbots can assist in interpreting and validating candidate responses in real-time too, reducing the interviewer bias.

Onboarding

After the interview, new joiner onboarding programmes can be customised for the individual through AI. This might include virtual reality where new joiners can be guided through various office processes and layouts and even enjoy a tour of a physical space if the organisation has an office presence. Such an experience would fast-track the learning and settling in process for new employees, ensuring that they are productive from the start (Sivathanu and Pillai, 2018).

Development

In team development, psychometric tests can be used to evaluate employees in relation to skills and personality assessments and to support team building. AI can be used to personalise coaching in relation to market trends, company needs and employee development plans. Chatbots can provide professional guidance and mentorship to each employee, customising support to the needs of everyone. Privacy and confidentiality are important areas of concern for the design of these interventions. Gamification and virtual reality are used in corporate training to arguably improve the employee learning experience.

Retention strategies

There are a number of ways in which technology can support the retention of staff. With the advent of cloud-based technologies, HR has been able to implement self-service technology where HR self-service, sometimes called employee self-service, allows staff to access their own documents and details through a portal. This provides 24/7 access to be able to check pensions, pay, training data and more. Employees are also able to update their personal details, book holiday and add training they have completed to their profile.

AI can be used to predict salaries for those missing from traditional data sets and support organisations in planning compensation when expanding into new markets where traditional compensation data is not available for those roles that do not yet exist. Rathi (2018) suggests that AI can support companies with their retention strategies by identifying employees who are at risk of leaving the company. For example, the tech company Veriato has developed a variety of AI platforms to support managers in monitoring their staff through software that tracks employee computer activity (emails, keystrokes, internet browsing etc.) and stores it for 30 days. The software can report on exceptions to the employer. It is able to identify changes in the overall tone of employee communications to predict when employees might be thinking of leaving the organisation. Machine learning can be up to 17 times more accurate than other methods at predicting who will resign (Bain & Co, 2018).

AI can also be used in decision-making about workforce planning and talent management. Machine learning can be used to judge employee performance by analysing employee software use, communications and service delivery censors. Audio and video images provide the data to more accurately and fairly make decisions in relation to resourcing, promotion and pay to support retention.

Offboarding

The intention to leave the organisation can now be predicted through the analysis of employee profiles (Sivathanu and Pillai, 2018). This data can support HR so that proactive steps can be taken to prevent high performers leaving the organisation, for example, through the provision of better opportunities internally. Low performers can be identified based on past job performance year on year and training outcomes, instead of relying on line manager decisions which may be subject to bias. Technology to support the offboarding process should be managed with care, however. The following case example provides an insight into the challenges of relying solely on data.

CASE STUDY: AMAZON

Amazon has in place warehouses to track, pack, sort and shuffle orders for delivery. It has been criticised for the strenuous conditions of workers with some being required to pack hundreds of boxes per hour and losing their jobs if they do not meet the output requirements. Between 2017 and 2018, Amazon fired about 300 full-time associates for inefficiency, averaging a termination rate of 10 per cent solely for productivity. The process for termination is automatically tracked and warnings and terminations are given to employees automatically in relation to their productivity without input from supervisors (although Amazon says that supervisors can override the process). Lecher (2019) reports that workers feel as if they are treated like robots due to the way they are monitored and supervised by automated systems. Any time away from the job is recorded and there are reports that some workers avoid bathroom breaks for fear of not adhering to expected timelines. Amazon has attracted a series of bad press for its use of algorithms which design work in such a way that the pace and intensity of work have led to workers sustaining injuries as well as becoming physically exhausted by the pace set.

RISKS AND CHALLENGES OF AI

Despite the benefits discussed in this chapter, there are also a number of risks and challenges posed by the use of technology in people management. Firstly, there are a number of financial barriers to entry and many organisations will be unable to fund the investment required to achieve competitive advantage. This may result in varying levels of digital skill acquisition across the profession.

As noted earlier in the chapter, there are risks associated with the transparency and interpretability of data. For example, as noted in the Veriato example above, to what extent are staff aware that their emails, keystrokes and internet browsing are being closely monitored and used to inform performance management? There are clearly a number of ethical considerations required when using AI (see the next chapter for further discussion of ethics and data analytics). Whittaker (2021) argues that one of the challenges of AI is that developers are overly focused on technical and commercial priorities, and they neglect the wider ethical impact of their work. To use AI effectively, all stakeholders will need to be trained so that they are able to not only use AI effectively but also offer challenges where appropriate.

Furthermore, although AI has the potential to reduce human bias, the narrow focus of AI developers may mean that their own biases are inherent in the systems that they design. Biased AI is not inevitable, and there are tools and methods available now to ensure that AI is free from bias. However, AI can only be ethical if it is based on consultations and involvement of the stakeholder group (employees and prospective employees). Ultimately, the user of the system must be able to understand and question the recommendations of the system to ensure they maintain control. This is also an important aspect of skills development for people professionals who will need to become experts in AI ethics so that they are able to take a lead role in the development and implementation of systems.

REGULATING AI

One of the major concerns regarding AI has been the lack of regulation which has resulted in employers having to decide themselves how to manage risk associated with AI. A number of European countries have laws which state that algorithmic management tools can only be introduced if agreed with worker representatives through co-determination processes but until recently there was little formal regulation. Roberts and Floridi (2021) discuss the EU Commission's proposed 'AI Act' which outlines a risk-based framework for governing AI. Systems deemed to be of unacceptable risk, such as manipulative or social scoring systems, will be prohibited; high-risk systems that could have an adverse impact on safety or fundamental rights are subject to a number of specific governance requirements, limited risk systems will be subjected to transparency requirements and minimal risk systems are encouraged to follow codes of conduct.

In the UK, the government published a pro-innovation approach to regulating AI in July 2022 and then an AI national strategy in September of the same year (GOV.UK, 2022). The Information Commissioner's Office published guidance and an AI risk toolkit in the form of an Excel spreadsheet risk assessment in September 2022. This focuses on best practices for data protection compliance and a methodology for auditing AI applications to ensure that personal data is fairly processed.

In the US, there has been greater hesitancy in introducing legal restrictions comparable to those of the EU. From early 2021, the steady introduction of limited governance is evident with the National AI Initiative Act of 2020, passed in January 2021, which mandates for the establishment of a number of bodies to provide federal-level guidance, the most notable of which is the 'National Artificial Intelligence Initiative Office' (Roberts and Floridi, 2021). The US approach emphasises the promotion of innovation to maintain US global leadership in AI.

SUMMARY POINTS

- The rapid development of new technology provides people professionals with the opportunity to reduce the time spent on mundane repetitive administration tasks in order to maximise the value and potential of the people team in supporting the organisation in achieving and maintaining competitive advantage.

- AI generally refers to an artificial creation of human–like intelligence that can learn, reason, plan, perceive or process natural language. AI is an umbrella term which encompasses machine learning and cognitive computing.
- From candidate attraction to the alumni stage, technology is having a significant impact on every aspect of the employee lifecycle.
- Chatbots can automate routine processes that are time consuming whilst simultaneously providing more access to HR for employees.
- Natural language processing can be used on job descriptions to reduce bias (so long as the algorithm is carefully designed).
- There are a number of financial barriers to exploiting the opportunities offered by technology, and many organisations will be unable to fund the investment required to achieve competitive advantage. This may result in varying levels of digital skill acquisition across the people profession.
- Algorithms may suffer from the inherent bias of developers in the systems that are designed although increasingly tools and methods are being designed to counter this bias.
- One of the major concerns regarding AI has been the lack of regulation which has resulted in employers having to decide themselves how to manage risk associated with AI. The UK government has published a pro-innovation approach to regulation in an attempt to balance data protection compliance and to promote further technological developments.

SELF-TEST QUESTIONS/REVIEW QUESTIONS

- To what extent can AI improve the employee experience at each stage of the employee lifecycle?
- Evaluate the case for greater regulation of AI. What are the advantages and disadvantages of implementing legal restrictions and governance?

A CASE EXAMPLE: AMAZON

Review the Amazon case study in this chapter. Amazon has clearly invested large sums to enhance efficiency in its warehouse operations. Evaluate the use of AI in the warehouse for all stakeholders (senior managers, line managers, employees, customers, suppliers). What recommendations would you make to Amazon regarding the use of AI in its business units? Consider the value that AI is adding to the organisation.

REFLECTION

Reflect on your own experience of using chatbots (perhaps in a recruitment situation from the candidate perspective or as a customer, or you may prefer to interview a family member or friend about their experience). What are the benefits of using a chatbot? What are the drawbacks? To what extent do you agree with the statement, 'using chatbots will revolutionise the employee experience at every stage of the employee lifecycle'? Consider each stage of the lifecycle and how chatbots are being used or have the potential to be used.

References

Agrawal, A., Gans, J. and Goldfrarb, A. (2018). *Prediction Machines: The Simple Economics of Artificial Intelligence*. Harvard Business Press.

Bain & Co. (2018). *HR's New Digital Mandate*. Bain & Co. Available at: https://www.bain.com/insights/hrs-new-digital-mandate/. (Accessed 14 June, 2022).

Booth, R. (2019). Unilever saves on recruiters by using AI to assess job interviews. [online] *The Guardian*. Available at: https://www.theguardian.com/technology/2019/oct/25/unilever-saves-on-recruiters-by-using-ai-to-assess-job-interviews. (Accessed 14 July, 2022).

Charlwood, A. and Guenole, N. (2022). Can HR adapt to the paradoxes of artificial intelligence? *Human Resource Management Journal, 32*(4). https://doi:10.1111/1748-8583.12433.

CIPD (2021). Technology and the future of work. CIPD. 6 Jan. Available at: https://www.cipd.co.uk/knowledge/work/technology/emerging-future-work-factsheet#gref (Accessed 2 July, 2022).

Dattner, B., Chamorro-Premuzic, T., Buchband, R. and Schettler, L. (2019). The legal and ethical implications of using AI in hiring. *Harvard Business Review*, 25 April. Available at: https://egn.com/dk/wp-content/uploads/sites/3/2020/06/The-legal-and-ethical-implications-of-using-AI-in-Hiring.pdf. (Accessed 3 October, 2022).

Deloitte. (2018). *Machine Learning Operations for Business*. Deloitte United States. Available at: https://www2.deloitte.com/us/en/pages/consulting/articles/machine-learning-operations-for-business.html. (Accessed 15 June, 2022).

Fernandez, V. and Gallardo-Gallardo, E. (2020). HR analytics conceptualization and adoption: Key issues. *Academy of Management, 2020*(1). https://doi.org/10.5465/AMBPP.2020.12180abstract.

GOV.UK (2019). A guide to using artificial intelligence in the public sector. Available at: https://www.gov.uk/government/collections/a-guide-to-using-artificial-intelligence-in-the-public-sector. (Accessed 1 August, 2022).

GOV.UK (2022). National AI strategy. Available at: https://www.gov.uk/government/organisations/office-for-artificial-intelligence. (Accessed 15 July, 2022).

Guenole, N. and Feinzig, S. (2018). The business case for AI in HR. With insights and tips on getting started. [pdf] IBM Corporation. Available at: https://forms.workday.com/content/dam/web/en-us/documents/case-studies/ibm-business-case-ai-in-hr.pdf. (Accessed, 15 July, 2022).

Heric, M. (2018). HR new digital mandate. Digital technologies have become essential for HR to engage top talent and add value to the business. Bain & Company. [pdf] Available at: https://www.bain.com/contentassets/3dea09cc27fd426abfb35f9 caa0e97dc/bain_brief_-hrs_new_digital_mandate.pdf.

IBM (2022). Available at: https://www.ibm.com (Accessed 13 August, 2022).

Kavanagh, M.J., Thite, M. and Johnson, R.D. (Eds.) (2015). *Human Resource Information Systems*. 3rd edn. Thousand Oaks: Sage.

Kew, J. and Stredwick, J., (2016). *Human Resource Management in a Business Context*. 3rd edn. London: CIPD.

KPMG (2020). The future of HR 2020: Which path are you taking? [online] *KPMG Global*. Available at: https://home.kpmg/xx/en/home/insights/2019/11/the-future -of-human-resources-2020.html. (Accessed 15 August, 2022).

Lebovitz, S. Levina, N. and Lifshitz-Assaf, H. (2021). Is AI ground truth really 'true'? The dangers of training and evaluating AI tools based on experts' know-what. *MIS Quarterly*, pp.1501–1525. Available at: https://papers.ssrn.com/sol3/papers.cfm ?abstract_id=3839601. (Accessed 15 August, 2022).

Lecher, C. (2019). How Amazon automatically tracks and fires warehouse workers for 'productivity'. 25 April. Available at: https://www.theverge.com/2019/4/25 /18516004/amazon-warehouse-fulfillment-centers-productivity-firing-terminations (Accessed 3 August, 2022).

Mahesh, B. (2018). Machine learning algorithms-a review. *International Journal of Science and Research (IJSR)*. *[Internet]*, *9*, pp.381–386. Available at: https://www .researchgate.net/profile/Batta-Mahesh/publication/344717762_Machine_Learning _Algorithms_-A_Review/links/5f8b2365299bf1b53e2d243a/Machine-Learning -Algorithms-A-Review.pdf?eid=5082902844932096. (Accessed 1 June, 2022).

Nankervis, A., Connell, J., Cameron, R., Montague, A., Prikshat, V. (2019). 'Are we there yet?' Australian HR professionals and the Fourth Industrial Revolution. *Asia Pacific Journal of Human Resources*. *59*. https://doi.org/10.1111/1744-7941.12245.

Rathi, R.A. (2018). Artificial intelligence and the future of HR practices. *International Journal of Applied Research*, *4*(6), pp.113–116. Available at: https://www .allresearchjournal.com/archives/?year=2018&vol=4&issue=6&part=B&ArticleId =5054. (Accessed 15 June, 2022).

Roberts, H. and Floridi, L. (2021). The EU and the US: Two different approaches to AI governance. University of Oxford. Available at: https://www.oii.ox.ac.uk/news -events/news/the-eu-and-the-us-two-different-approaches-to-ai-governance/ (Accessed 1 June, 2022).

Roberts, H., Cowls, J., Hine, E., Mazzi, F., Tsamados, A., Taddeo, M. and Floridi, L. (2021). Achieving a 'Good AI society': Comparing the aims and progress of the EU and the US. *Science and Engineering Ethics*, *27*(6). https://doi.org/10.1007/s11948-021 -00340-7.

Sivathanu, B. and Pillai, R. (2018). Smart HR 4.0: How industry 4.0 is disrupting HR. Human Resource Management International Digest, *26*(4), pp.7–11. https://doi.org /10.1108/HRMID-04-2018-0059.

Tripathi, P, Masood, G., Pitroda, J.R., Jaiswal, S. and Kumar, K.S. (2021). Impact of machine learning on economic crisis for HR managers during Covid-19. *Turkish Online Journal of Qualitative Inquiry (TOJQI)*, *12*(6) July, 2021, pp.4882–4890 (Accessed 15 June, 2022).

Whittaker, M. (2021). The steep cost of capture. *ACM Interactions, XXVIII*(6), pp.50–55.

People analytics and value creation

Chapter 10

INTRODUCTION

This chapter takes a practitioner focus on the use of people analytics in order to aid decision-making and strategic planning in the workplace. It provides an introduction to people analytics terminology including qualitative and quantitative data, descriptive, predictive and prescriptive analytics to solve complex problems. Metrics are explored through the stages of the employee lifecycle so that readers are able to understand how data can be utilised to enhance people practices and gain competitive advantage. The chapter explores how organisations can solve problems using insights gained from analytics to draw causal links. Data analytics tools are introduced along with issues of data privacy, transparency, security and ethics. Consideration of how to communicate and present data using dashboards and storytelling in order to inform decision-making for different stakeholders is provided.

DEFINING PEOPLE ANALYTICS

HR departments have for some years collected data about their employees. The largest fixed cost for most organisations is their human capital so from a business perspective people analytics is integral to efficient operations. The extent to which people teams have analysed people data to gain insights in support of business planning has been rather limited, however. A 2017 human resources trends survey by Deloitte found that only 9 per cent of surveyed companies confirmed that they had a good understanding

DOI: 10.4324/9781003342984-11

of talent and performance in their organisations, although 71 per cent of companies considered people analytics to be a high priority for their businesses (Deloitte, 2017). A 2019 study by KPMG found that analytics initiatives remain a low priority among HR leaders and their businesses with respondents ranking a commitment to analytics near the bottom of ten potential HR initiatives (KPMG, 2018). However, the 2018 Global Human Capital Trends survey found that 84 per cent considered people analytics as being important or very important, making it the second highest ranked HR trend (Deloitte, 2018). This may indicate that people professionals note the importance of people analytics but some are yet to prioritise action in relation to investment and implementation of the supporting infrastructure. Either way, Green (2019) highlights that companies with advanced capability in people analytics have 30 per cent higher stock prices, 79 per cent higher return on equity and 56 per cent higher profit margins emphasising the priority that should be given to people analytics in any HR function.

People analytics is about analysing data about people to solve business problems. Data analytics is already used by other functions, namely IT, marketing, finance, operations, sales and so on, to support decision-making. Boudreau (2017) suggests that people analytics are useful for drawing conclusions from data through the use of statistics and research design that goes further than just identifying problems and collecting data. Interest in people analytics has grown considerably over the last five years or so as good practice examples have emerged of how data can be used to support organisations in their recruitment, retention and performance management strategies. People analytics supports organisations to make more effective decisions at each stage of the employee lifecycle, thus increasing efficiencies, improving performance and making cost savings.

PEOPLE ANALYTICS TERMINOLOGY

Rather than referring to a technology, people analytics focuses on an evidence-based, data-driven approach to managing the workforce using a range of quantitative and qualitative data.

QUALITATIVE DATA

Qualitative data is collected through observation, interviews, focus groups, audio, images and is analysed in words rather than numbers. Qualitative data is the outcome of research undertaken that seeks to answer questions of how and why. It provides a deeper level of analysis into different perspectives and is subjective and biased. Reports generated through qualitative analysis will provide a rich narrative to support decision-making, for example, employee survey feedback and employee preferences.

QUANTITATIVE DATA

Quantitative data is expressed numerically, for example, staff turnover and absences. It is objective and measurable and is used in relation to costs, usage, length etc. Any information that is measured can provide statistical analysis.

Data can be used to analyse each stage of the employee lifecycle. HR metrics should be aligned to the HR strategy and will be unique to each organisation. Examples might include the percentage cost of the workforce (as a total of all company costs), percentage of holiday days used (to support well-being), absenteeism rates, number of staff (to identify growth), turnover, length of time in post, average time to fill a vacancy, training costs per individual and internal promotion rates. Using a mix of both quantitative and qualitative data will support organisations most effectively in their decision-making.

DESCRIPTIVE, PREDICTIVE AND PRESCRIPTIVE ANALYTICS

The CIPD (2022) explains that descriptive, predictive and prescriptive analytics are terms used to describe the maturity of an organisation's people analytics capability. It argues that whilst most organisations have the capability to provide descriptive analytics, only a few have the technology to support prescriptive analytics.

Descriptive analytics provide historical trends such as employee turnover, absence and perhaps a combination of engagement scores and leadership effectiveness. Marler and Boudreau (2017) contend that information technology provides the tool from which people professionals are able to use descriptive, visual and statistical data analysis to aid decision-making in relation to human capital, organisational performance and external economic benchmarks.

Predictive analytics is used to predict future trends and is possible when organisations use large data sets from employees to predict future outcomes. This might include candidate sourcing where people professionals use candidate selection tools based on a predictive model. These are built using algorithms which use current employee data, for example, performance reviews, employee surveys and attrition data. It is important that the data is used to support human decision-making, not replace it. Data needs to be relevant, high quality and robust to ensure reliability.

Prescriptive analytics uses descriptive and predictive analytics to automatically recommend actions, for example, an online learning platform that recommends courses to a learner based on their previous learning and goals (CIPD, 2022).

Companies already hold a vast amount of information about staff with most people professionals collecting data on performance, retention and engagement in some form. People analytics supports organisations to understand their workforce, their departments, work groups and individuals through deeper insights into areas such as workforce turnover rates to predict (and reduce if desirable) future churn, assessing and understanding organisation culture (including identifying inefficiencies) and exploring the effectiveness of leadership.

CASE STUDY: CREDIT SUISSE

Credit Suisse is a financial services company based in Switzerland, employing 47,000 employees. The organisation was exploring ways to reduce staff turnover. The company has a strong commitment to collecting data, and it was concerned at the costs of turnover which were estimated to be between 30 and 400 per cent of an employee's salary depending on the seniority of the grade and the experience required for the role. The company used people analytics to predict which employees were most likely to leave the company and when. With the data collected, the company was able to analyse who left the company, why and their length of tenure with the company (Ankum, 2022). In order to understand the reasons why staff were leaving the company, the organisation tracked 40 variables prior to the point of departure for each employee including performance ratings and the size of the employee's team. The predictive people analytics model that was built provided the company with the data to accurately predict how likely an employee is to leave the organisation in the next year based on as few as ten indicators. With this data, the company is able to identify and respond to the risk factors identified (Credit Suisse, 2022).

BIG DATA

Big data is data that cannot be handled using traditional tools and techniques due to its high volume, variety, velocity, value and veracity

(Elgendy & Elragal, 2016). Big data refers to the wealth of data accessible through computers, mobile devices and machines which can be used to drive decisions, improve policies and processes and ensure that experiences and services are employee focused. Essentially, big data is a database used for massive data analysis. This concept applies to all information that cannot be collected, processed or analysed through traditional software tools. Big data is not just vast, it is also complex and requires AI and machine learning technologies (as discussed in the previous chapter) to provide actionable and timely data which will add value to the organisation. Large organisations will particularly benefit from the insights that big data can provide due to the vast nature and complexity of data that is collected (although any organisation will find the deeper insights made possible by big data beneficial).

DATA ANALYTICS SKILLS

One of the challenges of adopting an effective people insight strategy is the skillset required to manage and analyse data. The CIPD's view is that people analytics forms a fundamental element of evidence-based HR, which requires people professionals to understand organisational data (CIPD, 2022). People analytics is outlined as one of the nine specialist disciplines in the CIPD HR profession map (CIPD, 2021). It focuses on gathering and using data and information to provide insights into people issues and to guide decision-making. This involves understanding research design, framing questions and using quantitative and qualitative techniques which can help organisations address issues or challenges. The CIPD explains that people analytics is about exploring issues and problems in a methodical way in order to shape solutions. To do this effectively requires a knowledge of statistical analysis, the ability to interpret data and present it in a meaningful way. People analytics aids decision-making and supports people professionals in making informed and actionable recommendations (ibid.).

Some larger organisations benefit from a digital data specialist or team of specialists that can support people professionals as subject matter experts. Koontz (2017) argues that the skillsets of data engineers and HR experts rarely overlap, and in order to develop a data-driven culture, organisations must first focus on capability (ensuring that staff have the right skills and knowledge) and the confidence to implement analytics. Training interventions to support analytical development in the organisation are key to embedding an evidence-based culture.

CASE STUDY: CHEVRON

Chevron was experiencing falling oil prices and was seeking ways in which to maintain its above-average profitability and revenue per employee. The organisation decided to centralise its data analytics team so that people metrics reports were standardised to improve the quality of reporting. The company was keen to understand workforce productivity more clearly, and the localised reports that were being produced resulted in variability of reporting and sometimes duplication of the same reports. The company business mission was redefined to focus on better, faster workforce decisions informed by data. An analytics team of 295 members across the world was created consisting of HR business partners, specialists and analysts. With standardisation of analytics and development for all stakeholders, to improve data analytics competency (for HR and non-HR staff), the team have been able to develop a strong team who are now consulted in relation to all strategic business decisions (Fineman, 2017).

PEOPLE ANALYTICS THROUGH THE EMPLOYEE LIFECYCLE

Key performance indicators (KPIs) provide the framework for driving strategic decisions. KPIs need to be set in alignment with the organisational strategy and goals. They should follow the SMART acronym, in that they should be specific (clear), measurable (trackable), attainable (achievable), relevant (to the organisation) and timely (set within a realistic timeframe). Some examples of the metrics that might be used across the stages of the employee lifecycle are included below in Table 10.1. This list is by no means exhaustive but it does highlight the importance of setting metrics relevant to the organisation across the employee journey.

DATA ANALYSIS TOOLS

Many organisations start to track people data manually initially, perhaps through a spreadsheet, although this is not feasible when working at scale. Manual-based reports are labour intensive to compile and whilst they can be effective if the information is unlikely to change, there is a limit to the number of reports that can be generated. People analytics tools provide people professionals with the opportunity to gather, store and analyse people data for future analysis. Monitoring data provides people professionals with the opportunity to track problems early so that improvements can be implemented, for example, to manage turnover

Table 10.1 People Analytics through the Employee Lifecycle

Attraction	Cost per quality applicant: how much does it cost to yield a quality applicant? Sourcing channel efficiency: this metric allows organisations to track where their candidates are sourced from to ensure that the most effective channels benefit from appropriate investment.
Recruitment	Time to hire: tracking the length of time from application to offer stage. Time to fill: the number of days it takes from posting a job to a candidate accepting the offer (measures the time when a candidate enters the candidate pool). Interview to offer ratio: the time it takes to offer and reject a candidate (this should be as low as possible to maximise the candidate experience). The quality of new recruits: might be measured through the ratings given in the probationary period and/or performance review. Equality, diversity and inclusion: link to gender and ethnicity balance targets within the organisation, for both recruitment and promotion.
Onboarding	90-day quit rates or first-year turnover rates: the first-year turnover rate calculates the number of employees who resign in less than one year. This may indicate a mismatch between the new employee and the company which will mean a review of the onboarding and recruitment process is required.
Development	Developmental effectiveness: all training and development should be measured to ensure that it reaches the intended goals. Workplace productivity: this relates to the output in terms of organisation growth, accuracy, speed etc. and it can be more challenging to measure. However, organisations should define a metric relevant to them based on the total value of the output divided by the total costs to obtain that output.
Retention	Net promoter scores: this measures the degree to which someone would recommend working for the organisation. Employee engagement: this is measured through engagement surveys. Benefits satisfaction: the degree to which employees are satisfied with the employee benefits. Absence rates: calculated by dividing working days lost by the total number of working days. Associated costs should also be tracked.
Offboarding	Turnover rate: turnover refers to the percentage of employees that have left over a certain period. This might be calculated for both voluntary and involuntary turnover.
Alumni	Metrics might relate to the number of ex-employees who have recommended a high-performing employee or who have supported events.

effectively. Automated reports can be created using specialist software and this is where organisations can benefit from predictive analysis to support strategic decision-making.

There are now many platforms that can support organisations with the collection of real-time analytics which are used for surveying employees and measuring organisation health. Some platforms provide the facility for people professionals to build secure employee databases that facilitate HR reports, charts and records on individual employees. Others focus more on employee engagement and well-being using employee net promoter scores, surveys, well-being pulse surveys, exit interviews etc. to support analysis of employee turnover and to focus on increasing employee engagement. Platforms can equip people professionals with the tools to make predictions, analyse data in relation to industry benchmarks and assess organisation change, month by month and year by year. Popular choices of people analytics tools at the time of writing are Lattice, BambooHR, intelliHR and Visier People. Tableau and Power BI are tools used to analyse and visualise data. These tools can be customised to organisation needs and requirements such as key performance indicators. Visuals can be exported into spreadsheets and PowerPoint slides in order to support the presentation of datasets and insights.

COMMUNICATING AND PRESENTING DATA

In order to communicate effectively to an audience, it is first necessary to understand their needs. When this is clear, data can be gathered and visualised. Communicating in an interesting and concise way that appeals to the stakeholders concerned is more likely to encourage engagement and discussion of the data being presented.

Data can be presented using a range of visuals using HR dashboards containing infographics. The HR metrics dashboard is a tool used for tracking workforce metrics to identify trends and any emerging concerns. For example, it can support employee retention at organisational and departmental level, assisting managers to focus on problem areas in relation to resourcing and retention. Dashboards provide enhanced visibility of past and current trends enabling organisations to forecast with more accuracy. To be effective the HR dashboard should focus on key performance indicators so that the data is both relevant and manageable to support trend analysis. Indeed, too much data is less effective for decision making as Google found. Initially, when Google began their people analytics journey they were keen for all people decisions at the company to be based on data and analytics. However, the volume of data produced was time consuming to digest and so they focused only on relevant information to inform more effective decision-making (Penny, 2019).

STORYTELLING WITH DATA

Providing a narrative with data allows complex information to be simplified to meet the needs of your audience. This approach also encourages engagement so that stakeholders will have the understanding and confidence to ask questions which may decrease the time it takes to agree critical decisions. Data storytelling involves the presentation of collated data in the form of infographics to support a defined purpose. It should include an introduction and conclusion, time for questions and an action for your audience (for example, to agree a proposal or plan). It is important to present both sides of the argument and focus on patterns, trends and findings in an objective manner. This approach works effectively when presenting through a HR dashboard as discussed above.

DATA PRIVACY, TRANSPARENCY, SECURITY AND ETHICS

The evolving nature of HRM practices to people analytics provides a shift in the power of relations between leaders and employees as organisations seek to optimise their workforce (Tursunbayeva et al., 2022). The ability to harvest, analyse and visualise complex information about individuals, teams, divisions and the workforce as a whole provides insights into performance, skills, aptitudes, weaknesses, threats and potential.

As we have discussed earlier in this book, the ability to capture data through AI and machine learning presents both opportunities and challenges. With the right technology in place, organisations can now monitor employees' personal emails, social media activity, interactions with digital devices and apps. Some organisations might argue that this is necessary to inform actions that will enhance the employee experience and employee well-being. Humu, founded by former Google executive Lazlo Bock, collects data through emails and questionnaire responses to build algorithms in order to understand performance patterns. This enables personalised messages to be sent to employees to shape or 'nudge' behaviour including reminders that encourage staff to save for retirement or opt for healthier snacks (Wakabayashi, 2018). A key concern with this use of data is the degree to which organisations are transparent in relation to its collection and use. There are several ethical questions that arise when using data in relation to a users' information rights, the impact on personal autonomy and the mechanisms in place to protect individuals from manipulation (ibid.).

Giermindl et al. (2021) argue that the use of people analytics can reduce employee autonomy leading to a dehumanisation of the worker experience and a loss of individuality. One of the problems identified is that managers and people professionals have an illusion that they are in control but in actual fact their faith in the algorithms prevents them from identifying errors. Relying on data to inform predictions without operating human judgement and where decisions and actions are incomprehensible for employees and managers results in a lack of accountability and a feeling of powerlessness.

One of the benefits highlighted in the business case for using people analytics is the ability data has for offering objectivity in decision-making. As discussed in the previous chapter, algorithms must be built with care. Systems are designed by humans and as such have the potential for prejudice and bias. The example below highlights how this can be problematic for organisations.

CASE STUDY: AMAZON

In 2018, Amazon stopped using its AI- and machine learning-based recruitment system after the company discovered that the algorithm used in the selection process was biased against women. Amazon's AI tool was programmed to vet candidates by observing patterns in resumes and it learnt who to select after analysing applications to the company over a ten-year period. The majority of those candidates had been men, which led the system to favour male candidates over female candidates (Dastin, 2018).

AI does offer the potential for a more cost-effective, targeted and efficient approach to selection in the longer term, but it is important that HR users are involved in the development of future technologies to remove the potential for bias and to ensure appropriately sized datasets are used (ibid)

Tursunbayeva et al. (2022) found that ethical considerations for people analytics have received relatively little attention compared to data analysis in education or medicine despite the fact that their research suggests there has been an increase in monitoring and surveillance of the workforce. For example, organisations are now using nudge prompts (as discussed above), pre-employment checks (including credit reports), driving records and criminal records even before a candidate joins an organisation. Within the workplace, monitoring and surveillance may continue through email, video, audio, location surveillance, social media messages, health data and more.

The degree to which employees are accepting of increased surveillance and monitoring is largely linked to the approach used by organisations to persuade employees that it is in their interest to share data. Organisations need to be transparent with regard to the data being collected and the way it is used. Using data on its own is likely to be problematic as it will not provide the full story of an event (for example the reason behind a staff member taking time out for creative thought). That is why using a mix of both quantitative and qualitative data in organisations is most effective.

Trust is fundamental to the employee experience, and the way staff perceive the organisation's ethics will impact every aspect of the employee lifecycle. Being clear and transparent about the organisation's approach to collecting data, how it is collected and how the data will be used is key to reducing the potential stress that employees might endure as a result of being monitored. Educating, communicating and agreeing on fair performance metrics with employees is key. Organisations must commit to clear ethical standards. Indeed, many professions set their own professional body standards as is the case for the CIPD where members must adhere to the CIPD code of professional conduct which includes a section on ethical standards and integrity requirements.

HR teams will need to operate within the data privacy laws of their own country. In the UK personal employee data comes under the General Data Protection Regulation (UK GDPR). The Information Commissioner's Office provides a guide to the UK GDPR and how it applies to organisations and businesses in the UK. It sets out key definitions of GDPR and the seven key principles (lawfulness, fairness and transparency, purpose limitation, data minimalisation, accuracy, storage limitation, integrity and confidentiality (security) and accountability. Favaro (2019) suggests that it is difficult for employers to embrace the opportunities that technology offers whilst complying with the GDPR, however, as the nature of big data and some AI technologies comes into direct conflict with the fundamental principles of GDPR compliance. Therefore, employers will need to balance the interests of their data subjects with their own interests in investing in new technology.

SUMMARY POINTS

- People analytics is about analysing data about people to solve business problems. It supports organisations to make more effective decisions at each stage of the employee lifecycle.
- Most organisations have the capability to provide descriptive analytics but few have the technology to support prescriptive analytics. Predictive models work most effectively when used to support human decision-making.
- One of the challenges of adopting an effective people insight strategy is the skills set required to manage and analyse data. This works effectively when analytics teams are formed consisting of both data analysts and subject matter experts in people practice.
- KPIs should align to the organisation strategy and be SMART. They should track each stage of the employee lifecycle so that early intervention to address problems can be undertaken if required.
- HR dashboards provide enhanced visibility of past and current trends enabling organisations to forecast with more accuracy, and they can be used to support the communication of data. Providing a narrative with data in the form of a story allows complex information to be simplified to meet the needs of an audience.
- The increasing use of people analytics in organisations is shifting the power balance back to organisations. The degree to which employees are accepting of increased surveillance and monitoring is largely linked to the approach used by organisations to persuade employees that it is in their interest to share data.

SELF-TEST QUESTIONS/REVIEW QUESTIONS

- How can organisations justify investment in technology that provides the capability for people analytics? What benefits can people analytics provide? How can a small organisation benefit from people analytics when they do not have the budget for sophisticated technology?
- One of the challenges of implementing a people analytics strategy discussed in this chapter is the skillset required to analyse data. Explore ways in which people professionals can prepare themselves effectively to take advantage of people analytics. Consider recommendations for large multinationals and smaller organisations.

A CASE EXAMPLE: AMAZON

Review the Amazon case study in this chapter. Amazon stopped using its AI- and machine learning-based recruitment system after the company discovered that the algorithm used in the selection process was biased against women. What could Amazon have done to prevent this bias in the selection process? What recommendations would you make to Amazon in their future building of algorithms?

REFLECTION

With the right technology in place, organisations can now monitor employees' personal emails, social media activity, interactions with digital devices and apps. How comfortable do you feel in the knowledge that your organisation is monitoring your activity within your role and even beyond the workplace? Reflect on the extent to which you would agree to any monitoring and surveillance by your organisation. What recommendations would you make to your organisation so that they are able to balance a need for data to improve business efficiency and gain competitive advantage with your need for privacy? You may wish to interview a family member or friend about their experience.

References

Ankum, M. (2022). People analytics: 5 real case studies. 4 March. Available at https://www.effectory.com/knowledge/people-analytics-5-real-case-studies/. (Accessed 28 July, 2022).

Boudreau, J. (2017). HR must make people analytics more user-friendly. [online] *Harvard Business Review*. Available at: https://hbr.org/2017/06/hr-must-make-people-analytics-more-user-friendly. (Accessed 13 July, 2022).

CIPD (2021). New profession map. [online] CIPD. Available at: https://peopleprofession.cipd.org/profession-map. (Accessed 1 June, 2022).

CIPD. (2022). Digital transformation: Practical insights from the people profession. [online] CIPD. Available at: https://www.cipd.co.uk/knowledge/work/technology/digital-transformation-insights.

Creditsuisse (2022). Available at https://www.credit-suisse.com/us/en.html (Accessed 13 August, 2022).

Dastin, J. (2018). Amazon scraps secret AI recruiting tool that showed bias against women. 11 October. Available at: https://www.reuters.com/article/us-amazon-com-jobs-automation-insight-idUSKCN1MK08G. (Accessed 3 September, 2022).

Deloitte (2017). Rewriting the rules for the digital age. *Deloitte Global Human Capital Trends*. Available at: https://www2.deloitte.com/content/dam/Deloitte/global/Documents/About-Deloitte/central-europe/ce-global-human-capital-trends.pdf. (Accessed 14 July, 2022).

Deloitte (2018). The rise of the social enterprise: 2018 Deloitte Global Human Capital Trends. Available at: https://www2.deloitte.com/content/dam/Deloitte/au/Documents/human-capital/deloitte-au-hc-human-capital-2018-120419.pdf. (Accessed 22 January 2023).

Elgendy, N. and Elragal, A. (2016). Big data analytics in support of the decision making process. *Procedia Computer Science*, 100(2016), pp.1071–1084. https://doi:10.1016/j.procs.2016.09.251.

Favaro (2019). People analytics and GDPR: The challenge for HR. *Future of Work Hub*. 28 October. Available at: https://www.futureofworkhub.info/comment/2019/10/28/people-analytics-and-gdpr-the-challenge-for-hr. (Accessed 13 July, 2022).

Fineman, D.R. (2017). People analytics: Recalculating the route. [online] *Deloitte Insights*. Available at: https://www2.deloitte.com/us/en/insights/focus/human-capital-trends/2017/people-analytics-in-hr.html. (Accessed 1 June, 2022).

Giermindl, L.M., Strich, F., Christ, O., Leicht-Deobald, U. and Redzepi, A. (2021). The dark sides of people analytics: Reviewing the perils for organisations and employees. *European Journal of Information Systems*, 31(3), pp.1–26. https://doi:10.1080/0960085x.2021.1927213.

Green, D. (2019). Six factors for the adoption of people analytics. [online] *myHRfuture*. Available at: https://www.myhrfuture.com/blog/2019/6/28/six-factors-influencing-the-adoption-of-people-analytics. (Available 13 July, 2022).

Koontz, K. (2017). People analytics. *Best's Review*, 18. Available at: http://tsuhhelweb.tsu.edu:2048/login?url=https://search.proquest.com/docview/188305651

KPMG (2018). HR data and analytics. Available at: https://home.kpmg/xx/en/home/insights/2018/11/hr-data-and-analytics.html. (Accessed 30 August, 2022).

Marler, J.H. and Boudreau, J.W. (2017). An evidence-based review of HR Analytics. *The International Journal of Human Resource Management*, 28(1), pp.3–26. Available at: https://www.tandfonline.com/doi/abs/10.1080/09585192.2016.1244699?journalCode=rijh20. (Accessed 13 September, 2022).

Penny, C. (2019). Case study: How Google uses people analytics. 1 Dec. Available at: https://www.sage.com/en-au/blog/case-study-how-google-uses-people-analytics/. (Accessed 3 September, 2022).

Tursunbayeva, A., Pagliari, C., Di Lauro, S. and Antonelli, G. (2022). The ethics of people analytics: Risks, opportunities and recommendations. Personnel Review, 51(3), pp.900–921. https://doi.org/10.1108/PR-12-2019-0680.

Wakabayashi, D. (2018). Firm led by google veterans uses A.I. to 'nudge' workers toward happiness. [online] *The New York Times*. (Published 31 Dec. 2018) Available at: https://www.nytimes.com/2018/12/31/technology/human-resources-artificial-intelligence-humu.html. (Accessed 3 October 22).

Putting employee well-being at the centre of performance management

Chapter 11

INTRODUCTION

This chapter focuses on the relationship between employee well-being and performance. It argues that well-being works most successfully when it is an integral part of organisation culture. It explores the role of leaders and managers in promoting well-being as the norm in the workplace through behaviours and involvement with well-being activities. It considers the role of the people professional in well-being strategy formulation and implementation. The notion of performance is explored and the culture and behaviours required for high performance are identified. The framework for workplace well-being is considered along with the business case and how the strategy can be measured and evaluated. Case study examples are provided to highlight how organisations can create a culture of well-being that promotes high-performance working through regular open and honest catch-ups, access to the right support and opportunities for staff to provide feedback.

DOI: 10.4324/9781003342984-12

WELL-BEING IN SOCIETY

Good health and well-being are increasingly being recognised as integral to sustainable growth at individual, organisation and policy level. Indeed, the United Nations includes good health and well-being as one of the 17 sustainable development goals (SDG 3), which is linked to SDG 8 that focuses on decent work and economic growth. The World Health Organization (WHO, 2017) explains that health is determined by our environment, income, education, gender, age as well as our socio-economic status. They also recognise that social support networks play an important part in our overall health.

THE PILLARS OF WELL-BEING

Adams et al. (1997) found six dimensions of wellness in their perceived wellness survey, including emotional, intellectual, physical, psychological, social and spiritual. The researchers explain that individuals who score high on perceived wellness are physically more healthy, have a greater sense of meaning and purpose in life, expect that positive things will occur in their lives no matter what the circumstances, are more connected with family or friends, are more secure and happy with who they are and are intellectually vibrant. Sfeatcu et al. (2014, p.123) argue that

> wellbeing is in general a term used to describe a condition of an individual or a group, with reference to the social, economic, psychological, spiritual or medical attention. A high level of wellbeing is related to the positive experiences of an individual or group. Similarly, a low level is associated with negative experiences.

In a workplace setting, companies might invest in well-being activities and services that are designed to promote good health and wellness for employees. Initiatives might include health awareness and education (for example, programmes to address specific health risk behaviours such as smoking), healthy eating, mental health, encouraging exercise and generally encouraging healthier lifestyles.

The quality of working life (QWL) concept proposed by Walton (1973) includes a framework of eight categories for analysing and measuring the quality of our working lives. Although written almost 50 years ago, the essential components of the framework remain as relevant today as they have always been. The pillars include:

1. Adequate and fair compensation: does the income meet socially determined standards of sufficiency or the subjective standard of the

recipient? Is it fair in relation to job evaluation, supply and demand and ability to pay by the employer?

2. Safe and healthy working conditions: are physical conditions safe and free from hazards and are hourly arrangements unduly detrimental to health?

3. Immediate opportunity to use and develop human capacities: to what extent does a worker have autonomy over the job role and the opportunity to plan activities, the ability to use a wide range of skills and abilities and information about the total work process so that a holistic overview of the role is possible?

4. Future opportunity for continued growth and security: is there opportunity for development, to expand skills and knowledge, to progress career and to achieve income security?

5. Social integration in the work organisation: what is the potential for upwards mobility free from prejudice, is there a sense of community and interpersonal openness and support to share ideas and feelings?

6. Constitutionalism in the work organisation: to what extent is a worker's right to personal privacy respected, is there opportunity to share views with leaders without fear of reprisals, is there equitable treatment in all matters (for example, compensation and reward) and equality of opportunity?

7. Work and total life space: to what extent is there opportunity for work and life balance?

8. The social relevance of work life: Is the organisation socially responsible in relation to its products, environmental concerns, marketing and employment practices? (Organisations that engage in socially irresponsible activities will cause employees to deprecate their work which impacts worker self-esteem).

The CIPD (2022a) in its contemporary framework on the same theme identifies seven inter-related domains of employee well-being including:

1. Health: physical health and safety and mental health focussing on stress management, risk assessments, health promotion, employee assistance programmes, occupational health, managing disability, personal safety

2. Good work: working areas that are open and inclusive, effective line manager training and people management policies, autonomy, effective communication, involvement and fair and transparent pay and reward

3. Values/principles: values-based leadership, clear mission, health and well-being strategy, governance, corporate social responsibility, inclusion and diversity
4. Collective/social: employee voice through communication, consultation and involvement and positive relationships, team working, healthy relationships
5. Personal growth: career development opportunities, positive relationships, financial well-being, lifelong learning and creativity through open and collaborative culture
6. Good lifestyle choices: opportunity for physical activity through walking clubs, lunchtime yoga, healthy eating, recipe clubs, menu choices if office based
7. Financial well-being: fair pay and benefit policies, pay rates above minimum, retirement planning and employee financial support

The notable developments between the models are the integration of mental health, employee assistance programmes and a move from safety to health promotion. Working hours are specifically mentioned in the QWL model and this continues to be a challenge for health and well-being today. Hesketh and Cooper (2019) make the point that stress at work is rising year on year with long working hours seemingly becoming the norm. They suggest that this is not only having a detrimental effect on employee health, happiness and productivity, but also impacting the organisation's bottom line. The CIPD has added financial well-being to its well-being domains. The CIPD (2022b) is encouraging employers to recognise the moral and business case of implementing support for employee financial well-being. Indeed, 65 per cent of employees say it is important that their next employer has a financial well-being policy in place according to the 2022 CIPD Reward Management Survey (CIPD, 2022c). Brown (2019) found that financial well-being strategies were only evident in a tenth of employers surveyed and employee financial guidance was not provided by two-thirds of employers in the Institute of Employment Studies research. However, financial well-being strategies were on the HR agenda of more than half of employers surveyed by Willis Towers Watson (WTS, 2017) although little progress appears to have been made by 2022 with just 18 per cent of organisations reporting to have a financial well-being policy in place, either as part of a wider employee health and well-being policy (14 per cent) or as a standalone financial well-being policy (4 per cent). A further 20 per cent plan to implement a financial well-being policy in 2022.

THE BUSINESS CASE

There are three broad arguments for investing in workplace well-being: the legal case, the moral case and the business case. The legal case is mandatory and provides a baseline standard. Just as organisations recognise their obligation to provide physical health and safety standards, they must also recognise mental health and safety standards (Daniels et al., 2022). There is a strong moral case for well-being and employers should take a holistic approach to employee physical health and safety and mental health. The business case for well-being relates to whether productivity improvements or future cost savings occur as the result of improving well-being which outweigh the initial and ongoing costs.

Stress, depression or anxiety and musculoskeletal disorders accounted for the majority of days lost due to work-related ill health in 2019/20 in the UK with 17.9 million and 8.9 million days lost, respectively (HSE, 2020). In 2020/21 stress, depression or anxiety accounted for 50 per cent of all work-related ill health (ibid.). Indeed, the HSE states that the total costs of workplace self-reported injuries and ill health in 2018/19 was £16.2 billion. According to Westfield Health, mental health-related workplace absenteeism cost the UK £14 billion in 2020 (Westfield Health, 2020). Deloitte (2020) found that poor mental health costs UK employers up to £45 billion each year. This is a rise of 16 per cent since 2016, an extra £6 billion a year. The research also explored ways in which employers could further support their staff's mental health. On average, for every £1 spent on supporting their people's mental health, employers get £5 back on their investment in reduced presenteeism, absenteeism and staff turnover (ibid.). A case example demonstrating the return on well-being investment at Anglia Water is provided below.

CASE STUDY: ANGLIAN WATER

Simpson (2017) reporting in the *Financial Times* found that Anglian Water were spending £2 million per year on medical cover which was predicted to rise by 10 per cent every year in 2005. Sickness levels averaged ten days per employee per year. The company changed its focus from a health and safety approach to a holistic well-being philosophy where it focused on the happiness and health of its workforce. Using the Workwell model (from the Mental Health at Work charity), well-being was placed at the centre of boardroom discussions which supported the employer brand and customer engagement. Staff absence was reduced and productivity rose. The company gained £8 back from every £1 spent. The focus on well-being also helped to improve safety standards.

WELL-BEING STRATEGY

Many companies are now developing a strategy for their employee's health, safety and wellness. Indeed, Hesketh and Cooper (2019, p.5) report that 'an effective well-being strategy, implemented well and evaluated, can prove highly valuable. It also leads to a strong bond forming with the workforce, one in which they feel understood, valued and part of the organisation'. According to the Future Workplace strategic priorities survey in 2021 (where 200 HR leaders were asked about changes they were making to their people strategies), employee well-being was on the top list of five priorities for the future together with diversity, equality and inclusion, employee experience, agility and digital HR (Meister, 2021).

A well-being strategy will be unique to each organisation. A strategy provides a holistic approach to well-being which will enable it to become embedded as part of company culture. Effective workplace well-being is far more than a series of ad-hoc activities (for example, exercise classes and awareness raising), and a strategy will help to drive forward initiatives in order to increase employee morale and engagement, provide a healthier and inclusive culture and reduce sickness absence (CIPD, 2022a). A strategy might be built around the CIPD 7 key pillars, as discussed above. It will align to other HR strategies such as equality, diversity and inclusion, reward, flexible working, corporate social responsibility and training and development strategies. It will bring together employee assistance programmes, training and the work environment as an open and inclusive space. It will also support social and group activities, non-financial recognition, job design, flexible working, career development, performance management, corporate social responsibility and more.

PROMOTING WELL-BEING THROUGH CULTURE AND BEHAVIOURS

People professionals have recognised that workforce well-being is an important aspect of increasing engagement and reducing turnover for some time. Indeed, well-being forms part of the employee experience specialist knowledge in the CIPD HR profession map (CIPD, 2021). The Society of Human Resource Management survey on employee health and wellness found that employees are about 40 per cent more engaged at work if employers take the time to care about their well-being and health (Gurchiek, 2020).

Well-being in organisations works most effectively when embedded in the company culture, where staff are treated well and recognised for their efforts. When staff experience less stress, they will be more engaged and feel psychologically safe to be their true selves. As a result, they will want to stay with the organisation. However, a study of 1,000 HR leaders by Virgin Pulse indicates that workplace culture is one of the greatest barriers to increased employee well-being and engagement (Kohl, 2018). This is usually due to a mismatch between strategy and culture where company values do not align to well-being. Well-being strategy and values must align. Organisation leaders will need to role-model the values and healthy behaviour in every aspect of company life, including how staff and customers are treated. Further focus on a supportive culture through strong leadership and feedback has the power to impact well-being but also influences organisational outcomes such as job satisfaction. Organisation values are brought to life through behaviours that set out how to work and provide accountability. The Virgin Money case study below provides an example of how company values and behaviours are embedded into organisational life (Virginmoney, 2022).

CASE STUDY: VIRGIN MONEY

Company values and behaviours:

Heartfelt service: we are warm, honest and authentic. We care and aspire to deliver the best for our customers.

Insatiable curiosity: we are open minded, ask questions and keep on learning. We keep searching for the best ideas, approaches and solutions.

Smart disruption: we are innovative, focused and shake up the things that matter, together. We explore new boundaries and balance this with risks.

Red hot relevance: We are inclusive, bold and progressive. We lead the way today and anticipate for tomorrow.

Straight up: We are straightforward, build trust and act with positive intent. We work together to make money simpler and easier.

Delightfully surprising: We look at the little things that make a big difference. We have fun and deliver experiences that make people feel happier.

Note the language and tone used and the focus on authenticity, trust, caring, inclusivity, collaboration and fun.

The following case study describes how Aviva has embedded well-being strategic intent into its company culture. It engages line managers and well-being champions as the key stakeholders in the implementation of the well-being strategy with mechanisms for two-way feedback built into the delivery plan.

CASE STUDY: AVIVA

Aviva believes that well-being needs to be much more than a strategy. To make a lasting difference, it contends that well-being must be embedded into the culture of the workplace and embraced from within the business. Line managers are instrumental to the well-being programme as they may already be familiar with the benefits well-being can bring and will be influential and motivated to deliver the strategy in order to avoid difficulties caused by absenteeism. Employees who are happier, healthier and able to manage stress stay with the company, therefore reducing staff turnover and saving money on recruitment costs as well as retaining experience within the company. Aviva uses well-being champions to organise and promote regular events such as healthy eating, financial education, volunteering and socialising as well as encouraging openness on subjects such as mental health. Through regular check-ins, possibly by webinars, champions provide feedback so that the company gets insights across the business and ensures that champions are recognised and rewarded (Aviva, 2022).

MEASURING WELL-BEING

Well-being initiatives have tended to focus on employee benefits and resources including fitness challenges, physical and emotional health discussion boards and training, employee assistance programmes and informal social events. Lieberman (2019) argues that the creation of health apps and the adoption of worksite wellness programmes by corporations large and small have been implemented to support productivity, but they may not produce the results that organisations and wellness companies are seeking. Song and Baicker (2019) found in their research of a large US company that after 18 months, employees on the workplace wellness programme self-reported greater rates of some positive health behaviours when compared with those employees not on the programme but there were no significant differences in clinical measures of health and employment outcomes at the end of the period. One of the reasons for this might be that these well-being initiatives tend to attract those that are already committed to healthy behaviours. Self-reported health is widely recognised as an indicator of personal well-being and this is prone to bias impacting the reliability of the data. When implementing a well-being strategy, it is important to consider how effectiveness will be measured including how behaviours have changed, as a result of an intervention or conversation for example. Staff surveys, pulse surveys, customer satisfaction rates, sickness absence, staff performance evaluations, occupational health referrals and data dashboards in relation to health and well-being frameworks will provide data from which to evaluate well-being strategy.

WELL-BEING AT THE CORE OF PERFORMANCE

High-performance working

Implementing a well-being strategy aligned to the pillars and frameworks discussed above provides the foundations for staff to flourish and for organisations to increase productivity thus achieving a competitive advantage. A strategy built on the good practices outlined provides the basis for a high-performance culture. Wilton (2016, p.438) defines high-performance work systems as a 'form of best practice HRM which stresses the importance of specific bundles of HR practices – such as continual skills development, employee participation in decision-making and high pay'. It relates to how people are led and managed within their organisations, the design of their job roles, the opportunity to use skills and knowledge and the degree to which they are able to participate within the organisation. When organisations implement high-commitment and trust-building work practices, employees in return will experience higher levels of job autonomy and involvement. As discussed above, these are essential ingredients for well-being. Organisations that implement high-performance working have robust selection processes and provide learning and development to support continuous learning compared to those organisations that don't have such practices. In addition, organisations adopting high-performance working are likely to implement performance appraisals, team working and opportunities for collaboration.

PERFORMANCE MANAGEMENT

Performance management has long since been an area of much discussion in both academic and practitioner circles, being praised for its efficiency or more usually criticised for its demotivational, unfair and tick-boxing process. It is a way for organisations to align the strategic objectives of the organisation with employee goals. Brown (2019) notes that performance management, in all its guises, occurs across all organisations whether formally through an official organisational process or informally through daily dialogue. Performance management refers to the cycle of continuous process of planning, measuring and developing performance of all employees in alignment with the strategic goals of the organisation.

The main principles of performance management are provided by Armstrong and Taylor (2014, p.335) citing the work of Armstrong and Baron (1998, 2004). Performance management is:

- About how we manage people, it's not a system
- What managers do: a natural process of management
- A management tool that helps managers to manage
- Driven by corporate purpose and values
- A way to obtain solutions that work
- Only interested in things you can do something about (to make improvements)
- Focused on changing behaviour rather than paperwork
- Based on accepted principles but operates flexibly
- Focused on development, not pay
- What the organisation needs to be in its performance culture

FEEDBACK MECHANISMS

Many companies are abandoning the traditional appraisal process in favour of ongoing dialogue and more informal systems. Traditionally, line managers met with each member of staff formally once a year to look back at whether objectives had been achieved and forward in relation to developmental objectives. Organisations are now focusing on developmental objectives that will support employees with career growth goals whilst also balancing organisation needs for added value and high performance. Indeed, in order for employees to provide high performance, they will need to develop the right skills and capabilities to do their job. Ongoing developmental opportunities should be provided in relation to SMART objectives to allow employees to focus on their skills and knowledge development whilst also being clear about what is expected of them in their role. The shift in performance management practices sees a move towards systems that are more comprehensive, holistic and ultimately more developmental in nature.

Rock and Jones (2015) found that approximately thirty large companies, such as Adobe, Deloitte and General Electric have changed their performance management systems, moving away from rating structures, annual performance goals and forced rankings (which traditionally set employee against employee for a higher rating), towards the use of shorter-term goals. This new structure encourages ongoing discussions between employees and their managers and underlies the changing nature of work which is increasingly team based. This is an important element of the employer brand, and the current trend is designed to attract, develop and retain employees through more frequent feedback which is likely to facilitate engagement and development. The structure of the performance management system should align to organisation culture.

As we have discussed in previous chapters, trust in the workplace is integral to staff engagement. If trust is at the core of organisation culture, well-being and performance will follow allowing staff to support organisational growth. The following case study provides an example of how forward-thinking organisations are changing their performance management systems to emphasise trust as the basis of effective working relationships.

CASE STUDY: MONEY AND PENSIONS SERVICE

We know that you want to perform at your best, so we've created a performance development approach. You will also have greater ownership of – and accountability for – the process. This is no longer about one or two appraisals a year. This is about an ongoing dialogue and your growth. With this approach we want to make things easier for everyone involved and more relevant to what we do and how we do it, moving away from completing 'tick-box' practices and towards a more fluid approach that works better for all.

Performance Development calls for less focus on the past and more focus on the present. We need to think less about 'How have I done?' and more about 'How am I doing?' You also need to take a step back from the detail of your job description and think more broadly about how your individual objectives contribute to the objectives of your team and the organisation as a whole. This means you will have more responsibility for:

- Establishing what doing a great job looks like for you;
- Reviewing how your work – and your behaviours – stack up against this;
- Identifying what gets in the way of you doing your best work and what you need to overcome these obstacles; and
- Maintaining an ongoing dialogue with your manager to guide your progress and receive the support that you need

Through regular progress conversations you will have an opportunity to review how you are doing, identify any support you may need and, if necessary, adjust your work priorities.

Source: Published with kind permission of Jenny Liebenberg, People, Culture and Skills Executive Director, Money and Pensions Service.

Leaders are fundamental to workforce well-being and instrumental in providing opportunities for staff to engage with the organisation. This might be achieved by providing mechanisms for listening to employees' ideas and incorporating those ideas into decision-making. Inclusive leadership will encourage commitment, satisfaction, conflict resolution, engagement, performance, innovation and resilience.

SUMMARY POINTS

- Well-being at work extends to all aspects of working life including the physical environment, physical health and safety, mental health, fair pay and benefits, opportunities for personal growth, opportunities for collective and social consultation and involvement, effective management practices, corporate social responsibility, inclusion and diversity.
- There is a strong moral and business case for well-being, and evidence suggests that employers that invest in well-being achieve a valuable return on investment.
- A well-being strategy should take a holistic approach and align to all other HR strategies.
- Well-being strategy will only be effective if embedded within the culture of the organisation. Organisation leaders should role-model the values and healthy behaviours in every aspect of organisation life.
- Clear performance measures will allow the effectiveness of the well-being strategy to be evaluated.
- High-performance working is closely aligned to well-being. The implementation of high-performance work systems supports well-being.
- Performance management occurs across organisations, formally and informally, and provides the framework for aligning strategic goals to employee objectives and measuring progress.
- Ongoing discussions are increasingly favoured in place of annual appraisal reviews with a focus on skills and knowledge and personal development.

SELF-TEST QUESTIONS/REVIEW QUESTIONS

- To be effective, a well-being strategy needs to be embedded into the organisation culture. Assess the ways in which this might be achieved, from an organisation, team and individual perspective.
- You are tasked by your senior management team to explore ways in which well-being strategy can be measured. Outline your recommendations in relation to your own organisation context or one with which you are familiar.

A CASE EXAMPLE: VIRGIN MONEY

Review the Virgin Money case study in this chapter. Reflect on the company values and behaviours in place. To what extent does the organisation embed the good practice pillars of well-being into their culture?

REFLECTION

Reflect on your experience of appraisal and one–to-one meetings with your line manager (or you may prefer to interview a family member or friend about their experience). What are the benefits and drawbacks of moving from an annual appraisal review to an ongoing dialogue with line management? Which system would you prefer and why?

References

Adams, T., Bezner J. and Steinhardt, M. (1997). The conceptualization and measurement of perceived wellness: Integrating balance across and within dimensions. *American Journal of Health*. Jan-Feb; 11 (3), pp208-18

Armstrong, M. and Baron, A. (1998). *Performance Management Handbook*. London: IPM.

Armstrong, M. and Baron, A. (2004). *Managing performance: Performance management in action*. London: CIPD.

Armstrong, M. and Taylor, S. (2014). *Armstrong's Handbook of Human Resource Management*. 13th edn. London: Kogan Page.

Aviva (2022). Available at: https://www.aviva.co.uk/business/business-perspectives/ featured-articles-hub/wellbeing-culture/. (Accessed 14 October, 2022).

Brown, D. (2019). *2019: A Totally Rewarding Year?* Institute for Employment Studies (IES). [online] 2019: a totally rewarding year? | Institute for Employment Studies (IES). Available at: https://www.employment-studies.co.uk/resource/2019-totally -rewarding-year.

CIPD (2021). HR profession map. Available at: https://peopleprofession.cipd.org/ profession-map#gref. (Accessed 14 August, 2022).

CIPD (2022a). Wellbeing at work. CIPD. 12 April. Available at: https://www.cipd.co .uk/knowledge/culture/well-being/factsheet#19075. (Accessed 3 July, 2022).

CIPD (2022b). Employee financial wellbeing. CIPD. 13 April. Available at: https:// www.cipd.co.uk/knowledge/culture/well-being/employee-financial-well-being #gref (Accessed 4 July, 2022).

CIPD (2022c). Reward management survey. CIPD. 22 April. Available at: https://www .cipd.co.uk/Images/reward-management-survey-2022_tcm18-108776.pdf (Accessed 4 July, 2022).

Cooper, C. and Hesketh, I. (2019). *Wellbeing at Work: How to Design, Implement and Evaluate an Effective Strategy*. London: Kogan Page.

Daniels, K, Connolly, S., Woodard, R, van Stolk, C, Patey, J, Fong, K, France, R, Vigurs, C. and Herd, M (2022). NHS staff wellbeing: Why investing in organisational and management practices makes business sense. *Economic and Social Research Council*. June.

Deloitte (2020). Poor mental health costs UK employers up to £45 billion a year. Available at: https://www2.deloitte.com/uk/en/pages/press-releases/articles/poor -mental-health-costs-uk-employers-up-to-pound-45-billion-a-year.html. (Accessed 19 August, 2022).

Gurchiek, K. (2020). SHRM research: Covid 19 takes a toll on employees mental wellbeing. SHRM, 11 May. Available at: https://www.shrm.org/hr-today/news/hr-news/pages/shrm-research-covid-19-takes-a-toll-on-employees-mental-well-being.aspx. (Accessed 13 August, 2022).

Hesketh, I. and Cooper, C. (2019). *Wellbeing at Work: How to Design, Implement and Evaluate an Effective Strategy*. London: Kogan Page.

HSE (2020). Health and safety at work: Summary statistics for Great Britain 2020. Available at: https://www.hse.gov.uk/statistics/overall/hssh1920.pdf. (Accessed 13 August).

Kohl, A. (2018). The biggest roadblock to improving employee wellbeing. Forbes, 18 September.

Lieberman, C. (2019). What wellness programs don't do for workers. *Harvard Business Review*, 14 August. Available at: https://hbr.org/2019/08/what-wellness-programs-dont-do-for-workers. (Accessed 4 September, 2022).

Meister, J. (2021). Five strategic HR priorities for 2021. Future Workplace Academy. Available at: https://futureworkplace.com/author/jeanne-meister/. (Accessed 4 August, 2022).

Rock, D. and Jones, B. (2015). Why more and more companies are ditching performance ratings. *Harvard Business Review*, 8 September.

Sfeatcu, R., Cernuşcă-Miţariu, M., Ionescu, C., Roman, M., Cernuşcă-Miţariu, S., Coldea, L., Bota, G., Burcea, C. C. (2014). The concept of wellbeing in relation to health and quality of life. *10*, pp.123–128.

Simpson, P. (2017). Reaping the benefits of a focus on wellbeing. *Financial Times*. 13 September. Available at: https://www.ft.com/content/1f06288a-898d-11e7-afd2-74b8ecd34d3b. (Accessed 19 July, 2022).

Song, Z. and Baicker, K. (2019 Apr 16). Effect of a workplace wellness program on employee health and economic outcomes: A randomized clinical trial. *JAMA*, 321(15), pp.1491–1501. doi: 10.1001/jama.2019.3307. Erratum in: JAMA. 2019 Apr 17; PMID: 30990549; PMCID: PMC6484807.

Virginmoney (2022). Available at: https://www.virginmoneyukplc.com/our-people/values-culture-and-behaviour/. (Accessed 13 July, 2022).

Walton, R. E. (1973). Quality of work life: What is it? *Sloan Management Review*, *15*(1), pp.11–21.

Westfield Health (2020). Coping with Covid: The hidden cost to businesses (and their people). Westfield Health. Available at: https://www.westfieldhealth.com/docs/marketing/covid-19/coping-with-covid/coping-with-covid-report.pdf. (Accessed 3 July, 2022).

WHO (2017). Determinants of health. 3 February. Available at: https://www.who.int/news-room/questions-and-answers/item/determinants-of-health. (Accessed 3 October, 2022).

Wilton, N. (2016) An introduction to human resource management. 3rd edn. London: Sage.

WTS (2017). 2017 UK benefit trends survey. 7 December. Available at: employers surveyed by Willis Towers Watson. (Accessed 13 August, 2022).

Reconceptualising the employee experience

Chapter 12

INTRODUCTION

With unprecedented societal and business changes in the way people work, how employees experience work has become increasingly important. This chapter explores how people teams are taking design thinking and employee journey maps to understand the complete experience of the multi-generation workforce. Moving beyond the narrow focus on employee engagement and culture, this chapter considers the use of pulse feedback tools and feedback apps, integrated employee self-service tools and employee net promoter scores to support the people team in understanding and improving the overall employee experience. The chapter explores the challenges associated with delivering excellence in the employee experience with organisation case study examples of where this has been achieved using cohesive design models that integrate data, processes, technology and HR.

DEFINING EMPLOYEE EXPERIENCE

Organisations have for some time invested in programmes to gather feedback from staff about their experience in the organisation, concentrating on engagement levels as the key metric from which to assess current levels of job satisfaction and productivity. Indeed, Pangallo et al. (2022) argue that engagement is one critical outcome (alongside others such as inclusion and well-being) that is the product of the employee experience. Engagement and experience are terms that tend to be used interchangeably. Whilst organisations were initially focused on employee engagement, this

DOI: 10.4324/9781003342984-13

has now evolved into employee experience. Indeed, many organisations now incorporate employee experience at the core of their employee engagement strategy.

Employee experience is about the daily interactions that an individual has in the workplace, whether that be remote or in-person throughout each stage of the employee lifecycle from the first contact that a prospective candidate has during the attraction stage of the recruitment cycle to the alumni phase. The employee experience relates to alignment with culture, facilities, communication, IT, risk and compliance and every aspect of the organisation. It is about the alignment of our values to the organisation and it will be different for each and every one of us depending on our own personal circumstances. It is about how employees find meaning in their work as well as how they perceive, interact and respond to internal practices.

Employee experience is included as specialist knowledge in the CIPD HR profession map (CIPD, 2021). The CIPD states that employee experience is about understanding the role that line management and trust play in the employment relationship, and how to design and develop approaches to employee engagement that enable people to have a voice. It also looks at other factors which impact the worker experience, such as well-being, employer brand and the way communication channels are used. Ultimately, employee experience is about creating a great work environment for people and helping them to be their best. It emphasises all interactions between an organisation and an employee (Morgan, 2017) at every stage of the lifecycle and each will influence employee productivity. Employee experience is therefore more akin to the input which impacts our engagement.

In 2009, David MacLeod and Nita Clarke produced a report for the Department of Business, Innovation and Skills on employee engagement (MacLeod and Clarke, 2009). The report found more than 50 definitions of engagement but eventually settled on

> a workplace approach designed to ensure that employees are committed to their organisations' goals and values, motivated to contribute to organisational success and at the same time to enhance their own sense of wellbeing. Engaged organisations have strong and authentic values, with clear evidence of trust and fairness based on mutual respect, where two-way promises and commitments between employers and staff are understood and are fulfilled.
>
> *(ibid., p.9)*

The four drivers of engagement were summarised as employee voice, leadership, engaging managers and integrity. Alfes et al. (2010, p.5) building on this research in a CIPD-commissioned report identified that engagement has three key dimensions: intellectual engagement (thinking about the job and how it might be undertaken more effectively), affective engagement (positive feelings associated with doing a good job) and social engagement (opportunities to discuss work-related issues). The report went on to cite six drivers of engagement including meaningfulness at work, employee voice, senior management and vision, line management, person-job fit and supportive work environment.

THE BUSINESS CASE FOR EMPLOYEE EXPERIENCE

The MacLeod and Clarke report found that highly engaged organisations averaged 18 per cent higher productivity and 12 per cent higher profitability than those with low engagement with engaged staff 87 per cent less likely to leave the organisation than the disengaged (Macleod and Clarke, 2009). Darbyshire (2021) argues that organisations in the top quartile for employee experience are typically 25 per cent more profitable than competitors in the bottom quartile. Indeed, in 2021 McKinsey and Company research found that employees working at companies committed to the employee experience are inclined to surpass work expectations, having a 40 per cent higher level of discretionary effort (Emmett et al., 2021). With 42 per cent of workers citing that they would like to work from home at least two days a week and 70 per cent of employees expecting their employer to be supportive of working from home, it is no wonder that 65 per cent of organisations are investing resources into transforming the employee experience (Darbyshire, 2021).

In this chapter, we focus on exploring employee experience as the input measure to an engaged workforce, noting that a great employee experience creates higher employee engagement. In turn, organisations with positive employee experiences grow significantly faster with higher profit margins (Morgan, 2017).

DESIGNING THE EMPLOYEE EXPERIENCE

Design thinking

Design thinking is a human-centric approach that is solutions focused. It is an innovative methodology that relies on a combination of skills, processes and mindsets. Wrigley and Straker (2015) suggest that design thinking refers to an ability to combine empathy, creativity and rationality to analyse and fit solutions to particular problems. Design thinking is helpful for dealing with ill-defined problems which are referred to as wicked as they are wickedly difficult to solve (Rittel and Webber, 1973.) The design thinking approach in relation to the employee experience focuses organisations on employees in order to frame problems and design solutions around them. This involves asking questions, brainstorming, challenging taken-for-granted assumptions and exploring the implications. For example, instead of focusing on the reasons for a drop in productivity, design thinking might encourage a focus on employee engagement. Focusing on the experience of the employee ensures that design thinking is an iterative process which focuses on specific needs rather than hypothesised ones. It is a helpful process for reframing problems from the employee perspective. People professionals using design thinking are able to take a 'hands-on' approach to challenge assumptions and redefine problems in order to find alternative solutions.

Schmiedgen et al. (2015) found that design thinking is practised in organisations of all sizes across all industry sectors and offers organisations a way of developing original products and services that provide competitive advantage. Martin (2009) agrees and contends that design thinking helps business become more innovative through knowledge development which in turn provides competitive advantage.

As a process, design thinking is a series of steps taken to solve a problem. There is no clear agreement on the number of steps, however. Brown and Wyatt (2010) describe it as optimisation across three elements: user needs, technology and business advantage. Stickdorn and Schneider (2012) argue that design thinking consists of five stages including empathy, identification, comprehension, model creation and testing. My personal preference is the five-stage design thinking model proposed by the Hasso Plattner Institute of Design at Stanford (d.school, 2022). The five stages include empathy, define, ideate, prototype and test. Empathy is about understanding the problem you are trying to solve, perhaps through observation and an immersion into the user environment. In the definition stage, it will be necessary to organise the information that has been collected and to define the problem from the perspective of the employee. In the third stage, ideate, the focus is on the design thinking approach using the understanding gained from earlier observations and analysis. You might start by considering what are the worst possible ideas and then brainstorm for ideas, use opposite thinking (looking at the opposites of each experience), analogy thinking (a comparison to show

how two things are similar), storyboarding (telling the story of the employee journey), cards and software such as Miro and Scamper (online collaboration tools to support innovation). The focus is on generating as many ideas as possible. Use as many ideation techniques as possible. When sufficient ideas have surfaced, the best ones can be summarised. Stage four is the prototype and the team will now build inexpensive versions and prototypes that can be shared and discussed to get a sense of the benefits and the limitations. The final stage is where new ideas are tested. As this is an iterative process, the feedback from this final stage is often used for revisiting, redesigning and retesting other ideas following refinement of earlier ideas.

EMPLOYEE SEGMENTATION

In order to get the most value from a design thinking approach in relation to the employee experience, it is helpful to firstly segment staff into different clusters to gain deeper insights through rigorous research about their experience. Segmentations might be by way of employee demographics such as an analysis of the multi-generation workforce which focuses on age or crude measures such as grade, gender or location. The problem with such analysis is that it tends to make broad assumptions about individual preferences. Increasingly, organisations today are looking at attitudinal data to segment employees. Using analytics, it is now possible to segment across demographics, role and length of time in role, attitudes towards life (future orientation versus present) and attitudes towards work (work-life balance, attitudes towards retirement, motivation for staying in job) and what an employee needs from the employer (career development, salary, benefits, work culture). Demographics can still prove useful when analysing the data but are less helpful if used as a guiding principle.

Using the employee lifecycle (as discussed in Chapter 1) is helpful to journey map the experience of different employee groups through the various transitions. Working through each stage of the employee journey stages, from attraction to alumni to assess the employee experience from their perspective. Organisations will need to collect data at each stage of the interaction to facilitate this process. Following this preparatory work, the phases of ideating, prototyping, testing and implementing experiences can begin to support the intended outcomes. Employee engagement surveys continue to be a helpful measure to get an in-depth view of the relationship across each stage of the employee journey (see below). Companies will need to understand and experiment with work design across different groups to understand how roles might become more flexible.

MULTI-GENERATION WORKFORCE

Changing demographics has resulted in a workforce where five generations coexist. The silent generation (or traditionalists) (born 1925–1944) make up about 2 per cent of the workforce, baby boomers (born 1945–1964), generation X (born 1965–1979), generation Y (or millennials) (born 1980–1994) and generation Z (born 1995–2015). There has been much research on the generational differences which exist and how differing values impact engagement. Popular descriptions have been depicted of the different traits across the generations such as traditionalists as dependable, straightforward, tactful and loyal, baby boomers as optimistic, competitive, workaholics, team oriented, generation X as flexible, informal, sceptical and independent, millennials as competitive, open minded, achievement oriented and generation Z as global, entrepreneurial, progressive and less focused. The CIPD (2020) suggests that it is time to stop talking about generational differences, however, as gross generalisations are not helpful and are rarely evidenced based. Instead, we should focus on life stages as a more effective determinant of managing people effectively. This is an important consideration in the way organisations segment their workforce to understand the employee experience.

USING TECHNOLOGY TO SUPPORT THE EMPLOYEE EXPERIENCE

Anderson and Patton (2022) argue that in a hybrid world, it is technology that is defining the employee experience. How employees communicate, collaborate and connect are fundamental qualities of the employee experience. Employees are 230 per cent more engaged and 85 per cent more likely to stay beyond three years in their jobs if they feel they have the technology that supports them at work, according to Qualtrics (2022) in their top workplace trends survey. Technology is the foundation in managing the new way of work as well as improving the employee experience.

There is an increasing diversity of technology to support the employee experience (see chapter 9) from video conferencing, scheduling software, asynchronous communication, collaboration tools, workplace apps (for example, wellness), solutions that support recruitment and onboarding etc.

The critical point, however, is whether staff receive sufficient training to enable them to utilise technology effectively. Frustrations with technology can negatively impact the employee experience and organisations should support staff in their use of technology.

For example, many organisations now use a human resource self-service system to provide managers and employees with the capacity to upload changes to their personal details such as change of address or additional qualifications and to be able to manage holiday entitlement, absenteeism, performance management, learning and development. These self-service tools enable employees to view and update personal information, apply for training, leave or holidays and choose or renew flexible benefits packages. Managers tend to have more access and authorisation privileges to systems than employees, and can access employee information, authorise HR transactions and generate relevant reports online. Self-service platforms are popular due to anticipated cost savings and other efficiency-related benefits. The degree to which staff will engage with technology is dependent on the way it is implemented, the perceived usefulness of the system and managerial pressures that encourage staff to use the system. Although a self-service system can be empowering and has the opportunity to enhance the employee experience, appropriate training is required for both managers and staff to ensure that users are able to maximise the potential of the system. Its usefulness, functionality and alignment to other systems should also be regularly reviewed.

CASE STUDY: MCDONALD'S

When global restaurant chain McDonald's designed their new engagement platform they focused on a platform that was accessible, allowing restaurant employees to engage on their mobile phone, whether to complete a training course during down time in a shift, or to build social connections with co-workers. The platform needed to be intuitive, allowing crew and managers to easily adjust to the new tool and to quickly communicate using the tool in order to drive team connection. Additionally, McDonald's needed to be able to incorporate the tool into its highly integrated secure current ecosystem. The implementation of modern technology has been a catalyst in evolving the way restaurant teams communicate, streamlining processes and creating team connections. Communication and training were key to the effective implementation of the platform.

MEASURING THE EMPLOYEE EXPERIENCE

Annual engagement surveys

The annual engagement survey is a common method of measuring employee engagement. It is a way of measuring engagement among employees at one point in time and should be designed with the strategic goal in mind with survey questions aligned to the organisation requirements. Employees are more likely to engage with a survey when they are confident that their responses are anonymous (Wilkie, 2018) and that is why many organisations now appoint independent companies to run their surveys. An essential part of the annual engagement survey is feeding back the results and actions that the organisation will take in response to the feedback. Feedback and action planning work most effectively when the people team work closely with the senior management team and line managers to organise and communicate plans. The action planning process of the engagement survey is a common reason why engagement surveys fail and this is largely due to the fact that managers do not spend enough time communicating with their teams on the organisational action plan in relation to the survey (Cava & Fernandez, 2017) resulting in a negative impact as employees feel their voice is being neglected.

PULSE SURVEYS

Many organisations now use pulse surveys to gain feedback from staff in addition to an annual staff survey. This is a short survey that checks on how an employee is feeling about employee satisfaction, their job role, communication, relationships, the work environment, belonging, equality, growth, reward and recognition for example. It is feedback in real time. Employees are asked to respond to between 5 and 15 questions on a quarterly/bimonthly cycle that leaves time for analysis of the data and a response. Getting feedback from staff is a critical way of measuring the employee experience (Welbourne, 2016). Pulse surveys are more limited in scope however than an annual engagement survey so employers need to understand their goals in collecting feedback and also to ensure the optimal timing of implementation.

Employee feedback enables an organisation to make improvements where elements of the employee experience are not working. Feedback can help to shape a strong company culture (that attracts more staff based on shared company values) and can decrease employee turnover (Huebner, 2021).

Organisations might ask employees for feedback on virtual meetings, hybrid working experiences and technology to support the user experience. It is essential that employers respond to employee feedback and confirm what actions the organisation is taking to improve the employee experience. There are many organisations now offering simple-to-use apps and survey platforms to support the administration and management of the pulse survey (for example, People Insights, Lattice, Qualtrics). Platforms are customisable so that organisations can include their own branding and are usually simple to use and mobile so that employees can offer feedback across a range of platforms. Pulse surveys are only useful however when implemented as part of a well-developed metrics strategy linked to the business plan (Welbourne, 2016). It is essential that training is provided for all involved and that effective communication complements the roll out plan (ibid.).

EMPLOYEE NET PROMOTER SCORE

Employee engagement has generally replaced the satisfaction metric in many organisations as it is a more rigorous test of how employees think, feel and behave towards an organisation. Satisfaction is rather a passive measure. Engagement category scores are increasingly replacing the satisfaction score using the employee net promoter score (eNPS). The net promoter score is calculated on a scale of one to ten and falls into three groups – promoters, passives and detractors – to determine the official eNPS score. If an employee scores the organisation nine or ten they are a promoter, seven or eight they are passive, six or below signifies a detractor. The eNPS score is calculated by taking the percentage of promoters and subtracting the percentage of detractors.

Net promoter score (NPS) is a loyalty metric developed by (and a registered trademark of) Fred Reichheld, Bain & Company, and Satmetrix. It was introduced by Reichheld in his 2003 *Harvard Business Review* article, 'One number you need to grow' (Reichheld, 2003). NPS can be as low as −100 (everybody is a detractor) or as high as +100 (everybody is a promoter). An NPS that is positive (i.e., higher than zero) is felt to be good, and an NPS of +50 is excellent.

As with annual engagement surveys and pulse surveys, the metric in itself is meaningless, it is the improvements that are implemented as a result of the metric that drives improvement. Fannah et al. (2022) argue that the eNPS is an important tool in employee engagement and employee experience as it measures a programme or a service within the organisational context and can help to quantify problems (Fannah et al., 2022). Shevlin (2019) argues that the problem with the employee net promoter score is that it measures intention not behaviour with Safdar and Pacheco (2019) reporting in the *Wall Street Journal* that the results are too easy to manipulate.

GLASSDOOR

Many organisations consider employee reviews as important as customer feedback. High performing organisations have adopted an 'employee-first' approach and translated customer experience principles to talent management and development areas in HR (Itam and Ghosh 2020). Employees and ex-employees are now able to rank their experience with an employer on Glassdoor, a platform that lists insights about jobs and companies. Glassdoor reports that it has 59 million visitors a month and holds 114 million reviews on salaries across 2.2 million companies (glassdoor.com). Glassdoor offers insights into the employee experience. All data is shared by employees. Job seekers on Glassdoor are informed about the jobs and companies they apply to and consider joining. A poor rating on Glassdoor might have implications for the attraction of new talent to the organisation. The following case example provides an insight into how Airbnb integrated the employee experience into 'business as usual'.

CASE STUDY: AIRBNB

Airbnb, based in San Francisco, California, operates an online marketplace which focuses on short-term homestays and experiences. The company acts as a broker and charges a commission from each booking. The company was founded in 2008.

From its early years, the company's executives made employee experience a cornerstone of its operating philosophy. It created an employee experience department that addressed every aspect of the employee life cycle, from the interviewing process to onboarding protocols, host and guest engagement, annual strategic planning additionally including office design and decoration. On Glassdoor (discussed above), 85 per cent of the 2,200 reviews about the company would refer the company to a friend and 87 per cent approve of the CEO (October, 2022). Airbnb has gone beyond hybrid working with its 'work anywhere' policy. Employees can work anywhere across the country they live in or for up to 90 days in another.

Airbnb has developed a culture of belonging through three key pillars:

1. Fostering a welcoming culture

Prior to the coronavirus the company designed their head office to inspire community and belonging. The building includes a 'landing zone' where staff can recharge laptops and leave their belongings and then they can team up with colleagues and work from anywhere in the building.

2. Inspiring a mission beyond us

The Airbnb mission is to create a more connected world. Airbnb perceives itself to be a pioneer of the sharing economy. The mission has faced criticism for helping private home owners earn excessive money and avoid taxes. Airbnb appears to remain adaptive to change and has convinced its shareholders of its purpose. The mission and values of the organisation are built into the Airbnb culture. The company focuses on recruiting people with values that align to the company mission. For example, 'being a host is one of our most important values, and it is how we behave both with one another, and everyone else'. The company's mission is also at the heart of its volunteering programme. Through this programme, employees have the opportunity to volunteer four hours per month by spending time in neighbourhoods with hosts and even guests.

3. Building trust and autonomy

Airbnb states that it believes in its people and delegates responsibility to individual employees. For instance, engineers are expected to be self-driven and take initiative: 'At the core, our philosophy is this: engineers own their own impact. Each engineer is individually responsible for creating as much value for our users and for the company as possible'. Employees are encouraged to feedback on what the company does well and what it could improve on. Listening to employees is a central part of the Airbnb culture and is a way of communicating trust. Airbnb builds trust and autonomy through teams, with employees typically working in groups of ten people or less.

When the Covid-19 epidemic drastically reduced vacation travel, the company laid off a quarter of its workforce. The company offered generous severance terms and provisions and CEO Brian Chesky communicated the changes to employees in a transparent and compassionate way.

EMPLOYEE ENGAGEMENT KEY PERFORMANCE INDICATORS

There are many ways in which organisations might measure employee engagement. Apart from net promoter scores, pulse surveys, engagement surveys and Glassdoor as discussed above, organisations might also focus on absenteeism where high levels and repeat cases of absenteeism can indicate if something is wrong. Attrition rates compare the numbers of desired turnover with actual levels and can be analysed across departments to determine the location of the area that requires further focus. Wellness metrics need to take a long-term approach to evidence changing behaviour, for example, engaging in exercise or taking advantages of other organisation wellness benefits. Engaging in benchmarking activity can also be helpful in order to assess how the organisation is comparing to competitors in the sector.

SUMMARY POINTS

- Employee experience is about the daily interaction that an individual has in the workplace whether they are working remotely, in the office or a mixture of both.
- Highly engaged organisations are more proactive and are more profitable than their competitors.
- Design thinking is a methodology which can support organisations to reframe problems and design solutions. It is an approach that can be used to support organisations transition to hybrid working effectively.
- Employee segmentation of the workforce is necessary in order to design an experience that is tailored to the employee lifecycle, attitudes and preferences.
- The generation segmentation approach is prone to generalisation and is not effective as a strategy for effectively tailoring the employee experience.
- Technology is an enabler of the employee experience but must be implemented with care with appropriate training and support available.
- Measuring the employee experience is essential for analysing progress. There are many tools available to support analysis including

engagement surveys, pulse surveys, Glassdoor, net promoter scores and qualitative techniques such as focus groups and interviews.

SELF-TEST QUESTIONS/REVIEW QUESTIONS

- McDonald's was looking for a platform to share information more effectively and to foster community by connecting, informing and empowering teams. How can design thinking help?
- Summarise the pros and cons for each of the employee experience evaluation methods discussed above. Analyse the factors that might be considered when selecting the most appropriate methods in different organisation contexts.

A CASE EXAMPLE: AIRBNB

Review the Airbnb organisation case study example discussed above. Using the employee lifecycle framework, analyse how Airbnb incorporates an employee-first philosophy in the organisation?

REFLECTION

Reflect on your own employee experience (or interview a member of your family or a friend about their experience) of using technology in organisations. Consider the employee lifecycle and how you/they engage with the organisation through technology at each stage of the employee journey. How did technology enhance or detract from your employee experience? Analyse the strengths and limitations of technology used in organisations. What could be improved and how?

References

Alfes, K., Bailey, C., Soane, E., Rees, C. and Gatenby, M. (2010). *Creating an Engaged Workforce (CIPD Research Report)*.

Anderson, B. and Patton, S. (2022). In a hybrid world, your tech defines employee experience. *Harvard Business Review*. 18 February. Available at: https://hbr.org/2022/02/in-a-hybrid-world-your-tech-defines-employee-experience (Accessed 13 August, 2022).

Safdar, B. K. and Pacheco, I. (2019). The dubious management fad sweeping corporate America. *Wall Street Journal, 1–10*(2019). Available at: https://www.wsj.com/articles/the-dubious-management-fad-sweeping-corporate-america-11557932084. (Accessed 27 July, 2022).

Brown, T. and Wyatt, J. (2010). Design thinking for social innovation. *Stanford Social Innovation Review*. Winter. Leland Stanford Jr. University, Stanford Graduate School of Business.

Cava, J. and Fernandez, C. (2017). Case study: Starwood hotels: From descriptive to impact: Linking the employee engagement survey to the guest experience. *Human Resource Planning Society, People and Strategy, 40*(4). Available at https://www.shrm.org/executive/resources/people-strategy-journal/Fall2017/Pages/guest-experience.aspx. (Accessed 22 January 2023).

CIPD (2020). Should we stop talking about generational differences? CIPD. 13 March. Available at: https://www.cipd.co.uk/news-views/changing-work-views/future-work/thought-pieces/generational-differences#gref. (Accessed 14 August, 2022).

CIPD (2021). Explore the profession map. Available at: https://peopleprofession.cipd.org/profession-map#gref. (Accessed 3 August, 2022).

Darbyshire, R. (2021). Employee experience: How to design a more engaging and productive Future of Work. Deloitte. 26 July. Available at: https://www2.deloitte.com/uk/en/blog/future-of-work/2021/employee-experience-how-to-design-a-more-engaging-and-productive-future-of-work.html (Accessed 3 July, 2022).

Dschool (2022). Available at: https://dschool.stanford.edu/. (Accessed 13 July, 2022).

Emmett, J., Komm, A., Moritz, S., Schultz, F. (2021). This time it's personal: shaping the 'new possible' through employee experience. Mckinsey and Company. 30 September. Available at: https://www.mckinsey.com/capabilities/people-and-organizational-performance/our-insights/this-time-its-personal-shaping-the-new-possible-through-employee-experience (Accessed 30 September, 2022).

Fannah, J. A., Ismaili, S. A., Jahwari, F A., Mohamed, O. and Awaidy, A. (2022). Improving the process of employee recognition: An exploratory study. *Journal of Hospital Administration, 10*(6). doi: 10.5430/jha.v10n6p19.

Huebner, L.A. and Zacher, H. (2021 Dec 9). Following up on employee surveys: A conceptual framework and systematic review. *Frontiers in Psychology, 12*, p.801073. doi: 10.3389/fpsyg.2021.801073. PMID: 34956026; PMCID: PMC8696015.

Itam, U. and Ghosh, N. (2020). Employee experience management: A new paradigm shift in HR thinking. *International Journal of Human Capital and Information Technology Professionals, 11*. doi: 10.4018/IJHCITP.2020040103.

MacLeod, D. and Clarke, N. (2009). Engaging for success: Enhancing performance through employee engagement. A report to Government. Available at: https://engageforsuccess.org/wp-content/uploads/2020/12/engaging-for-success.pdf. (Accessed 13 August, 2022).

Martin, R. (2009). *The Design of Business: Why Design Thinking is the Next Competitive Advantage*. Boston: Harvard Business School Publishing.

Morgan, J. (2017). *The Employee Experience Advantage*. New Jersey: Wiley.

Pangallo, A., Atwell, T., Roe, K. and Boissy, A. (2022). Understanding modern drivers of the employee experience in healthcare. *Patient Experience Journal, 9*(2), pp.46–61. doi: 10.35680/2372-0247.1710.

Qualtrics (2022). What flexibility means in the new world of work. 9 February. Available at: https://www.qualtrics.com/blog/flexible-working-statistics/. (Accessed 13 July, 2022).

Reichheld, F. F. (2003). The one number you need to grow. *Harvard Business Review*, December. Available at: https://hbr.org/2003/12/the-one-number-you-need-to-grow. (Accessed 3 July, 2022).

Rittel, H. W. J. and Webber, M. M. (1973). Dilemmas in a general theory of planning. *Policy Science. Policy Series*, *4*, pp.155–169.

Schmiedgen, J., Rhinow, H., Koppen, E. and Meinel, C. (2015). *Without a Whole: The Current State of Design Thinking in Organisations*. Stanford: HPI. Technical reports, 97. ISSN 1613-5652.

Shevlin, R. (2019). It's time to retire the net promoter score. *Forbes*, May 21. Available at: https://www.forbes.com/sites/ronshevlin/2019/05/21/its-time-to-retire-the-net -promoter-score/?sh=1533a46a6bbb. (Accessed 3 July, 2022).

Stickdorn, M. and Schneider, J. (2012). *This Is Service Design Thinking: Basics, Tools, Cases*. New Jersey: Wiley.

Welbourne, T. M. (2016). The potential of pulse surveys: Transforming surveys into leadership tools. *Employment Relations*, Spring, *43*(1), pp.33–39.

Wilkie, D. (2018). Employee engagement surveys: Why do workers distrust them? 5 January. SHRM. Available at: Employees are more likely to engage with a survey when they are confident that their responses are anonymous. (Accessed 3 July, 2022).

Wrigley, C. and Straker, K. (2015). Design thinking pedagogy: The educational design ladder. *Innovations in Education and Teaching International*, *54*(4), pp.374–385. doi: 10.1080/14703297.2015.1108214

Business continuity planning and people management

Chapter 13

INTRODUCTION

This chapter explores the elements of business continuity planning and the types of threats that may impact on business. It considers the relationship between business continuity and the strategic planning process together with how organisations can prepare themselves for crisis and disruption. Using a range of frameworks and case examples in different sectors, the chapter reviews varying approaches to business continuity planning. Research undertaken during the coronavirus pandemic found that data had been prioritised over people in contingency planning. To be effective, business continuity plans should place people at the very centre of crisis management and the benefits of doing so are explored. The employee lifecycle as a framework for analysing business continuity planning is introduced to ensure that every aspect of people practice is examined at the pre-crisis stage.

DOI: 10.4324/9781003342984-14

WHAT IS BUSINESS CONTINUITY?

Planning for business continuity is necessary for all types of business. Business continuity is a process driven approach to support the organisation in maintaining its operations as far as possible in an unplanned and disruptive event. It requires organisations to consider what might cause disruption to critical activities and what contingencies can be put in place to minimise the disruption. The International Organization for Standardization (ISO) defines business continuity as the

> holistic management process that identifies potential threats to an organization and the impact to business operations that those threats, if realised, might cause, which provides a framework for building organisational resilience with the capability of an effective response that safeguards the interests of its key holders, reputation, brand and value-creating activities.
>
> *(ISO 22301:2019, p. 5)*

Mukherjee et al. (2020) define business continuity planning as essential for maintaining control and capabilities for managing organisations' overall ability to continue to operate during disruptions. Business continuity planning is a part of an organisation's business resilience approach which also includes crisis management. Business continuity is therefore a planned response to disruption. A business continuity plan should also consider disaster recovery. Business continuity planning is essential for responding to crisis situations which might be defined as 'a serious threat to the basic structures or the fundamental values and norms of a social system, which under time pressure and highly uncertain circumstances necessitates making critical decisions' (Rosenthal & Kouzmin, 1997, p. 279).

BUSINESS CONTINUITY AND STRATEGIC PLANNING

Business continuity planning is a key element of strategic management and it impacts on every organisation, regardless of size and at every stage of growth (Holland et al., 2022). Indeed, Mukherjee et al. (2020) argue that business continuity planning establishes the strategic objectives and guiding principles for the organisation in a crisis, and is expected to integrate safe industrial standards for resilience. Business continuity is a key strategic priority and organisations must consider their strategic vulnerabilities so that they can plan and prioritise their resources in order that they can manage effectively in a crisis (Fischbacher-Smith, 2017). Strategic priorities provide an effective structure for a business continuity plan.

THE NEED FOR BUSINESS CONTINUITY PLANNING

The causes of emergency situations vary but may include anything from a loss of power, drinking water, traffic congestion to wind damage, flooding, earthquakes, pandemics, chemical spills, cyberattacks, terrorist activity or social, political or military unrest and may have short- or long-term impacts The main focus in each of these situations is to ensure the safety of people and the maintenance of essential business operations. The continuously changing environment necessitates the formulation of a business continuity plan and a set of procedures to minimise disruption and enhance resilience. The case study below provides an example of the implications when a business continuity plan is not in place or when it is not fit for purpose.

CASE STUDY: NORTHERN LINCOLNSHIRE AND GOOLE NHS FOUNDATION TRUST

On 30 October, 2016, a computer virus infected a network of hospitals in the UK, known as the Northern Lincolnshire and Goole NHS Foundation Trust. The virus attacked its systems and halted operations at three separate hospitals for five days. Patients had to be turned away and sent to other hospitals. More than 2,800 patient procedures and appointments were cancelled due to the attack. Only critical emergency patients, such as those suffering from severe accidents, were admitted. It is unclear as to whether a continuity plan was in place but reports that suggest there was one consider that it was outdated. A clear business continuity plan with comprehensive measures for responding to a critical IT systems failure would have prevented such disruption.

A FRAMEWORK FOR BUSINESS CONTINUITY

There are a number of models that have been developed to understand and manage crisis management with varying numbers of stages. One of the most widely used is the three-stage model, which consists of pre-crisis, crisis and post-crisis. Building on this three-stage model, Burnett (1998) developed a model that focused on identification, confrontation and reconfiguration and within each step highlighted a number of other steps including goal formation, environmental analysis, strategy formulation, strategy evaluation, strategy implementation and strategic control. Fink (1986) refers to a four-stage model of crisis management that consists of prodromal, acute, chronic and resolution. Mitroff (1994) has been working on the development of stages for some years with colleagues Pauchant and Shrivastava (Pauchant and Mitroff 1992). In 2005, Mitroff proposed that the five stages should start with detecting signals that indicate an impending crisis in an organisation setting, for example, a rising amount of customer complaints (Mitroff, 2005). The second step is then to engage in crisis preparation to manage the crisis event. The containment phase involves limiting the damage to the organisation and communication with all stakeholders. The recovery phase focuses on back to business and recovery, reassuring stakeholders. Mitroff (ibid.) argues that organisations should engage in no-fault learning after the event so that experience can be reviewed and business continuity processes redesigned to support any future crisis.

Smits and Ally (2003) argue that planning and preparation should in fact come first in the management of crisis and disruption in order to create behavioural readiness. In reality, business continuity planning is unlikely to be a linear process as changes will need to be made following simulation tests and updates in business objectives. The redesign phase may be enacted with each of the other stages. Nonetheless, Smits and Ally's (ibid.) argument does highlight the importance and case for business continuity planning. Organisations with a business continuity plan in place will gain an advantage in times of disruption as they will be in a position to minimise losses. However, according to the PWC (2021) Global Crisis Survey, only 67% of organisations applied a business continuity plan as part of their response to the Covid-19 pandemic. This is concerning as Cloudman and Hallahan (2006) found that employees working for organisations with crisis plans had greater confidence in their ability to respond to a crisis event and this impacts on staff retention.

THE ABSENCE OF PEOPLE IN BUSINESS CONTINUITY PLANNING

Business continuity plans tend to focus on policies, procedures, data and offices, and there is often too little focus on people. Indeed, I found this in my own research exploring how people professionals delivered well-being through the coronavirus pandemic (Maddox-Daines, 2021). I found that the focus of business continuity planning, if it did exist (and often it didn't), was too generic and concentrated on access to data, namely staff records and payroll information rather than people. Little prior analysis had been undertaken to assess the possible impact of crisis on resourcing, inducting and onboarding, performance management, learning and development and reward. As a result, HR professionals responded to the coronavirus pandemic 'in the moment', and this had implications for a coherent response to employee well-being. Failure to develop crisis policies in advance impacts the effectiveness of the response. As a result, lack of preparation limited the opportunity for HR professionals to respond strategically. The importance of people in business continuity planning is emphasised in the revisions to the ISO business continuity standard (2019) which stress that when developing a business continuity plan it is essential to have contingencies for people, processes and technology (ISO, 2019). The case study below provides an insight into business planning from a risk management rather than a people perspective. It takes a holistic organisation approach through the appointment of business continuity champions.

CASE STUDY: UNIVERSITY OF READING, UK

The university lists disruptions such as loss of staff, denial of access to place of work, loss of a supplier or contractor, disruption to gas, water, electricity supply, loss of telephonic or computer system and disruption to supply chains as areas that require development of business continuity plans. The university requires each school to identify a business continuity champion to prepare a business continuity plan for the school and then to notify the risk management and business continuity officer of the business continuity champion. Each champion is responsible for preparing a business impact analysis and business continuity plan, which are then reviewed by the business continuity officer. The champion is required to train their team in the contingencies within the plan once it is approved by the risk management and business continuity offer. Plans are updated when changes occur and tested every two years. The champion is also required to engage in corporate emergency exercises. A business continuity guide and relevant templates are provided.

PEOPLE PROFESSIONALS AND BUSINESS CONTINUITY PLANNING

The pandemic has highlighted how important it is for people professionals to be active in business continuity management. Indeed, Premeaux and

Breaux (2007) identify that a common deficiency evident in continuity planning is failing to consider an organisation's policies, procedures, systems and infrastructure and the subsequent impact on staff. HR play an important role in ensuring that employees' needs are considered pre, during and after a crisis. The people team are well placed to support leaders with identifying the emotional and interpersonal support required in the planning stages and the potential impact on people at each stage of the employee lifecycle. They will also be able to keep employees updated and informed about business continuity planning and will play a key role in crisis communication systems. This is important as employees seek effective communication and transparency about what they know and what they do not know and more information about resources for emotional and mental health in dealing with stress and anxiety.

Nizamidou and Vouzas (2018) conclude that people professionals play an important role in business continuity at each stage of crisis. In the planning stage they act as a mentor and can focus on preparing employees for a potential crisis and explaining to them what will be expected of them during a crisis. In the event of a crisis, the HR team will support employees to cope with and recover from the disruption, supporting them to return to work. Finally, they suggest that HR will provide leadership and remind employees that they have survived the crisis and that they are now stronger, united and better prepared for similar critical events in the future (ibid.).

In preparing for crisis, Balaouras (2015) found in their research that the top lessons learned by organisations following a crisis situation focused on three key areas. Firstly, there had not been enough training and awareness across the company. Secondly, plans did not adequately address internal communication and collaboration requirements. Thirdly, plans did not take into account communication and collaboration with strategic partners and other third-party dependents. This is an important learning point, and exploring the impact of crisis on all stakeholders is key to effective business continuity.

It is clear that people professionals need to take an active role in each stage of a crisis, and their involvement in business continuity is integral to the successful preparation and implementation of the plan. At the preparation stage, people professionals will be able to highlight the impact of a crisis on employees in stakeholder discussions, to emphasise staff needs and requirements including support and training, the physical and psychological impact of a crisis and health and safety requirements. There are various ways in which a plan might be compiled, and this will differ across organisations, from a list of activities across the organisation to a departmental or functional plan that may feed into a central plan. Every process should include planning, communication and training, and this works most effectively when a business continuity team, consisting of representatives across the organisation, meets regularly to review and test the plan.

BUSINESS CONTINUITY AND THE EMPLOYEE LIFECYCLE

The employee lifecycle framework might be used to support business continuity planning from a people perspective. A detailed HR business continuity plan might feed into the organisational plan depending on the size of the organisation. Business continuity is about adding value to the organisation by limiting the potential damage of a crisis. People professionals are able to support each area of the business to minimise disruption through crisis. The needs of every employee in a hybrid workforce should be considered. The framework below offers some initial ideas for exploring business continuity across the lifecycle beyond the protection and accessibility of data which have traditionally been the main focus in organisations.

There is an indication that companies are starting to recognise the importance of people in their business continuity planning. The case study below provides an example of an organisation putting employees as top priority in their business resilience programme. Note the strategic approach that the organisation takes and how it embeds business resilience into its continuity management.

CASE STUDY: CISCO

Cisco is an IT, networking and cybersecurity company. It achieves resilience through three principal areas of focus: business resilience, incident management and IT. Cisco maintains readiness by proactively assessing operational risks, establishing contingency plans and administering incident response training. Cisco assesses and mitigates potential business disruptions through the Global Business Resiliency (GBR) programme. Under this programme, all corporate business units are required to maintain and exercise alternate operation strategies. The Global Business Resilience programme office validates that each business unit's resilience strategies

Table 13.1 Business Continuity through the Employee Lifecycle

Attraction	Business continuity planning is essential for protecting the employer brand. In times of crisis, it is important that the organisation retains its presence in the marketplace and is true to its values. Developing relationships with potential candidates should not stop in a crisis. The organisation will continue to need talented staff after the crisis. Continuity will prepare the organisation for business recovery.
Recruitment	A crisis situation does not necessarily mean a reduction in staff will be required. Depending on the nature of the crisis and how it impacts the business, it may result in a higher demand for the organisation's service or products. For example, consider the high-growth sectors of education technology, online retailing and pharmacy stores during the coronavirus pandemic. Whether or not a company continues to recruit will depend on the impact of the crisis. Organisations might consider recruitment from the perspective of the jobseeker and the uncertainty that they might be experiencing. Careful attention to the needs of the hybrid workforce will be required.
Onboarding	As onboarding is such an important part of the recruitment cycle, it is essential that careful thought be given to how this will be managed in a crisis. During the coronavirus pandemic, many organisations moved their onboarding online with varying success. Communication is key to helping people settle into their new roles and meet new colleagues. What will the people team do to support line managers in onboarding their new staff? What will need to change and how? What training might be required? How will the onboarding process accommodate the hybrid workforce?
Development	All staff will benefit from disaster preparedness and crisis management training so that they are equipped to implement the business continuity plans. Threat and risk assessment training will support staff with the skills and knowledge necessary to detect risks in the course of their work, for example cybersecurity. Business continuity training is also important so that each member of staff understands their role in terms of planning and crisis management, for example in relation to technology, loss of data, communication and preparedness for business as usual. Training should include simulation exercises so that participants get a real sense of how to manage in a crisis situation, and this should be designed in relation to the needs of the hybrid workforce. Leaders will benefit from specialist training focusing on security and safety and how to communicate effectively. Leading with empathy, compassion and authenticity with strong acknowledgement of the difficult situation will also prove useful preparation.

(Continued)

Table 13.1 Continued

Retention	Protecting the welfare of staff and their individual and social needs whilst tailoring support for individual cases will support retention. Communication is key and needs to be effective throughout the planning and crisis stage as well as after the event. A crisis communication plan should be shared with staff so that they are aware of the planned response at organisation and team level and their individual responsibilities. Providing opportunities for the hybrid workforce to participate in business continuity planning, perhaps through championing the plan within their teams and departments, will increase engagement. Embedding business continuity in the organisation culture by building resilience into values and behaviours and developing leadership capabilities will ensure that everyone is working towards the same goal. Business continuity might be added to job roles so that all employees are prepared.
Offboarding	There might be a requirement for a reduction in headcount as a consequence of the crisis. How will this be managed? There should be close alignment to organisation values and behaviours with a focus on compassion and support. People professionals might work with leaders to assess which roles might be impacted and how.
Alumni	It is important to ensure that communication with alumni continues throughout any crisis situation. Consideration of how the organisation will continue to communicate with alumni in times of crisis might be undertaken. For example, are alumni communications included in the organisation communication plan? What other methods will be used to stay in touch?

(Maddox-Daines, 2022)

are effective and meet the global policy requirements established by the programme office. For critical business operations, audits of business continuity plans are conducted and moderated through annual exercises to ensure plans are efficient and mitigate realistic disruptions. The business resilience programme is committed to providing a readiness state for the company that protects Cisco's top priorities: employees, business operations, customers and partners, community and shareholders. The business continuity management policy calls for reviews, updates and testing of business continuity plans at scheduled intervals.

SUMMARY POINTS

- Business continuity is a process-driven approach to support the organisation in maintaining its operations as far as possible in an unplanned and disruptive event.

- Business continuity planning is a key element of strategic management that demands organisations identify their vulnerabilities, priorities, critical resources and functions.
- There are numerous frameworks for managing any crisis. Each should include a planning stage, management of the event and a post-crisis stage for learning and reflection.
- People should be at the very centre of business continuity planning, and HR professionals are integral to the effective planning and implementation of business continuity.
- An effective business continuity process will include planning, communication and training, and this works most effectively when undertaken across the organisation involving representation from all stakeholders.
- The employee lifecycle might be used as a framework for examining business continuity from a people-first perspective.

SELF-TEST QUESTIONS/REVIEW QUESTIONS

- You have been asked to present to your senior management team on the benefits of business continuity planning. What key points would you include in your presentation?
- There are various approaches that organisations use for business continuity planning. Assess the essential elements that should be included to maximise the effectiveness of the process.

A CASE EXAMPLE: UNIVERSITY OF READING

Review the University of Reading case study discussed in this chapter. Evaluate the university's approach to business continuity planning. What other considerations might the university explore for embedding business continuity into organisational culture?

REFLECTION

Reflect on your own role or one you are familiar with (or interview a member of your family or a friend about their experience). What might you include in your own business continuity plan to ensure that you are able to undertake your role effectively in times of crisis? Assess whether business continuity planning should be included in job descriptions.

References

Burnett, J. J. (1998). A strategic approach to managing crises. *Public Relation Review, 24,* pp.475–488. 66.

Balarouras, S. (2015). The state of business continuity preparedness. *Disaster Recovery Journal,* Winter. Available at: https://drj.com/journal_main/the-state-of-business-continuity-preparedness-2021/. (Accessed 22 January 2023).

Cloudman, R. and Hallahan, K. (2006). Crisis communications preparedness among U.S. organizations: Activities and assessments by public relations practitioners. *Public Relations Review, 32*(4), pp.367–376. ISSN 0363-8111. https://doi.org/10.1016/j.pubrev.2006.09.005.

Fischbacher-Smith, D. (2017). When organisational effectiveness fails: business continuity management and the paradox of performance. *Journal of Organizational Effectiveness: People and Performance, 4*(1), pp.89–107. https://doi.org/10.1108/JOEPP-01-2017-0002.

Fink, S. (1986). *Crisis management: Planning for the inevitable.* New York, N.Y: American Management Association.

Holland, P., Bartram, T., Garavan, T. and Grant, K. (2022), Introduction: Work, workplaces and human resource management in a disruptive world. Holland, P., Bartram, T., Garavan, T. and Grant, K. (Ed.) *The Emerald Handbook of Work, Workplaces and Disruptive Issues in HRM.* Bingley: Emerald Publishing Limited, pp.1–9. https://doi.org/10.1108/978-1-80071-779-420221001

ISO (2019). Available at: https://www.iso.org/standard/72808.html (Accessed 13 August, 2022).

Maddox-Daines, K. L. (2021). Delivering well-being through the coronavirus pandemic: The role of human resources (HR) in managing a healthy workforce. *Personnel Review.* https://doi.org/10.1108/PR-04-2021-0224

Mitroff, I. I. (1994). Crisis management and environmentalism: A natural fit. *California Management Review, 36*(2), pp.101–113. https://doi.org/10.2307/41165747

Mitroff, I. I. (2005). *Why Some Companies Emerge Stronger and Better from a Crisis: 7 Essential Lessons for Surviving Disaster.* USA: New York, Amacom.

Mukherjee, M., Chatterjee, R., Khanna, B. K., Dhillon, P. P. S., Kumar, A. Bajwa, S., Prakash, A. and Shaw, R. (2020). Ecosystem-centric business continuity planning (eco-centric BCP): A post COVID19 new normal. *Progress in Disaster Science, 7.* https://doi.org/10.1016/j.pdisas.2020.100117

Nizamidou, C. and Vouzas, F. (2018). Providing a new perspective in HR in terms of crisis management. *Journal of Business Science and Applied Management, 13*(1), pp.15–25.

Pauchant, T. C., & Mitroff, I. I. (1992). Management by nosing around: Exposing the dangerous invisibility of technologies. *Journal of Management Inquiry, 1*(1), pp.70–78. https://doi.org/10.1177/105649269211012.

Premeaux, S. F. and Breaux, D. (2007). Crisis management of human resources: Lessons from Hurricanes Katrina and Rita. *Human Resource Planning, 30*(3), pp.39–47.

PWC (2021). Global crisis survey 2021. PWC. Available at: https://www.pwc.com/gx/en/issues/crisis-solutions/global-crisis-survey.html. (Accessed 3 July, 2021).

Rosenthal, U. and Kouzmin, A. (1997). Crises and crisis management: Toward comprehensive government decision making. *Journal of Public Administration Research and Theory, 7*, pp.277–304.

Smits, S. J. and Ezzat Ally, N. (2003). Thinking the unthinkable" — leadership's role in creating behavioral readiness for crisis management". Competitiveness Review, *13*(1), pp.1–23. https://doi.org/10.1108/eb046448

Managing equality, diversity and inclusivity in a hybrid world

Chapter 14

INTRODUCTION

In a new era of hybrid working, how will organisations ensure that everyone feels included and that they belong? Managing people effectively in a hybrid organisation requires a culture of inclusion whereby communication is purposeful, regular and transparent. This chapter will explore the theoretical knowledge base and skills to understand equality, inclusion and diversity. It will assess the notion of diversity in socially responsible organisations. It will consider how to build inclusive teams within the workplace, the impact of natural biases and presumptions and how these can be negated. The chapter will introduce the Equality Act and the protective characteristics and examples of how to build a harmonious, supportive workplace. An open and inclusive workforce has many benefits, both for individuals and the organisation and these will be assessed. Through the equality, diversity and inclusion strategic framework and action plan template, the chapter will reflect on and review workplace policies and atmosphere to assess its alignment to hybrid working.

DOI: 10.4324/9781003342984-15

DEFINING EQUALITY, DIVERSITY AND INCLUSION.

The Equality and Human Rights Commission (EHRC, 2022) describes equality as ensuring that every individual has an equal opportunity to make the most of their lives and talents. It also explains that no one should have poorer life chances because of the way they were born, where they come from, what they believe or whether they have a disability. Whilst equality focuses on ensuring that everybody has an equal opportunity, diversity recognises and celebrates difference. Indeed, Leatherbarrow and Fletcher (2018, p.428) argue that diversity has become one of the most important issues and challenges in the workplace. Armstrong and Taylor (2020, p.365) define diversity as the differences between people. The CIPD (2022) adds that diversity is about acknowledging the benefit of having a range of perspectives in decision-making and the workforce being representative of the organisation's customers.

Inclusion is the deliberate act of welcoming diversity and creating an environment where different kinds of people can thrive and succeed. 'Put simply diversity is what you have. Inclusion is what you do' (Armstrong and Taylor, 2020, p.365). Inclusion and diversity are not interchangeable, however. Inclusion focuses on creating a culture of openness for different perspectives, approaches and experiences so that both individuals and organisations can benefit. The CIPD (2022) explains that inclusion is where people's differences are valued and used to enable everyone to thrive at work. It's where everyone feels that they belong without having to conform, that their contribution matters, where they are able to perform to their full potential, no matter their background, identity or circumstances. Alexander, Dowling and Prince (2021) explain that inclusion is related to employee engagement. They emphasise the importance of developing models to support inclusion whilst the CIPD (2022) highlights the need for fair policies and practices to achieve an inclusive workplace as this enables a diverse range of people to work together effectively. A diversity and inclusion policy might include the organisation values, the commitment to eliminating bias throughout the employee lifecycle, the need to promote inclusion and details of how an inclusive environment will be achieved.

Working inclusively is one of the core behaviours in the HR profession map (CIPD, 2021). People professionals have a key role to play in working collaboratively and inclusively, as well as encouraging, facilitating and setting up cross-boundary working, building high-trust relationships and managing conflict constructively (ibid).

THE LEGAL FRAMEWORK

The Equality Act 2010 came into force in 2010 in Britain bringing together over 116 separate pieces of legislation to one Act. The law protects individuals from unfair treatment and promotes a fair and more equal society (EHRC, 2022). The Act makes it unlawful to discriminate against a person in any of the protective characteristics groups including age, disability, gender reassignment, race, religion or belief, sex, sexual orientation, marriage and civil partnership and pregnancy and maternity. It also provides protection from discrimination by association or perception.

PROTECTED CHARACTERISTICS
UNDER THE EQUALITY ACT 2010

Age: workers of all ages are protected from discrimination.

Disability: a worker is disabled under the Equality Act if they have a physical or mental impairment which has a substantial and long-term adverse effect (which has lasted or is likely to last for at least 12 months) on their ability to carry out normal day to day activities such as shopping, eating, walking).

Gender reassignment: protection is provided to transsexual workers who have started, are going to start or have completed a process to change their gender.

Marriage and civil partnerships: employees who are married or in a civil partnership are protected against discrimination but single people are not protected.

Pregnancy and maternity: women are protected against discrimination on the grounds of pregnancy and maternity during the period of their pregnancy and any statutory maternity leave.

Race: includes colour, nationality and ethnic or national origins.

Religion and belief: the Act protects workers against discrimination on grounds of their religion or belief or lack of religion or belief. A religion must have a clear structure and belief system. A 'belief' must be genuinely held and a significant and substantial aspect of human life and behaviour. It must not conflict with the fundamental rights of others.

Sex: both men and women are protected under the Act.

Sexual orientation: the Act protects bisexual, gay, heterosexual and lesbian people and also those who are discriminated against because of perceptions about their sexual orientation.

THE SOCIAL JUSTICE CASE

The CIPD (2022) argues that the social justice case for diversity is based on the belief that everyone should have a right to equal access to employment, training and development based solely on merit. Everyone should have the right to be free of any direct or indirect discrimination and harassment or bullying. This can be described as the right to be treated fairly, and the UK law, principally in the Equality Act 2010, sets minimum standards. Beardwell and Claydon (2010, p.201) refer to a 'moral obligation to treat employees with fairness and dignity'.

THE BUSINESS CASE

The Boston Consulting Group states that businesses with above-average diversity on their management teams report 19 per cent higher revenues from innovative products and services than those with less diverse leadership (Lorenzo, 2018). The UK Department for Business, Innovation and Skills in the Government Equalities Office's report 'The Business Case for Equality and Diversity' (2013) explains that external business benefits arise when firms better represent the world (and legislative environment) around them. For instance, having staff with roots in other countries and cultures can help a business address its products appropriately and sensitively to new markets. Consumers are becoming more diverse and firms may need to reflect this or risk losing out in important markets. Internal business benefits arise also from improving operations internally in the organisation. For example, a diverse workforce brings together a range of perspectives and this can improve creativity, problem-solving and flexibility.

Georgeac and Rattan (2022) point out that organisations should no longer be arguing the business case for diversity. In their research, they found that 80 per cent of organisations used the business case to justify diversity and yet when underrepresented participants read a business case for diversity (rather than a moral case) on average they felt 11 per cent less sense of belonging to the company. They were 16 per cent more concerned that they would be stereotyped at the company. Additionally, they were more worried that the company would view them as interchangeable with other members of their identity group.

The legal framework provides a minimum standard for equality protection. Organisations should encourage diversity beyond this minimum standard, however, as this is the way to create belonging which supports productivity and in turn creates business advantage. Diversity and inclusion are integral to job satisfaction and high-performance work, and a strategic approach is required to ensure that the organisation promotes a culture where everyone feels that they belong.

DIVERSITY AND INCLUSION STRATEGY

Creating an inclusive culture requires a diversity and inclusion strategy which aligns to the organisation values. Covering the characteristics of the Equality Act (discussed above) the strategy should focus on fairness and inclusion through each stage of the employee lifecycle. A clear indication of how the strategy will be delivered, for example through communication, training, diversity networks, and how it will be managed, for example through committees, working groups and other initiatives, is required.

CASE STUDY: FOOTBALL ASSOCIATION (FA)

Putting strategy into action

The FA has a three-year equality, diversity and inclusion strategy in place which outlines three key strategic commitments; lead the change, be the change and inspire the change.

Lead the change focuses on actively tackling discrimination on and off the pitch by delivering effective sanctioning and education, furthering efforts to tackle online abuse, creating safe venues and building trust in reporting mechanisms and disciplinary processes for incidents of discrimination.

Be the change focuses on building a diverse workforce through education, development and inclusive leadership. Codes are set to drive and promote inclusion such as the football leadership diversity code. Targets are set to increase diversity across the workforce with a focus on improving disability representation and increasing the ethnic diversity of England's women's coaching team.

Inspire the change uses the organisation's influence to positively impact every aspect of the game, including delivering core diversity programmes for historically underrepresented communities across the areas of gender, ethnicity, disability, faith and sexual orientation. It also focuses on providing career opportunities and addressing underrepresentation through positive action initiatives such as the Elite Coach Placement Programme.

Positive action

The FA case example above discusses positive action in the form of the Elite Coach Placement Programme. The Equality Act 2010 allows positive action to be taken if employers consider that employees or job applications who share a particular protected characteristic suffer a disadvantage connected to that characteristic or if their participation in an activity is disproportionately low.

Diversity networks

Diversity networks are also helpful for supporting groups for minority staff. The Bank of England supports diversity and inclusion through staff-run networks including LGBTQ+, disAbility Network, Mental Health Network, Bank of England Ethnic Minorities (BEEM) Network, Women in the Bank Network, Carers Network, Parents+, Bank employees that served (BETS), Christian Union, Jewish Network and Muslim Network. Networks provide support, events, activities, advice and information. The bank encourages staff to be themselves in order to achieve their full potential.

LEADERS DRIVE INCLUSIVE STRATEGY

Leaders are instrumental to the effective implementation of a diversity and inclusion strategy and embedding inclusion through organisation culture and values. As has been discussed in previous chapters, trust is key to engagement and retention and leadership behaviours that build trust facilitate belonging. Leaders that role model inclusivity and belonging are likely to report high-quality decision-making and higher levels of team cooperation (Bourke and Titus, 2019). Leaders should role-model the values of the organisation to promote and facilitate belongingness through regular meetings with their team.

As leaders are instrumental to the effectiveness of an inclusive culture it is important that they receive the training and support to equip them to run hybrid teams. Leaders will also need to be trained in areas such as making reasonable adjustments (*a* change that must be made to remove or reduce a disadvantage related to an employee's disability) and flexible working requests. Leaders that take the time to find out about the individual support requirements of each member of their staff will usually find that their team achieves higher levels of productivity. The case study below provides an insight into how the CEO is driving inclusion and performance through the organisation.

CASE STUDY: MITIE

Mitie is based in the UK and specialises in facilities management and professional services including technical services (engineering services, energy, water and real estate services), business services (security, cleaning and office services) and specialist services (care & custody, landscapes and waste management).

Mitie employs 47,500 people across the country with a diverse client base that includes a blue-chip customer base, from banks and retailers, to hospitals, schools and critical government strategic assets. It supports customers' people and buildings by deploying advanced technology and is using smart analytics to provide insights and deliver efficiencies for customers.

Its vision and values are built on the premise of 'The exceptional, every day', which is its commitment to both customers and colleagues. 'Our diversity makes us stronger' is one of Mitie's core values and a fundamental part of what it is as an organisation. This mindset has been driven from the top by the company's CEO emphasising support for people to be the best they can be as one of the core objectives. The company strives to create an inclusive, supportive and high-performing culture.

BUILDING INCLUSIVE CULTURE AND VALUES

Biased perceptions occur when people use stereotypes rather than factual information about individuals; for example, older workers not being so tech savvy or young workers not being as committed. It is negative bias that is problematic to building inclusive organisations. Unconscious bias training is now delivered in some form by many organisations, but this alone is unlikely to reduce barriers. Building inclusive behaviours that promote acceptance and respect and that genuinely value and support individual contributions will encourage a sense of belonging and an inclusive culture. Systems and processes within an organisation will need to be reviewed to ensure that there are no invisible barriers to high performance at each stage of the employee lifecycle.

Having a sense of belonging so that each of us is able to be ourselves in work is integral to well-being. It is also important for productivity. Henley (2022) reporting on the value of belonging at work explains that a sense of high belonging has been linked to a 56 per cent increase in job performance, a 50 per cent drop in turnover risk and a 75 per cent reduction in sick days. Yet Deloitte (2019) found in its 'Uncovering talent: a new model of inclusion' report that 93 per cent of respondents stated that their organisation articulated inclusion as one of its values but only 78 per cent believed that their organisation lived up to their values. This might indicate that the strategic intention is in place but company values have not been embedded through behaviours. The case study below provides detail of the initiatives undertaken to remove bias, create a sense of belonging and celebrate diversity at Bupa.

CASE STUDY: BUPA

Bupa is an international healthcare group with over 25,000 employees and serving over 5 million customers. Bupa Global & UK is a leader in the health insurance market, providing services including dentistry, care homes and health services. As well as services spread across the UK, Global offers international health insurance to over 450,000 customers across the globe. It is the biggest health insurer in the UK, with Bupa UK providing cover to 2 million members. Elsewhere it has over 470 dental practices, 49 health clinics, the Cromwell Hospital and over 120 care homes, treating 2.4 million patients and caring for over 7,000 residents respectively.

Bupa supports and celebrates diversity. Its existing campaigns continue to drive inclusion across the business. It promotes 'Be You at Bupa' and 'Everyone's Welcome', which are displayed at the entrance to Bupa sites across the UK and internationally. Both these initiatives act as a reminder that colleagues and guests alike are not only welcome but encouraged to express their true selves, and set clear expectations that individualities should be celebrated.

Bupa has a fully accessible careers website, removing barriers for applicants with disabilities, and it has updated its interview approach to focus on strengths over experience. It has also reviewed its recruitment process to help reduce unconscious bias and has provided inclusivity training for recruitment teams and hiring managers (including piloting anonymised CVs). Bupa has started to trial video interviews and the use of artificial intelligence in the recruitment process in order to reduce bias and increase diversity.

NEURODIVERSITY

Neurodiversity is a growing area of workplace inclusion. It refers to the natural range of differences in human brain function. In organisations neurodiversity is used to describe alternative thinking styles including dyslexia, autism and ADHD. Microsoft has built a specific neurodiversity hiring programme to support neurodivergent individuals and to strengthen their workforce with innovative and creative thinking solutions. Diverse teams are encouraged and the hiring programmes seek to attract neurodivergent candidates. Training and support is provided for career growth and success. Applicants engage in extended interviews that focus on workability, interview preparation and skills assessment.

EQUALITY, DIVERSITY AND INCLUSION IN A HYBRID WORKFORCE

The proportion of workers hybrid working in the UK has risen to 24 per cent in May 2022. The percentage working exclusively from home is 14 per cent in the same period (ONS, 2022). Howlett (2021) reports that more than two in five employers (41 per cent) will have adopted hybrid working in two years' time, with only 3 in 10 (30 per cent) businesses expecting to have their workforce fully back on site before 2023. As discussed earlier in this book, people have generally found that working more flexibly in a hybrid model is good for work and life balance, productivity and health. However, a challenge for organisations is the tension between implementing hybrid working and a desire to treat people fairly. Some organisations are offering different levels of flexibility for certain job types and building this into new contracts. Others have prioritised equity, allowing all staff to have the same right to work from home whatever their role (Cherubini et al., 2021, p.18).

One of the key challenges for inclusivity when people are working from home is reduced visibility in the workplace which may result in different rates of progression. Those most affected may be individuals that already face disadvantage in the workplace, for example, disabled workers who may find working remotely more convenient as they are able to manage energy levels or their condition more effectively. Taylor et al. (2021) found in their research that disabled workers are 1.3 times more likely than non-disabled workers to be working remotely (57 per cent compared with 44 per cent). Working remotely for more of the time or full time can also create risks for women who might find that they are missing out on opportunities for progression. There is also a danger that women may regress towards more traditional role patterns (ibid). Taylor et al. (ibid.) also found that women were less likely than men to agree that their organisation is inclusive of remote workers in their day-to-day operations.

Younger staff (under 24 years old) may also be impacted by hybrid working patterns and may potentially miss out on networking, stretch projects or representing the organisation at external events (ibid.).

PEOPLE PROFESSIONALS AND THE INCLUSIVE WORKPLACE

Creating an inclusive workplace enables employees to thrive. Developing a diversity and inclusion strategy and policy provides a framework of principles and intention but this needs to be owned and embraced by every member of the organisation, from the senior team, to line managers and employees. This can be achieved through inclusive behaviours that deliver on the values of the organisation. People professionals should role model inclusive behaviours and work with all stakeholders to get their support in advocating the same. Diversity and inclusion should be aligned to each stage of the employee lifecycle and measured through metrics and feedback from representatives and champions. Two-way communication is integral to progress and creating opportunities for feedback are key. The people team are well placed to take the lead in coordinating initiatives and to provide support in the form of networks and training for all stakeholders. Such activities need to go beyond compliance to support real behaviour change.

SUMMARY POINTS

- Equality is about ensuring that every individual has an equal opportunity to make the most of their lives and talents.
- Diversity acknowledges the benefit of having a range of perspectives in decision-making and the workforce being representative of the organisation's customers.
- Inclusion is the deliberate act of welcoming diversity and creating an environment where different kinds of people can thrive and succeed.
- The Equality Act 2010 makes it unlawful to discriminate against a person in any of the protective characteristics groups including age, disability, gender reassignment, race, religion or belief, sex, sexual orientation, marriage and civil partnership and pregnancy and maternity.
- Having a diversity and inclusion strategy that aligns to organisation values and covers the requirements of the legal framework will provide direction for diversity and inclusion but this needs to be embedded within the culture of the organisation.
- Leaders should role model inclusive behaviours and create an environment of trust to facilitate belonging. Training, development and support are essential to help leaders manage effectively.

- People professionals are inclusion and diversity role models and should work closely with leaders across the organisation to support the delivery of inclusive behaviours, challenging leaders where required. Arranging diversity and inclusion training and development for all staff, leaders, the senior management team and the board that goes beyond compliance to behaviour change is key.

SELF-TEST QUESTIONS/REVIEW QUESTIONS

- You have been asked by your senior team to present the business case for diversity and inclusion. What key points would you make?
- You have written a diversity and inclusion strategy and a policy but organisation metrics suggest that some staff still don't feel a sense of belonging in the organisation. You are concerned about staff retention. What actions might you take?

A CASE EXAMPLE: FA

Review the FA case study discussed in this chapter. Assess the initiatives that are discussed in the diversity and inclusion strategy. Which stakeholders are discussed in the strategy? How might the effectiveness of the strategy be measured?

REFLECTION

Reflect on your own role or one you are familiar with (or interview a member of your family or a friend about their experience). Does your organisation have a diversity and inclusion strategy in place? How effective is it? How does the organisation measure its effectiveness? What else might be done?

References

Alexander, A., Dowling, B. and Prince, S. (2021). Reimagining the virtual workplace around inclusion and engagement. McKinsey, [online] April 12. Available at: https://www.mckinsey.com/business-functions/people-and-organizational -performance/our-insights/the-organization-blog/reimagining-the-virtual -workplace-around-inclusion-and-engageme

Armstrong, M. and Taylor, S. (2020). *Armstrong's Handbook of Human Resource Management Practice.* 15th edn. London: Kogan Page.

Beardwell, J. and Claydon, T. (2010). *Human Resource Management: A Contemporary Approach.* https://lib.ugent.be/catalog/rug01:002070678

Bourke, J. and Titus, A. (2019). Why inclusive leaders are good for organisations and how to become one. *Harvard Business Review.* 29 March. Available at: https://hbr.org /2019/03/why-inclusive-leaders-are-good-for-organizations-and-how-to-become -one. (Accessed 1 July, 2022).

Cherubini, F., Newman, N. and Nielsen, R. S. (2021). Changing newsrooms 2021: Hybrid working and improving diversity remain twin challenges for publishers. University of Oxford and Reuters Institute. Available at: ttps://ora.ox.ac.uk/objec ts/uuid:bcc6ec6f-3935-49ad-ac4b-015a3bf143a7/download_file?safe_filename=Ch erubini_et_al_2021_changing_newsrooms_2021.pdf&file_format=pdf&type_of _work=Report. (Accessed 19 June, 2022).

CIPD (2021). HR profession map. Available at: https://peopleprofession.cipd.org/ profession-map#gref. (Accessed 13 July, 2022).

CIPD (2022). Inclusions and diversity in the workplace. CIPD. 24 August. Available at: https://www.cipd.co.uk/knowledge/fundamentals/relations/diversity/factsheet. (Accessed 13 June, 2022).

Deloitte (2019). Uncovering talent: A new model of inclusion. Available at: https://www2 .deloitte.com/content/dam/Deloitte/us/Documents/about-deloitte/us-about-deloitte -uncovering-talent-a-new-model-of-inclusion.pdf. (Accessed 13 July, 2022).

Department for Business, Education and Skills (2013). *The Business Case for Equality and Diversity: A Survey of the Academic Literature*. BIS Occasional Paper No 4. January. Available at: https://assets.publishing.service.gov.uk/government/uploads/system/ uploads/attachment_data/file/49638/the_business_case_for_equality_and_diversity .pdf. (Accessed 19 July, 2022).

EHRC (2022). Available at: https://equalityhumanrights.com/en (Accessed 13 June, 2022).

Georgeac, O. A. M. and Rattan, A. (2022). The business case for diversity backfires: Detrimental effects of organizations' instrumental diversity rhetoric for underrepresented group members' sense of belonging. *Journal of Personality and Social Psychology*. Advance online publication. https://doi.org/10.1037/pspi0000394

Henley, D. (2022). The secret to creating a sense of belonging at work. *Forbes*. 20 March. Available at: https://www.forbes.com/sites/dedehenley/2022/03/20/the -secret-to-creating-a-sense-of-belonging-at-work/?sh=3bba59c17a88. (Accessed 3 June, 2022).

Howlett, E. (2021). Two in five employers will embrace hybrid working by 2023, poll finds. *People Management*. 24 August. Available at: https://www.peoplemanagement .co.uk/article/1745148/two-in-five-employers-will-embrace-hybrid-working-poll -finds. (Accessed 4 August, 2022).

Leatherbarrow, C. and Fletcher, J. (2018). *Introduction to Human Resource Management: A Guide to HR Practice*. 4th edn. London: Kogan Page CIPD.

Lorenzo, R. (2018). How diversity leadership teams boost innovation. BCG. January 23. Available at: https://www.bcg.com/publications/2018/how-diverse-leadership -teams-boost-innovation. (Accessed 13 June, 2022).

ONS (2022). Available at: https://www.ons.gov.uk/employmentandlabourmarket/ peopleinwork/employmentandemployeetypes/articles/ishybridworkingheretostay /2022-05-23. (Accessed 1 August, 2022).

Taylor, H., Florisson, R. and Hooper, D. (2021). Making hybrid inclusive: Key priorities for policymakers. *Policy Brief*, Chartered Management Institute and Work Foundation. [online] Available at: https://www.managers.org.uk/wp-content/ uploads/2021/10/wf-cmi-making-hybrid-inclusive-policy-brief.pdf. (Accessed 19 July, 2022).

Environmental sustainability

Chapter 15

INTRODUCTION

Human activity is cited as the biggest cause of climate change with organisations contributing significantly too. Organisations emit greenhouse gases through their energy and resource use, transport and travel, waste management and supply chain. This chapter looks at the business case for acting urgently to reduce the impact on the environment. It assesses the negative impact of climate change on the organisation and how by making changes it will be possible to benefit from improvements in energy efficiency leading to reduced costs and innovations to inspire new products. The chapter will assess the role of the people professional in implementing environmental sustainability through all aspects of the employee lifecycle. It will include a number of case examples to illustrate how environmental sustainability can be built into organisational culture. Methods for measuring, monitoring and reporting progress will be explored.

CLIMATE CHANGE

Climate change refers to the increasing changes in temperatures and weather patterns. Human activity is the main cause of climate change as a result of burning fossil fuels (oils, coal, natural gas) that emit greenhouse gases which prevent the sun's heat from leaving the atmosphere. Agriculture is the largest driver of deforestation resulting in carbon emissions that contribute to climate change. The World Economic Forum argue that failure to mitigate climate change is the number one global risk to business (WEF, 2021). Indeed, Marchant (2021) reporting on the findings of the Swiss Re Institute found that the global economy could lose 10 per cent of its total economic value by 2050 due to climate change. The Paris Climate

DOI: 10.4324/9781003342984-16

Agreement of 2015, signed by 195 of the world's countries, committed governments to limiting climate change to well below 2° above pre-industrial levels (Coppola and Blohmke, 2019).

THE BUSINESS CASE FOR SUSTAINABILITY

Companies now have the opportunity to not only mitigate risks but to take advantage of the new opportunities presented by reducing greenhouse gases and taking significant action on climate change. For example, Coppola and Blohmke (2019) argue that companies can improve their resource productivity by increasing energy efficiency, thereby reducing costs. Climate change can also encourage the development of new products and services that are less carbon intensive and enhance the resilience of supply chains by reducing reliance on price-volatile fossil fuels. Indeed, focusing on environmental health, social well-being and the organisation's financial success and resilience, in the form of the triple bottom line (people, planet and prosperity) can reap rewards (Elkington, 1994). The following case studies provide examples of two organisations that have managed to balance social, environmental and financial priorities.

CASE STUDY: THE LEGO GROUP

The Lego Group is a toy production company based in Denmark employing just over 20,000 staff. The company has been exploring alternatives to oil-based plastic bricks for a number of years. In 2018, the company set a target to manufacture all of its products from sustainable materials by 2030. In 2021, the company unveiled a new Lego brick prototype made from recycled plastic bottles. They are also now rolling out fully recyclable paper packaging inside all Lego sets. This is not only in response to environmental concerns but also to teach and help children understand the importance of recycling. Lego experienced considerable growth in 2021 with revenues increasing by 27 per cent and operating profit by 32 per cent.

CASE STUDY: NATURA &CO

Natura & Co is a global, purpose-driven, multi-channel and multi-brand cosmetics group which includes Avon, Natura, The Body Shop and Aesop. The company aims to source sustainable ingredients in the rainforest while achieving social, environmental and financial outcomes. The company has been carbon neutral since 2007 and is also preserving almost 1.8 million hectares of Amazonian forest. While Natura has been called a 'champion of the earth' by the UN, it has also been labelled the world's third strongest brand in cosmetics after Neutrogena and Johnson&Johnson. It is also very profitable; since 2012, Natura has doubled its revenues to US$3.32 billion.

CSR AND ESG

Corporate social responsibility (CSR) has been on the agenda of many organisations for some time (Fatima and Elbanna, 2022). CSR is an all-encompassing term for sustainable, socially conscious business practices. It refers to corporate citizenship which seeks to have a positive impact on all business stakeholders including the wider community, employees, consumers and the environment. CSR activities might include recycling policies, the reduction of carbon emissions, staff volunteering and environmental awareness sessions. The case study below emphasises the community focus of the CSR strategy at Jaguar.

CASE STUDY: JAGUAR LAND ROVER

- Jaguar Land Rover is the holding company of Jaguar Land Rover Limited and a subsidiary of Tata Motors Ltd, employing over 44,000 staff. The global corporate social responsibility strategy emphasises the company's commitment to playing an active role in the communities in which it operates in order to make a positive impact, by investing resources in and addressing key issues which affect its communities and its business alike. The company's CSR programme aims to create opportunities for 12 million people in the local and global communities by 2020. It operates through projects in areas such as education and talent, design and technology and well-being and health.

CSR activities are self-regulated and usually included in the company's annual report (Fatima and Elbanna, 2022). However, increasingly a number of organisations are being accused of not 'walking the talk' meaning that their CSR claims on environmental or social issues have not been followed, a practice commonly known as 'greenwashing' (Gatti et al., 2019). The scope of CSR is disputed and has shifted over time. One of the key challenges has been the lack of standardised metrics which has impacted on comparative analysis.

Environmental, social and governance (ESG) performance is the collective term for measuring the business impact on environment and society as well as the robustness of its governance. ESG requires organisations and businesses to consider their environmental impact. It also focuses on how an organisation treats and values their employees, and the principles and policies an entity uses to make decisions (Khalid et al., 2021). Gerald (2019) argues that whilst CSR encompasses the first two elements of ESG, the environmental and the social conduct of the firm, ESG combines the environmental and social impact of the company, with its corporate governance focus. The social elements of ESG include a focus on human rights, contribution to community, labour and employment, consumer safety and protection and social contribution (Jin and Kims, 2022).

There is an ever-increasing investor interest in corporate social responsibility (CSR) generally, and environmental social governance (ESG) in particular. Khalid et al. (2021) note that an ESG framework is not an altruistic goal, rather it meets the dual aim of financial success whilst supporting a sustainable future for all involved in a company's ecosystem. Hazen (2021) reports that the emergence of the ESG framework has provided a renewed focus on CSR by embracing the use of metrics to measure a company's commitment to socially responsible behaviour. Indeed, Pollman (2019) argues that corporate leaders and investors are increasingly recognising the importance of social responsibility and sustainability. The case study below outlines the core elements of the Siemens Group ESG strategy. Note how the strategy is designed to 'empower customers' and 'benefit all stakeholders'.

CASE STUDY: SIEMENS GROUP

Siemens is a technology company that employs 303,000 people globally. Their ESG strategy is focused on transforming the everyday to create a better tomorrow.

> We empower our customers to drive sustainable growth and transform their industries. With our degree framework (based on six fields of action that drive sustainability and are dynamic and continuously evolving), we set strategic ambitions for the benefit of all our stakeholders on the key topics of environment, social and governance.
>
> *(Siemens, 2022)*

The Siemens Group degree framework represents the areas that the organisation has focused on and created targets. These include decarbonisation, ethics, governance, resource efficiency, equity and employability. The company argues that it does this by providing customers with the software and the hardware of a smarter and greener future. For example, through the Mireo Plus Battery trains that provide emission-free passenger transport for commuters in Baden-Württemberg (Germany). These trains achieve up to 25 per cent energy savings throughout operations compared to previous models and 95 per cent of the components can be recycled at the end of the lifecycle.

SUSTAINABLE DEVELOPMENT GOALS

The 2030 agenda for sustainable development adopted by all United Nations member states in 2015 has at its core 17 sustainable development goals (SDG2 s) (UN, 2022) (see Table 15.1). The SDGs provide a broad framework for the examination and promotion of the three ESG pillars. Many of the SDGs are relevant to HRM practitioners, for example the goals for decent work and economic growth, gender equality, good health and well-being, reducing inequalities and developing partnerships for the achievement of these goals (Kramar, 2022).

MEASURING, MONITORING AND REPORTING

A variety of systems have been developed to measure organisational sustainability outcomes. The SDGs provide a framework for measuring the effectiveness of goals in the areas of economy, society and the environment. Metrics and measurements are important for assessing progress but to be effective need to be embraced by all stakeholders. At the organisation level, there are several reporting mechanisms that companies might use, for example the Global Reporting Initiative (GRI), the FTSE4Good Index Series and the Dow Jones Sustainability Index (DJSI). The GRI provides standards for sustainability reporting and supports decision-making and action planning that can benefit all stakeholders. The FTSE4Good Index Series is designed to measure the performance of companies demonstrating specific Environmental, Social and Governance (ESG) practices. The Dow Jones Sustainability World Index (or DJSI World) represents the top 10 per cent of the biggest 2,500 companies in the Standard and Poor's (S&P) Global Broad Market Index based on long-term environmental, social and governance criteria. The GRI reporting system is used more than other reporting systems, with 75 per cent of the world's 250 largest organisations reporting (KPMG 2017) and thousands of organisations in 93 countries using it worldwide. Many organisations are now reporting

Table 15.1 Sustainable Development Goals

1	No poverty	2	Zero hunger	3	Good health and well-being	4	Quality education	5	Gender equality	6	Clean water and sanitation
7	Affordable and clean energy	8	Decent work and economic growth	9	Industry, innovation and infrastructure	10	Reduce equalities	11	Sustainable cities and communities	12	Responsible consumption and production
13	Climate action	14	Life below water	15	Life on land	16	Peace, justice and strong institutions	17	Partnerships for the goals		

on economic, social and environmental measures in sustainability reports. Kramar (2022) argues however, that the move towards sustainable outcomes is an evolutionary process requiring system-wide change. To date, the use of tools as measurement devices has not been effective in creating sufficient change towards sustainability and the achievement of SDGs.

B CORP CERTIFICATION

From a movement that started 15 years ago, the non-profit B lab has seen a rapid rise in the number of companies seeking certification which stands at over 5,000 across 79 countries at the time of writing (B Lab, 2022). Certified B Corporations are for-profit companies that must meet established standards in ESG performance. These include accountability in terms of profit and purpose and transparency regarding operations and policies, such as sourcing and labour practices.

B Corporations aim to bridge the gap between not-for-profit organisations and profit corporations by requiring leaders to act in the interest of all stakeholders, including customers, employees, vendors and the local community (Butcher, 2022). As they are required to undergo the verification process every three years in order to recertify, they focus on continuous improvement, leading to their long-term resiliency. The case study below provides an insight into the sustainability journey of Bailey & Co.

CASE STUDY: BAILEY & CO

Bailey & Co is the producer of Baileys Irish Cream Liqueur. Based in Dublin, Ireland, the company is part of Diageo, a global leader in beverage alcohol. Baileys was launched in Ireland in 1974 and is now available in 153 markets worldwide. The company aims to make a positive difference to communities and the planet. Since it launched, the company has paid a premium for top-quality milk from farmer-owned co-operative dairy suppliers. This ensures the company supports the maintenance of high standards of animal welfare and traceability in the milk that transforms into Baileys Irish Cream Liqueur. In recent years, the company has reduced the amount of water used in its factories and switched to 100 per cent renewable electricity to power them. The company pays employees a living wage and ensures they have access to benefits such as six months' paid family leave for parents. B Corp certification is the latest milestone for Baileys in the brand's sustainability journey and supports the parent company's (Diageo) wider ten-year sustainability action plan.

SUSTAINABILITY AND THE PEOPLE TEAM

Although corporate social responsibility has been a part of business for some time, the degree to which people professions have been involved in sustainability work has been variable. Indeed, Gond et al. (2011) suggest that this is because HR managers have tended to delegate CSR and sustainability issues to other members of the organisation. Anwar et al. (2020) contend that environmental consciousness is an integral part of HRM arguing that HR teams need to support the workforce in understanding the impact of organisation practices and initiatives on the environment.

The people team should be involved in key sustainability decision-making in order to support the formulation of strategic priorities in sustainability and contribute to financial, social and ecological outcomes. For an organisation that is working towards sustainable goals, such as one that is aiming for B Corporation certification, HR will be instrumental to the large scale culture change process. Indeed, the sustainability agenda is an integral part of what HR does, impacting on both organisation performance and organisation success.

The CIPD (2022) argues that HR teams have an important role to play in building and maintaining ethical cultures within organisations. They should review corporate responsibility in each of the core HR processes throughout the employee lifecycle. For example, recruitment, terms and conditions, health and safety, communications, inclusive, diversity and fair treatment, learning and development, performance management and reward and benefits. Scrutinising employment arrangements for subcontractors and people employed throughout the supply chain, along with people involved in the gig economy is also important for sustainable HR practices (Kramer, 2022).

Although long-term job security might not be possible, companies can offer opportunities for skills development so that they are able to remain marketable as well as supporting high performance working. Getting feedback about policies and processes through participation and dialogue will ensure that they are not only devised in relation to sustainability principles, but perceived as fair with intentions clearly explained. Building people management systems that support ethical behaviours through appropriate reward and performance management systems is one example of this. Additionally, the people team might encourage decision makers to review the ethical dimensions of business decisions. Working in partnership with government bodies and non-governmental organisations that protect or represent stakeholder interests (ibid.) to enact policies that further support sustainability outcomes is an effective approach to partnership working (SDG 17). The people team might also work with external institutions and support them in the formulation of their own HRM policies.

Houghton (2019) highlights the need for HR professionals to create and capture value over the longer term and to be effective this must take into account the internal and external environment and the changing context. Stankeviciute and Savanevicien (2018) suggest that the essential HR considerations for effective sustainable practices include:

- Long-term orientation: workforce planning; assessing needs of future employees
- Care of employees: health, safety, well-being management; work–life balance
- Care of environment: fostering 'eco-career'; rewarding against environmentally sustainable behaviour
- Profitability: share programmes
- Employee participation and social dialogue: different forms of employee voice and employee participation
- Employee development: job rotation; training for skills development; employability
- External partnership: cooperation with key stakeholders
- Flexibility: flexible working arrangements; job rotation
- Compliance beyond labour regulations: involve employee representatives in decision-making where participation is a statutory requirement; financial and non-financial support
- Employee cooperation: teamwork; good relationships of managers and employees
- Fairness and equality: fostering diversity; respectful relationships; fairness as regards as remuneration; career

Taking a long-term perspective to sustainable people management requires a holistic approach to employees' working lives. It requires a focus on each stage of the employee lifecycle. An assessment of both positive outcomes and the potential harm caused by people practices on their stakeholders is required and this should be reviewed regularly. The CIPD (2019, p.2) in its UK Working Lives report argues that 'access to and opportunity for good work and jobs is a vital part of a healthy society and economy, whatever people's background, skills and experience'. This is SDG 8: decent work and economic growth. The CIPD (ibid.) describes good work as follows:

Good work is fairly rewarded.

Good work gives people the means to securely make a living.

Good work gives opportunities to develop skills and a career and ideally gives a sense of fulfilment. Good work provides a supportive environment with constructive relationships.

Good work allows for work–life balance.

Good work is physically and mentally healthy.

Good work gives employees the voice and choice they need to shape their working lives.

Good work should be accessible to all.

Good work is an achievable goal, but requires buy-in from both policymakers and employers. Sustainable work is a journey and HR professionals are well placed to shape the future of their organisations through the framework of the SDGs.

SUMMARY POINTS

- Climate change refers to the increasing changes in temperatures and weather patterns. Human activity is the main cause of climate change as a result of burning fossil fuels that emit greenhouse gases.
- ESG performance is the collective term for measuring the business impact on environmental and social factors and for examining organisational governance robustness.
- The 17 SDGs provide a broad framework for the examination and promotion of the ESG pillars.
- Metrics and measurements are important for assessing progress. They include FTSE4Good Index Series, Global Reporting Initiative and the Dow Jones Sustainability World Index (or DJSI World). The measures need to be embraced by all stakeholders in order to support strategic planning and intent.
- Certified B Corporations are for-profit companies that must meet established standards in ESG performance.
- Environment consciousness is an integral part of HRM, and people teams play an important role in building and maintaining ethical cultures within organisations.

- HR professionals should review each of the core organisation HR processes throughout the employee lifecycle against sustainability goals and provide mechanisms so that stakeholders can offer feedback.
- Working in partnership with government bodies and non-governmental organisations that protect or represent stakeholder interests and companies in the supply chain will provide opportunities for scrutinising good practice and further developing robust HR systems, processes and practices (SDG 17).

SELF-TEST QUESTIONS/REVIEW QUESTIONS

- You have been asked by your senior team to explain the differences and similarities between CSR and ESG. Prepare your main points for discussion.
- Examine the reasons for the rapid rise in the number of companies that are seeking Certified B Corporation status.

A CASE EXAMPLE: SIEMENS GROUPS

Review the Siemens Group case study discussed in this chapter. Take a look at the SDGs in more detail at https://sdgs.un.org/goals. Which SDGs can you map to the Siemens Group ESG strategy?

REFLECTION

Reflect on your own sustainable journey. Take a look at the WWF footprint calculator to assess your environmental footprint. Challenge yourself to make a difference https://footprint.wwf.org.uk/#/.

References

Anwar, N., Nik Mahmood, N. H., Yusliza, M. Y., Ramayah, T., Noor Faezah, J., and Khalid, W. (2020). Green human resource management for organisational citizenship behaviour towards the environment and environmental performance on a university campus. *Journal of Cleaner Production*. 256, p.120401. https://doi.org/10.1016/j.jclepro.2020.120401.

B Lab. (2022). *About B Lab*. [online] Available at: https://www.bcorporation.net/en-us/movement/about-b-lab. (Accessed 15 September, 2022).

Butcher, D. (2022). The rise of b corporations. *Strategic Finance*, *103*(9), pp.15–16. Available at: https://www.proquest.com/openview/db565b1376ef5caa431eb3f 2d55e8f3f/1?pq-origsite=gscholar&cbl=48426. (Accessed 14 August, 2022).

CIPD (2019). UK working lives. Available at: https://www.cipd.co.uk/Images/uk-working-lives-summary-2019-v1_tcm18-58584.pdf. (Accessed 13 August, 2022).

CIPD (2022). Corporate responsibility: An introduction. 28 March. CIPD. Available at: https://www.cipd.co.uk/knowledge/strategy/corporate-responsibility/factsheet #gref. (Accessed 27 August, 2022).

Coppola, M., Krick, T. and Blohmke, J. (2019). Feeling the heat? Companies are under pressure to act on climate change and need to do more.[pdf] *Deloitte*. Available at: https://www2.deloitte.com/content/dam/insights/us/articles/43123_feeling-the -heat/DI_Feeling-the-heat.pdf.

Elkington, J. (1994). Towards the sustainable corporation: Win-win-win business strategies for sustainable development. *California Management Review*, 36(2), pp.90–100. https://doi:10.2307/41165746.

Fatima, T. and Elbanna, S. (2022). Corporate social responsibility (CSR) iplementation: A review and a research agenda towards an integrative framework. *Journal of Business Ethics*. [online] https://doi:10.1007/s10551-022-05047-8.

Gatti, L., Seele, P. and Rademacher, L. (2019). Grey zone in – Greenwash out. A review of greenwashing research and implications for the voluntary-mandatory transition of CSR. *International Journal of Corporate Social Responsibility*, [online] 4(1), pp.1–15. Available at: https://ideas.repec.org/a/spr/ijocsr/v4y2019i1d10.1186_s40991 -019-0044-9.html#:~:text=Lucia%20Gatti%20%26%20Peter%20Seele%20%26 %20Lars%20Rademacher%2C.

Gerard, B. (2019). ESG and socially responsible investment: A critical review. *Beta*, 33(01), pp.61–83. https://doi:10.18261/issn.1504-3134-2019-01-05.

Gond, J.P., Igalens, J., Swaen, V. and El Akremi, A. (2011). The human resources contribution to responsible leadership: An exploration of the CSR–HR interface. In *Responsible Leadership* (pp. 115–132). Dordrecht: Springer. https://doi.org/10.1007 /978-94-007-3995-6_10.

Hazen, T.L. (2021). Social issues in the spotlight: The increasing need to improve publicly-held companies' CSR and ESG disclosures. [online] SSRN. https://doi.org /10.2139/ssrn.3615327.

Houghton, E. (2019). Sustainable HR: A 'green' fad, or a realistic model for change? [online] CIPD. Available at: https://www.cipd.co.uk/news-views/changing-work -views/future-work/thought-pieces/sustainable-hr. (Accessed 13 August, 2022).

Jin, M. and Kim, B. (2022). Effects of ESG Activity recognition factors on innovative organization culture, job crafting, and job performance. *Administrative Sciences*, 12(4), p.127. https://doi:10.3390/admsci12040127.

KPMG (2017). *The KPMG Survey of Corporate Responsibility Reporting 2017.* [online] KPMG. Available at: https://home.kpmg/xx/en/home/insights/2017/10/the-kpmg -survey-of-corporate-responsibility-reporting-2017.html. (Accessed 27 September, 2022).

Khalid, S., Hung, K. and Wiley, J. (2021). The ESG value opportunity: A decision point for utilities. *Climate and Energy*, 38(5), pp.10–17. https://doi:10.1002/gas.22261.

Kramar, R. (2022). Sustainable human resource management: Six defining characteristics. *Asia Pacific Journal of Human Resources*, 60(1). https:// doi:10.1111/1744-7941.12321.

Marchant, N. (2021). *This Is How Climate Change Could Impact the Global Economy.* [online] World Economic Forum. Available at: https://www.weforum.org/agenda /2021/06/impact-climate-change-global-gdp/. (Accessed 3 July, 2022).

Pollman, E. (2019). *Corporate social responsibility, ESG, and compliance.* [online] SSRN. Available at: https://papers.ssrn.com/sol3/papers.cfm?abstract_id=3479723. (Accessed 1 August, 2022).

Siemens (2022). Available at: https://new.siemens.com/global/en/company/sustainability.html. (Accessed 20 August, 2022).

Stankevičiūtė, Ž. and Savanevičienė, A. (2018). Designing sustainable HRM: The core characteristics of emerging field. *Sustainability, 10*(12), p.4798. https://doi:10.3390/su10124798.

UN (2022). Available at: https://www.un.org/sustainabledevelopment/sustainable -development-goals/. (Accessed 3 August, 2022).

World Economic Forum (2021). The global risks report 2021. Available at: https://www3.weforum.org/docs/WEF_The_Global_Risks_Report_2021.pdf. (Accessed 13 August, 2022).

Managing an international workforce

Chapter 16

INTRODUCTION

The hybrid workplace has facilitated a number of changes in the way that work is organised. Remote work has provided opportunities for organisations to recruit staff from different regions and to tap into talent that was not available in the traditional model. Managing people in a global environment requires different and often more complex considerations. This chapter will explore the way in which international HRM is structured through the use of a number of case examples to contextualise the discussion. It will explore the policy and practice preferences of organisations towards convergence and divergence. Understanding cultural diversity through training is discussed not just for expatriates but for all global employees. The effective management of expatriates is considered in relation to retention. The extent to which organisations will continue to invest in expatriates in the new world of work is unclear with the advance of digital technologies but it is clear that the global opportunities are plentiful and it will be those organisations that review existing practices and adapt that will reap the rewards.

Institutions are becoming increasingly globalised and business activities often transcend national boundaries. Globalisation incorporates complex processes such as the global flow of finance, knowledge and people (French, 2010). Global work arrangements are defined as situations in which employees who are collaborating with each other are culturally diverse and often also geographically distant from one another and thus embedded in

DOI: 10.4324/9781003342984-17

different national contexts (Hinds et al., 2011). Managing people in a global context today is a holistic process which far exceeds solely the management of expatriates. Managing in an international context is complex and organisations must navigate different legal, cultural and institutional situations, ensuring that practices are both effective and cost efficient.

International HRM policy needs to address a number of specific areas including organisation culture, cultural differences between countries where the company is active, differences in laws, regulations, rewards and labour conditions, differences in local, ethnic and religious standards and values and the relationship between head office and subsidiaries. Indeed, managing in an international organisation requires careful attention as to the extent to which parent company policies and practices should be adopted by subsidiaries.

INTERNATIONAL HRM STRATEGY

An international people strategy should provide a cohesive holistic plan to manage people effectively in a global environment. The plan will naturally be guided by the mission and vision of the organisation (as discussed in chapter 2). The organisation structure will provide the framework from which the global organisation operates which may be multidivisional in a large organisation where the company is split by product or entity or perhaps a matrix structure where employees report across both departments and divisions (for example, an employee might work in finance and product design). The strategy will need to focus on global hiring, management tools, payroll regulations, employee engagement and retention, the same as if operating on a national scale except with the added international complexity. The case study below is an example of an organisation structured to meet the needs of a large workforce.

CASE STUDY: SHELL

Royal Dutch Shell is an energy company which has more than 80,000 employees spread across the globe. Many of them are based in Asia and Singapore is the regional headquarters. The company has reviewed its HR strategy and implemented a new digital platform designed to create more business impact, a great employee experience and to reduce costs (Harper, 2020). The company engages in regular benchmarking with organisations of a similar size. The company has outsourced much of its operation through a shared business centre leveraging the HR IT platform. Shell has created global business operations centres integrating some of its HR functions. The four hubs are based in Krakow (Poland), Chennai (India), KL (Malaysia) and Manila (Philippines). Each hub has a slightly different speciality and serves different parts of the globe. The organisation employs 3000 HR staff globally with a third based in the operation centres which focus on HR account manager roles.

CONVERGENCE AND DIVERGENCE

The debate regarding the extent to which companies should take a convergence or divergence approach to employment relations around the world is key to international HRM policy. Convergence relates to the standardisation of policies and practices. Divergence relates to the extent to which overseas subsidiaries should be able to devise or modify the policies and practices of head office to suit the local context.

Ayentimi et al. (2018) found in their research that companies are taking a convergence approach and this is not so much because the host country has limited influence in decision-making, but rather that the bounded rationality argument for a 'global best practice model' is pursued in relation to the implementation of HRM practices that contribute to economic goals. Budhwar et al. (2016) concur, finding that global standardisation of HRM practices and policies (with local adjustments) is taking place in the Asia-Pacific context providing an indication of soft convergence. They also argue that there is emerging evidence that some of the country-specific HRM systems (e.g., the core pillars of Japanese management systems) are changing in favour of the global 'best practice' model, for example performance-based systems. In many cases, this is the result of the competitive forces of globalisation and competition, the need to attract talented staff and the preference of decision-makers to support 'best practice' models (ibid.).

The liberalisation of economies in China, India and Vietnam has resulted in a boom in foreign direct investment and the arrival of foreign firms in these economies has in some places forced local firms to rationalise their HRM practices to stay competitive (Ayentimi et al., 2018). Farndale et al. (2017) contend that in reality, convergence and divergence occur to different extents in relation to contextual and temporal situations where organisations operate. From an HR perspective, it is therefore necessary to determine what policies are common and global and which should be developed in relation to context and this needs to be reviewed regularly.

MULTINATIONAL ORGANISATIONS

A multinational enterprise (MNE) (also sometimes referred to as a transnational corporation) is one that is registered and operates in more than one country at a time, for example, Apple, Amazon and McDonald's. Usually, a corporation is headquartered in one country and operates wholly or partially owned subsidiaries in other countries. Worldwide, there are about 60,000 multinational companies (MNCs) controlling more than 500,000 subsidiaries. In Europe alone, 135,450 multinational enterprise groups operate employing over 42 million people. In other words, the influence of multinationals on employment relationships is significant. Pulignano and Keune (2015, p 8) suggest that

> employment policy within MNEs and their subsidiaries reflects a complex interaction between national institutions that enforce certain standards; the parent which attempts to impose home country rooted policies or practices; and negotiation between management and employee groups.

CULTURAL DIVERSITY

Many people now live and work in cultures that are different from their home country. People from different cultural and social backgrounds need to communicate effectively both face to face and in person. Understanding culture is complex as there are many subsets of culture from national, regional, community, organisations and so on. There have been a number of international studies that have been undertaken based on dozens of countries to help us understand how culture varies across different workplaces. For example, Hofstede (1980, 2005), Hall and Hall (1990), Trompenaars and Hampden-Turner (2004) and House et al. (2004). Hofstede's dimensions have remained the most popular with businesses and scholars. Much of Hofstede's work was undertaken with the IT company, IBM with data collected from surveys carried out with thousands of staff from 70 countries. The culture map has been developed over the years and today includes six dimensions, including:

- Power distance: how a society manages inequalities among people.
- Individualism/collectivism: the degree to which a society is focused on the individual who takes care of themselves and their immediate family and the collective, where the norm is for families to look after each other.

- Masculinity/femininity: societies that favour masculinity have a preference in society for achievement, heroism, assertiveness and material rewards for success. Society at large is more competitive. Its opposite, femininity, stands for a preference for cooperation, modesty, caring for the weak and quality of life. Society at large is more consensus-oriented.
- Uncertainty avoidance: the degree to which the members of a society feel uncomfortable with uncertainty and ambiguity. The fundamental issue here is how a society deals with the fact that the future can never be known.
- Long-term orientation versus short-term orientation: societies prioritise short-term focus on preparing for the future and long-term traditions and norms.
- Indulgence versus restraint: the degree to which societies enjoy relatively free gratification of basic and natural human drives related to enjoying life and having fun. Restraint stands for a society that suppresses gratification of needs and regulates it by means of strict social norms.

The Hofstede Insights website is a useful resource which includes a country culture comparison tool. To understand how the framework works in practice, see https://www.hofstede-insights.com/.

Hofstede's work has received a degree of criticism regarding the representativeness of the sample, the societal level focus rather than accounting for occupation, organisational influences and the exclusion of non-employed people in the surveys (McSweeney, 2002). Clegg et al. (2008) also question whether the methodology is valid as it resulted in average scores taken from national sample data. However, overall, noting its limitations the model does provide a helpful framework from which to understand how expectations in the workplace differ.

Other studies have undertaken similar dimensions of culture and although the descriptors might be different, essentially, they are underpinned with the same ideas and findings.

Cultural development training is an essential component of helping staff to interact effectively with each other in a global environment. Whether staff are relocating as an expatriate or working in an international organisation, training can help to improve communication, reduce the potential for conflict and enhance creativity and innovation. Language training might also be provided depending on the location. Tahir (2021) recommends that culture training is most effective when it is ongoing. The case study below provides an insight into cultural and linguistic experiences as a result of a change in strategic priorities.

CASE STUDY:

Rakuten is a global innovation company founded in 1997 with a head office based in Tokyo, Japan. Prior to 2010, Rakuten was a multilingual company and each subsidiary operated relatively autonomously with its own organisational culture. In 2010, CEO, Hiroshi Mikitani, established an English-only policy for the company's 10,000 employees. Mikitani felt that multilingualism was preventing the organisation from sharing knowledge across its global operations. The aim of the policy was to increase knowledge sharing in order to increase overseas revenue to help offset Japan's projected GDP decline (as a percentage of global GDP) and also enlarge its global talent pool.

The linguistic and cultural challenges of the policy were experienced differently depending on people's backgrounds and locations. Two groups had the most difficult transitions:

- Japanese employees – they were already fluent with Japanese concepts like kaizen (continuous improvement) but found becoming proficient in English challenging.
- American employees – they were fluent in English but struggled with cultural work routines and expectations from Japan.

Employees from countries like Brazil, France, Germany, Indonesia, Taiwan and Thailand – (who had to adjust to a new language *and* a new culture) found the transition the easiest.

MANAGING EXPATRIATES

There are three approaches for fulfilling staffing requirements across a multinational organisation: ethnocentric, polycentric and geocentric. Ethnocentric refers to the practice whereby key positions are filled by head office in the home country. The head office practices are prevalent as important decisions are made by a group of managers from the home country. Subsidiaries must then comply with the decisions of the home country (French, 2010). Polycentric refers to a policy where local managers are employed to implement strategies and subsidiaries are authorised to operate in more diverse ways including people management policies and practices. Geocentric is where staffing is undertaken on a worldwide basis and people practices are implemented consistently across headquarters and subsidiaries. Quality and availability are the determining factors. The company's strategy and vision are what shape the choice of approach.

Internationalisation of the economy has triggered expatriation where professionals change location with varying degrees of frequency for work (Gomez, 2014). Sometimes this involves travelling rather than moving home but for others, it will involve spending long periods of time abroad.

Traditionally, the ethnocentric approach would involve a pool of expats who are prepared for being sent abroad. Expatriation is a process whereby individuals relocate temporarily to a host country for work. There are now a number of common types of expatriates that include migrant workers who move overseas to take up a permanent job, global careerists that move from country to country and employer to employer and those that travel rather than move home.

An expat can cost up to twenty to forty times more than a local employee (Gomez–Mejia et al., 2015). As such, it is crucial that appointments are successful. The process of expatriation requires careful management including a formal selection process that focuses on performance and career, potential and talent, flexibility and technical knowledge (Gomez, 2014). Following selection, staff should be prepared through a variety of developmental interventions including coaching, informal discussions with current expatriates and visits to the country prior to taking up the post. Cross-cultural training and diversity and language skills will provide practical skills for settling quickly. The financial settlement will depend on the circumstances of the assignment but may include education for children, accommodation, a vehicle, medical insurance and such (ibid.). Monitoring, reviews, communication and support are integral to the successful management of the assignment.

Repatriation is the most complex phase of an assignment and careful management of expectations is required. The degree to which expatriation is successful is disputed by companies and expatriates with nine out of ten companies viewing expatriation as successful (based on only 5 per cent of expatriates not completing an assignment and 41 per cent choosing to extend it). However, 33 per cent of expatriates say that they didn't finish the agreed term and 17 per cent say that they changed companies on their return (Gomez, ibid.). A few of the challenges of working as an expatriate are revealed in the case study below.

CASE STUDY: INTELBRAS

Intelbras was founded in 1976 and is a leading Brazilian corporation in the production of telecommunications equipment. The company employs over 2,300 workers divided into five different producing facilities. In 2008, the company opened an office in Shenzhen, in the south of China. The office is mainly responsible for purchasing, controlling the quality of the company's suppliers, researching and developing new products and logistics. A review of the expatriation process revealed that the company had an expatriate manual in place but this focused on rules and duties that govern procedure rather than any specific repatriation programme or policy. Feedback from staff suggested that the 12-hour time difference and the lack of established procedures meant that expatriated employees very often receive business telephone calls from Brazil late at night which extends the working day and complicates communication between the head office and the subsidiary. This case study is based on the research undertaken by Meyer et al. (2016).

THE EMPLOYEE LIFECYCLE AND THE INTERNATIONAL MARKET

There will be a number of additional considerations to explore in an international market. People professionals will need to focus on each area of the employee lifecycle to ensure that policies and practices are effective. Some initial considerations are included below.

THE FUTURE

Whilst there may be changes to how expatriate assignments are designed in the future as a result of the evolving nature of the working environment, it is clear that hybrid models support international business. Organisations now have global reach in the digital economy. Indeed, some companies are now benefitting from considerably larger talent pools. The changing era means that the way we understand internationalisation may need to be redefined. This will present both opportunities and challenges and will undoubtedly require greater collaboration, discussion and development with all stakeholders.

Table 16.1 The employee lifecycle in an international context

Attraction	It may be necessary to amend existing candidate attraction tools to target staff in different country contexts depending on the organisation strategy. Explore international job boards, country-specific publications, social media channels and other more personalised approaches, for example, networking. Applicants may have different educational backgrounds and skills and consideration of how to amend campaigns to suit the audience will be required. Consider whether multilingual staff are required and, if so, which languages are needed.
Recruitment	Understanding the labour market, the rate of participation across different groups, and compensation and benefits packages will enable a competitive offer to be made. Global organisations might also reassess their selection framework and focus on hiring through cultural agility. Multicultural competencies might include tolerance for ambiguity, resilience and curiosity for all employees working multiculturally (Caligiuri et al., 2020). The recruitment and hiring process must comply with local laws.
Onboarding	Being clear about expectations and setting goals from the start is essential to effective working practices. Embedding new staff into the values of the organisation and ensuring that they understand the behaviours will support them in becoming productive members of the team. The HR team will need to ensure that all local regulations are complied with.
Development	Cross-cultural training is required to support the development of relationships. Leaders will benefit from training on how to use technology inclusively and how to set team-level ground rules for communication and work flow. Other training might include building harmonious teams through shared values in order to promote understanding and empathy. A focus on the development of both soft and technical skills will be beneficial, being aware that training needs may differ according to country context, education and background.
Retention	Staff that work on global cross-national teams in MNEs are required by the nature of their roles to be flexible and to operate across different time zones. Employees should be supported in their management of work-life balance. Alternative work models might be explored. Although, as discussed earlier in this book, many people have found working from home or in a hybrid model a positive experience, consider those international business travellers and globally mobile employees in MNEs that might not now enjoy the same frequent travel and associated benefits. Some job roles may require redesign to avoid all-day virtual meetings. Communication is key. Using the variety of technological platforms now available enables effective and efficient communication with global teams. Careful attention and consideration of the legal requirements for compensation and benefits are required and in particular how salaries will be determined along with any customary benefits and industry norms.

(Continued)

Managing an international workforce 229

Table 16.1 Continued

Offboarding	Gaining feedback from leavers about their experience can provide insightful comments that will support changes where required. Apart from communicating the offboarding process and timelines, a transition plan will also need to be implemented. This is especially true in the case of expatriates where it may take longer to recruit and prepare a replacement staff member. Investing time in thanking the team member for their efforts and recognising their achievements during their time in post is an important part of the process.
Alumni	If ex-employees receive a seamless offboarding experience, they are more likely to act as ambassadors for the company going forward. Departing employees in an international market will be in a position to promote (or otherwise) the employer brand which in turn will support referrals of new staff and customers.

(Maddox-Daines, 2022)

SUMMARY POINTS

- International HRM strategy should provide a holistic plan to managing people effectively in a global environment. It will need to focus on global hiring, management tools, payroll regulation, employee engagement and retention.
- Convergence relates to standardisation of policies and practices across the global business. Divergence relates to the extent to which overseas subsidiaries are able to devise and modify the policies and practices of head office.
- An MNE is one which is registered and operating in more than one country at a time, for example, Apple, Amazon and McDonald's.
- Understanding cultural diversity through training and development will improve communications, reduce the potential for conflict and enhance creativity and innovation.
- Expatriation is a process whereby individuals relocate temporarily to a host country for work. It requires careful management including a formal selection process that focuses on performance and career, potential and talent, flexibility and technical knowledge.
- There are a number of additional considerations when managing people in an international context. The employee lifecycle provides a framework for ensuring that international policy and practices are effective.

SELF-TEST QUESTIONS/REVIEW QUESTIONS

- Take a look at the Hofstede Insights website country comparison tool at https://www.hofstede-insights.com/. Compare the US and Japan. What are the key differences that you find?
- Your organisation has found that over half of its expatriates leave the organisation within six months of returning to head office. Your senior management team have asked you to present a report on key actions that the organisation must take to reduce the number of expatriates leaving the organisation. What key points will you include in your report?

A CASE EXAMPLE: RAKUTEN

Review the Rakuten case study discussed in this chapter. Based on your analysis of country comparisons between the US and Japan using the Hofstede country comparison tool as discussed above, assess why the American employees found it hard to adapt to work routines and expectations from Japan.

REFLECTION

Reflect on your own role or one you are familiar with (or interview a member of your family or a friend about their experience). To what extent do you liaise with colleagues globally? Have you undertaken any cultural diversity training? What might you do to prepare yourself effectively for working as a global employee?

References

Ayentimi, D.T., Burgess, J. and Brown, K. (2018) HRM practices of MNEs and domestic firms in Ghana: Divergence or convergence? *Personnel Review*, 47(1), pp.2–21. https://doi.org/10.1108/PR-05-2016-0116.

Budhwar, P.S., Varma, A. and Patel, C. (2016) Convergence-divergence of HRM in the Asia-Pacific: Context-specific analysis and future research agenda. *Human Resource Management Review*, 26(4), pp.311–326. https://doi:10.1016/j.hrmr.2016.04.004.

Caligiuri, P., De Cieri, H., Minbaeva, D., Verbeke, A. and Zimmermann, A., (2020) International HRM insights for navigating the COVID-19 pandemic: Implications for future research and practice. *Journal of International Business Studies*, 51(5), pp.697–713. https://doi.org/10.1057/s41267-020-00335-9.

Clegg, E.S., Kornberger, M. and Pitsis, T. S (2008) *Managing and Organisations: An Introduction to Theory and Practice*. 2nd edn. London: Sage.

Farndale, E., Brewster, C., Ligthart, P. and Poutsma, E. (2017) The effects of market economy type and foreign MNE subsidiaries on the convergence and divergence of HRM. *Journal of International Business Studies, 48*(9), pp.1065–1086. https://doi:10.1057/s41267-017-0094-8.

French, R. (2010) *Cross-cultural Management in Work Organisations.* 2nd edn. London: CIPD.

Gomez, S. (2014) How to manage expatriates. *IESE Business School,* Apr–Jun (133).

Gomez-Mejia, L.R., Balkin, D.B., Cardy, R.L. and Carson, K.P. (2015) *Managing Human Resources.* 7th ed. Amsterdam: Pearson/Prentice Hall.

Hall, E. and Hall, M.R. (1990) *Understanding Cultural Differences.* Yarmouth, Maine: Intercultural Press.

Harper, J. (2020) Shell's HR transformation journey. 29 January. *HRM Asia.* Available at: https://hrmasia.com/shells-hr-transformation-journey/. (Accessed 30 October, 2022).

Hinds, P., Liu, L. and Lyon, J., (2011) Putting the global in global work: An intercultural lens on the practice of cross-national collaboration. *Academy of Management Annals, 5*(1), pp.135–188. https://doi.org/10.5465/19416520.2011.586108.

Hofstede, G. (1980) *Cultural Consequences: International Differences in Work Related Values.* California: Sage.

Hofstede, G. (with G.J Hofstede) (2005) *Cultures and Organisation. Software of the Mind.* 2nd edn. New York: McGraw-Hill.

House, R.J., Hanges, P.J., Javidan, M., Dorfman, P.W. and Gupta, V. eds., (2004) *Culture, Leadership, and Organizations: The GLOBE Study of 62 Societies.* London: Sage publications.

McSweeney, B. (2002) Hofstede's model of national cultural differences and their consequences: A triumph of faith-a failure of analysis. *Human Relations, 55*(1), pp.89–118. https://doi.org/10.1177/0018726702551004.

Meyer, B., Jr, Victor, Silva Mathias, K.V. Da, Fernandes, L. (2016) Managing expatriates: analyzing the experience of an internationalized Brazilian Company. *Revista de Ciências da Administração, 18,* 137–147. https://doi.org/10.5007/2175-8077.2016v18n46p137.

Pulignano, V. and Keune, M. (2015) Understanding varieties of flexibility and security in multinationals: Product markets, institutional variation and local bargaining. *European Journal of Industrial Relations, 21*(1), pp.5–21. https://doi.org/10.1177/0959680114527880.

Tahir, R. (2021) Cross-cultural training: A study of European expatriates in New Zealand. *European Journal of Training and Development.* https://doi.org/10.1108/EJTD-01-2021-0013.

Trompenaars, F. and Hampden-Turner, C. (2004) *Managing People Across Cultures.* Oxford. Capstone publishing.

Index

Printed in the United States
by Baker & Taylor Publisher Services